PASSION & EXCESS

Passion

Blanchot, Bataille,

STEVEN SHAVIRO

& Excess

and Literary Theory

The Florida State University Press
Tallahassee

CONTENTS

ACKNOWLEDGMENTS

Much of this book was written with the help of stipends provided by the University of Washington Graduate School Research Fund, for the summers of 1985 and 1987. A version of the first chapter was originally presented to the Colloquium on Literary Theory sponsored by the Department of Comparative Literature at the University of Washington. Other sections have been presented in talks at conferences of the Modern Language Association, the International Association for Philosophy and Literature, and the Colloquium on Twentieth-Century Literature in French.

My greatest personal indebtedness is to Joseph Libertson, who first introduced me to the texts of Blanchot and Bataille. My own writing has been influenced by his teaching, and by his great book, *Proximity*, in more ways than I can possibly enumerate.

During the years I thought about and wrote this book, I was lucky to be able to discuss Blanchot and Bataille, and literary theory in general, with William Flesch; I could not have written what I did without the intellectual stimulation he provided. Laura Quinney carefully read and responded to my drafts, and provided the inestimable service—several times—of showing me where I was wrong. Ann

Smock helpfully commented on my manuscript. Hazard Adams was instrumental in uniting me with my publisher.

Among the many other friends and colleagues whose helpful and encouraging responses were important to me in the writing of this book, I wish particularly to thank Douglas Collins, Therese Grisham, Katurah Hutcheson, Vivian Kerman, Barry Schwabsky, Thomas Wall, Evan Watkins, and above all Faye Hirsch.

ABBREVIATIONS

To avoid a cumbersome apparatus of footnotes, I have given brief page references for my citations in the body of the text; full information can be found in the Bibliography. Quotations from Blanchot and Bataille are given both in French and [in brackets] in English; I have used existing translations whenever possible, but often silently modified them when necessary. The most frequently cited works by, and translations of, Blanchot and Bataille are indicated by the following abbreviations:

	Blanchot		Bataille
AM	*L'arrêt de mort*	IE	*Inner Experience*
DS	*Death Sentence*	OC	*Œuvres complètes* (followed by volume number and page number)
CI	*La communauté inavouable*		
EI	*L'entretien infini*		
EL	*L'espace littéraire*	VE	*Visions of Excess*
FJ	*La folie du jour*		
GO	*The Gaze of Orpheus*		
MD	*The Madness of the Day*		
MV	*Au moment voulu*		
PF	*La part du feu*		
SL	*The Space of Literature*		
UC	*The Unavowable Community*		
WT	*When the Time Comes*		

CHAPTER 1

Stop Making Sense

Introduction

It is happening, it has already happened, it has not yet happened, it is going to happen. Afterwards, we tell stories, we try to make sense of it. But something always goes wrong. Whatever we say about it seems curiously off the mark. It is neither effable nor ineffable: it happens only in the words we use to describe it, and yet these words are never the right ones. Something has happened; it is too overwhelming to be relegated to absence; and yet there is also no way to render it in the present, or into presence. Thus Blanchot's narrator in *La folie du jour* [*The Madness of the Day*]:

> Je faillis perdre la vue, quelqu'un ayant écrasé du verre sur mes yeux. . . . J'eus l'impression de rentrer dans le mur, de divaguer dans un buisson de silex. Le pire, c'était la brusque, l'affreuse cruauté du jour; je ne pouvais ni regarder ni ne pas regarder; voir c'était l'épouvante, et cesser de voir me déchirait du front à la gorge. . . . A la longue, je fus convaincu que je voyais face à face la folie du jour; telle était la vérité: la lumière devenait folle, la clarté avait perdu tout bon sens; elle m'assaillait déraisonnablement, sans règle, sans but. (*FJ*, 21–22)

I nearly lost my sight, because someone crushed glass in my eyes. . . . I had the feeling I was going back into the wall, or straying into a thicket of flint. The worst thing was the sudden, shocking cruelty of the day; I could not look, but I could not help looking. To see was terrifying, and to stop seeing tore me apart from my forehead to my throat. . . . In the end, I grew convinced that I was face to face with the madness of the day. That was the truth: the light was going mad, the brightness had lost all reason; it assailed me irrationally, without control, without purpose. (*MD*, 11)

Such is the violence, the madness, of the event. We are frightened by this happening, but frightened even more by our inability to give adequate words to it, to assign it a fixed place. The more-than-presence, the "face à face" of this encounter, defies expression and categorization. That is why it is so powerfully traumatic. But we cannot, we must not, we do not want to submit to this madness. And so we have recourse to hermeneutics. Interpretation is a means for mastering trauma. We "make sense" by discovering meanings, or by producing them. Everything is safe, once we can interpret the symptoms of madness, once we can envelop the event in a network of significations. We reassure ourselves that it is only something that we imagined. In Emily Dickinson's sarcastic phrase, "We dream—it is good we are dreaming—. . . . It's prudenter—to dream—" (*#531*). The event is something recounted in words, it is a work of art, it is allegorical, symbolic, representational. We have formally circumscribed the event, and established the possibility of *recognition*: whether the objects we recognize be experiences, concepts, powers of the mind, or simply signs. We speak of values, of beauty, and of truth.

But perhaps I'm getting it all backwards. What I am calling a happening, or an event, is not an originary perception or a founding experience; it is not something from which we can begin. If we capture the event within forms and significations, it is only because the forms and significations are already at hand. We can only begin to speak out of the contexts (linguistic, literary, cultural, social, political) which we use to encompass the event, and to which it is so ill adapted. Before anything happens, we already live in a world of significations, of values, of social roles, of political commitments, of ideals of beauty and of truth. The system of such a world is, like Dickinson's *aurora borealis*, "preconcerted with itself" (*#290*) prior to our finding ourselves within it. Modern thought assures us again and again that the system of contexts and significations *must* be adequate, that *"the limits of my language* mean the limits of my world" (Wittgenstein, *Tractatus*, 5.6), that, thanks to the "universal semantization of [social] usages . . . there is no reality except when it is intelligible" (Barthes, *Elements of Semiology*, 42), or that "there is no language [*langue*] in existence for which there is any question of its inability to cover the whole field of the signified, it being an effect of its existence as a language [*langue*] that it necessarily answers all needs" (Lacan, *Ecrits*, 150).

The sheer excessiveness of the event provokes anxiety. It does not fit easily into our schemes of understanding and representation. Yet since the possibility of comprehension is given in advance, the event can always somehow be recuperated as meaning. Thus, for Heidegger, the event is always already a movement of appropriation (*Ereignis*). The discord introduced by the event is only the unfolding of a "self-vibrating realm," a "self-suspended structure," the opening of a space within which the fundamental *"belonging* together [*Zusammengehören*]* of man and Being" is able to appear (*Identity and Difference*, 38 and passim). The rupture produced by the event is itself incorporated by the structures of language and of philosophical reflection, the better to foreclose any more radical possibility of the loss or escape of meaning. A similar process is already at work in Kant's account of the sublime. As Neil Hertz suggests, the "distress" of the imagination's breakdown in the experience of the sublime seems "slightly factitious, staged precisely in order to require the somewhat melodramatic arrival of Ethics" (*The End of the Line*, 50). Kant falls back on a rather creaky narrative machinery because everything has already been decided in advance. The failure of the imagination's power to order experience is prescribed and anticipated by Reason, that higher faculty that steps in to restore coherence and continuity. One cannot posit the rupture without the recuperation. The anxiety of the sublime can be capitalized, realized as profit, transformed into an edifying and ultimately self-congratulatory experience. For in such an experience "the mind can make itself sensible of the appropriate sublimity of the sphere of its own being, even above nature" (*Critique of Judgement*, 112).

One might relate the scenario of the Kantian sublime to Nietzsche's observation that "what really arouses indignation against suffering is not suffering as such but the senselessness of suffering" (*Genealogy of Morals*, 2:7, 68). Anxiety, suffering, even death, are tolerable once they can be converted into signification. We see, we know, we understand.

A clear line—the line which is clarity itself—passes from the immediacy of sight to the supremacy of the signifier or of the concept, conceived as "une vue affranchie des limitations de la vue. . . . une manière transcendante de voir [a sight liberated from the limitations of sight. . . . a transcendent way of seeing]" (*EI*, 40). We are not yet free of what Blanchot calls "cette exigence optique qui, dans la tradition occidentale, soumet depuis des millénaires notre approche des choses et nous invite à penser sous la garantie de la lumière ou sous la menace de l'absence de lumière [this optical exigency which, in the Western tradition, has subdued our approach to things for thousands of years, and which invites us to think under the guarantee of light or under the threat of the absence of light]" (*EI*, 38). Suffering is accepted and assimilated when it is given sense, and it is given sense when it is illuminated, pacified by the light—or by the dialectic of light and darkness, hiddenness and revelation, concealment and unconcealment.

Nothing is more important to Western tradition than the clarity and truth of vision: in the sublime moment, as Emerson puts it in a famous passage from his essay "Nature," "All mean egotism vanishes. I become a transparent eyeball; I am nothing; I see all" (*Selections*, 24). The narcissistic integrity of the ego is less important than the purity of sight itself: at such a moment, there is "no disgrace, no calamity (leaving me my eyes), which nature cannot repair." Yet Emerson's remarkable qualification suggests that, even after transparency has been attained, even after the Kantian recuperation or Hegelian *Aufhebung*, a certain anxiety remains. The light allows us to see, and therefore to understand, to possess, to rejoice in what we see: "je ne suis pas aveugle, je vois le monde, bonheur extraordinaire. Je le vois, ce jour hors duquel il n'est rien. Qui pourrait m'enlever cela? [I am not blind, I see the world—what extraordinary happiness! I see this day, and outside it there is nothing. Who could take that away from me?]" (*FJ*, 10; *MD*, 6). And this happiness is bolstered by the confidence that the day is everything, totality and tautology, that nothing (or only the nothing) lies outside it: "Et ce jour s'effaçant, je m'effacerai avec lui, pensée, certitude qui me transporte [And when this day fades, I will fade along with it—a thought, a certainty, that enraptures me]" (*FJ*, 10; *MD*, 6).

But what about that anxiety over "my eyes"? Is it really possible for me to be deprived of that immediacy of vision which is also my access to a world rich in mediations and meanings? If "intuitions without concepts are blind" (Kant, *Critique of Pure Reason*, 93), then can it be that my fear of the event is really a fear of (literal or metaphorical) blindness? ("Someone crushed glass in my eyes"). The loss of signification is far worse than any loss to which I can assign signification. And this is why my naive enjoyment of the transparency of the day, of the world in its totality, is predicated on my confidence that "je m'effacerai avec lui [I will fade along with it]." When menaced with blindness, I may think that I am going to die: "Parfois, je me disais: 'C'est la mort; malgré tout, cela en vaut la peine, c'est impressionnant' [At times I said to myself, 'This is death. In spite of everything, it's really worth it, it's impressive']" (*FJ*, 22; *MD*, 11). But my being impressed by my own death, my rescuing splendor and sublimity from it, is a self-deluding, defensive reaction. Living on in blindness, interminably not seeing, not signifying, is far more frightening than death.

Of course, the ambiguity of this formulation is that it wrongly designates, by the negative term of "blindness," that which a certain metaphysical-optical tradition simply cannot or will not see. Even the most empty or indeterminate designation can be a way of reducing the event to meaning (or to the absence of meaning, which comes to the same thing), and hence of mastering or circumscribing a source of traumatic anxiety. Absence always refers back to a correlative presence. It seems inevitable that "blindness" will continue to function, *within* the limits of our system of significations, in dialectical relation to "insight." Yet *La folie du jour* resists such inscriptions, insofar as the blindness which it invokes is not merely a deprivation of light. For the story asks us: what happens when we "see" the light itself? when the transparency that permits vision becomes in its turn disconcertingly visible? when there is an excess of light, when the light goes mad, an eruption of light violently "erasing sight—" (Dickinson, #601)?

We find ourselves not so much lost in darkness, as dazzled by "le plein jour de l'obscurité [the broad daylight of obscurity]" (Blanchot, *Le pas au-delà*, 97). Transparency, the medium which grants us limitless vision, has itself become the limit of vision, "la plus infranchissable des traverses [the most impassable of shortcuts]" (*Le pas au-delà*, 30). In the blinding excess or undefinable deficiency of the event, the eruption of a light no longer simply transparent, or the insinuation of a darkness no longer simply the privation of light, a new type of relation is at work. I am no longer able to see, but this inability is itself a source of ocular "fascination": "la relation que le regard entretient, relation elle-même neutre et impersonelle, avec la profondeur sans regard et sans contour, l'absence qu'on voit parce qu'aveuglante [the relationship—one that is itself neutral and impersonal—that the gaze maintains with the depths which have no gaze and no contour, the absence that one sees because it is blinding]" (Blanchot, *EL*, 27; *GO*, 76). Vision no longer seizes and dominates the world, but it is also unable to extinguish itself; it continues to be sustained in and by its own impossibility. My gaze is riveted precisely on that which limits or abolishes it. The blindness of the narrator of *La folie du jour* may be compared with that of the eponymous protagonist of *Thomas l'obscur*:

> C'était la nuit même. Des images qui faisaient son obscurité l'inondaient. Il ne voyait rien et, loin d'en être accablé, il faisait de cette absence de vision le point culminant de son regard. . . . Non seulement cet œil qui ne voyait rien appréhendait quelque chose, mais il appréhendait la cause de sa vision. Il voyait comme objet ce qui faisait qu'il ne voyait pas. (17–18)

> It was night itself. Images which constituted its darkness inundated him. He saw nothing and, far from being distressed, he made this absence of vision the culmination of his sight. . . . Not only did this eye which saw nothing apprehend something, it apprehended the cause of its vision. It saw as object that which prevented it from seeing. (*Thomas the Obscure*, 14–15)

Thomas seems to welcome this strange sightlessness, this apprehension of nonvision. But the dilemma of a blindness that infects sight from within, that cannot be figured as death or deprivation, is a scandal for Western rationality. Thus Sartre attacks the passage from *Thomas* that I have just quoted with the oddly Cartesian argument that "a thought which thinks that it does not know is still a thought" (*Situations*, 1:223). The bad faith of such an objection is evident; it takes for granted the very identity of vision with thought, and of both with spontaneity (the Cartesian, Kantian, or Husserlian constitutive activity of the subject), that Blanchot explicitly contests. What is really at stake in Sartre's objection? The radical exteriority intimated by the opacity of light or by the palpability of darkness must be resorbed at all costs within the immanence of the day: whether this immanence be figured as the immediacy of a founding *cogito* or as the systematicity of mediations and significations. What is intolerable to philosophical thought is that vision should be held captive by that which it cannot see, even as thought is haunted and obsessed by "quelque chose comme *une pensée qui ne se laisserait pas penser* [something like *a thought which will not let itself be thought*]." But why do we find "cette sorte de tache aveugle de la pensée [this sort of blind spot of thought]" (*EI*, 173) so disturbing? Deeper than our fears for ourselves is our intense, yet frivolous, anxiety over seeing that which we are powerless to see, thinking that which we are unable to think. It is on behalf of the world of pregiven significations, more than on our own accounts, that we are afraid when we suddenly find ourselves "face to face with the madness of the day."

At the very least, philosophical and critical discourse is continually marked by this anxiety. Heidegger says that care (*Sorge*) is a fundamental structure of our being in the world. He insists that the phenomenon of care, as a "primordial structural totality," precedes any constitution of the subject, or any distinction between theory and practice (*Being and Time*, 238). In our common caring, the usual oppositions between idealism and materialism, between mystification and demystification, between the individual and the collective, or between formalist and historicist approaches to art, simply break down. Care lies equally at the root of any philosophy of subjective spontaneity, and any philosophy of presubjective or transsubjective mediations and significations. As critics, we may identify ourselves as guardians of the sanctity of cultural tradition, as preservers of something at once infinitely precious and dangerously fragile. Or else we may regard ourselves as critical theorists, seeking to uncover the limitations, the biases, the exclusions, the hidden ideologies of that same cultural tradition. But once we are guided by care, once we posit the world of values and meanings as our concern, the crucial step has already been taken. It doesn't much matter, afterwards, whether truth is located in works of art themselves, or in the critique of them. What matters is that art has been subordinated to truth, in classical Platonic fashion. A sense of responsibility, a concern for values and meanings already distances and conditions our approach to the event.

Heidegger posits care as a universal, originary phenomenon. But isn't there something ridiculous in all this solemnity? Philosophers, theorists, and critics are always trying to "save the appearances," to account for how things hold together, as if they wouldn't hold together were not reason there to hold them together. Or else, in an opposite but symmetrical movement, we invoke negativity and critical rationality, as if change would never take place were not reason there to impel and direct it. Perhaps such fantasies merely reflect our too strong investment in our own academic methodologies. For despite such imaginings, things hold together all too completely and coherently on their own: and this is a political as well as an aesthetic observation. Foucault shows how easily even the strongest oppositional movements can be co-opted and absorbed by the mechanisms of power. The problem is not how to save the appearances, but how to escape from them; and not how to establish a rational, critical basis for change, but how to free the forces of change or of the event from the conceptualizations that constrain it. Let us ask, not how the coherence of the world is possible, but whether anything can interrupt or escape from this coherence. The radical possibility of metamorphosis need not be merely an occasion for our reactive anxieties. The violent intensity of sensation and passion allows or forces us to approach the unsituable event, to think outside the canons of coherence and truth.

If I have been approaching this prospect in what seems too negative a manner, defining the event largely in terms of what it is not, this is because contemporary literary criticism remains so dominated by projects of formalization and idealization. The difficulty is not one of language *per se*, but it is certainly one inherent to the particular language I find myself compelled to speak. I would like to reorient my discourse along the triple lines suggested by Foucault: "to question our will to truth; to restore to discourse its character as an event; to abolish the sovereignty of the signifier" ("The Discourse on Language," 229). But what could be more difficult? The languages of criticism that we all know and use take for granted the will to truth, repress the event by seeing discourse as a formal structure, and exalt the signifier. Even the self-consciously most 'advanced' forms of criticism practiced today participate in this dilemma. Thus, deconstruction traces the continual frustration of the will to truth, but never conceives any horizon for art and criticism other than that of such a will. It privileges language as a play of signifiers, thereby foreclosing any possibility of approaching discourse as an event. And thus it assumes and perpetuates the structural imperative, even as it rightly demonstrates that formalization can never be complete. In its narrowly linguistic and epistemological focus, and its complacently self-validating structure of argument, deconstruction appears as a massive hypostasis of the very tradition of academicism, idealism, and intellectualism whose futility it has so amply exposed. To dismantle critical language more radically, to dislodge the exigency of *Sorge*, to discover or invent what Deleuze and Guattari call "lignes de fuite [lines of flight]," other strategies must be adopted. It will be necessary for me to proceed indirectly, to question from yet another angle our culture's (and my own) devotion to the ideals of beauty and truth.

I have been suggesting that a significant death is less terrifying than a life which continues in blindness *to* signification. In this context, I would like to look more closely at the connections between death, beauty, and truth established by romantic and modernist tradition. Every process of formalization or idealization is founded upon the death of its object. It is already a kind of death when Kant (or Husserl, whose *epochē* reproduces the structure of Kantian aesthetics) disengages perception from any reference to the object's actual existence. A higher or purer imaginative awareness is obtained by negating the materiality of the thing. One step further, and the aesthetic impulse is encapsulated in the coldness and sterility of Keats's Grecian Urn; beauty is united with truth in a tautological short-circuiting of desire. The formalizing *epochē*, or the aesthetic state of purposiveness without purpose, eliminates the proximity of the object on the one hand, and the passion of the subject on the other. Aesthetics is predicated upon death precisely to the extent that it posits the free disinterested delight of a fixed and centered subject regarding the unity of a static object. Death in its perfection is "the bare form of finality" (*Critique of Judgement*, 63), the absence of purpose or affect that guarantees the efficacy of a higher intentionality or purposiveness. The price paid for idealization is that the completed art object is built around a corpse: the work of art is either the lifeless residue in which the process of creation is lost (Shelley), or the funerary monument in which it is preserved (Keats). But the corpse itself remains a problem. The difficulty, for the aesthetic tradition, is always one of articulating the idealization that produces beauty with the embarrassing necessity of having to dispose of the remains.

These points can be clarified by considering one of Dickinson's most familiar poems (#449):

I died for Beauty—but was scarce
Adjusted in the Tomb
When One who died for Truth, was lain
In an adjoining Room—

He questioned softly "Why I failed"?
"For Beauty," I replied—
"And I—for Truth—Themself are One—
We Brethren, are", He said—

And so, as Kinsmen, met a Night—
We talked between the Rooms—
Until the Moss had reached our lips—
And covered up—our names—

Dickinson pushes the logic of the Grecian Urn to the point where it dissolves into self-parody. It is only insofar as they are ironically "Adjusted in the Tomb," assigned their fixed boundaries under the power of death, that beauty and truth are one. "I died for beauty": does this mean that the speaker and her interlocutor died for the sake of beauty and truth (as martyrs or witnesses)? Or, more perversely, did they choose to die *in order that* they might thereby attain truth and beauty? A desire for death is perhaps the hidden *telos* of beauty and truth, ascetic ideals that predetermine their own failure ("Why I failed?"). In any case, we can only die for truth and beauty, and not live for them. Virtual images, devoid of literal or referential meaning, they do not, properly speaking, exist at all. Only death articulates the discourses of truth and beauty and allows them to circulate, at once distinguishing and uniting them. Yet this movement is highly ambiguous: if death generates the names "beauty" and "truth," death also effaces them.

Sharon Cameron notes, in this poem, "the capacity of voice to survive its limitations, hyperbolically figured in the apparent survival of its own death," so that, "although the voice tells us what silences voice, it is still talking, is *after* its end recounting its end" (*Lyric Time*, 209–10). The poem enacts a continual withdrawal of affect, "like the Distance / On the look of Death—" (#258). Yet this withdrawal is never completed; it never reaches the point of absolute emptiness. The movement of aestheticization remains impure. The murder requisite for idealization has not been completely successful; the corpses (as in Poe's stories) are still somehow alive. In its parodic force, the poem anatomizes the aesthetic impulse, identifying the presence of ascetic ideals, of a kind of death drive. But at the same time, the poem affirms an anti-aesthetic, anti-idealizing countermovement. As the dead people talk, achieving a derisory mutual recognition, the moss gradually covers up their names. They speak in vain of their ideals while, in a subtext which defies idealization and symbolization, their bodies interminably decay.

Keats maintains infinite potentiality at the price of eternal stasis; nothing can change even though (or, ironically, because) everything has been left open. The silence of death, which "tease[s] us out of thought," serves the ulterior purpose of purifying speech. A similar project animates Mallarmé's endeavor to purify poetic language: in "Le Tombeau d'Edgar Poe" (*Œuvres complètes*, 70), "Donner un sens plus pur aux mots de la tribu [To give a purer meaning to the words of the tribe]." The sonnet presents Poe "Tel qu'en Lui-même enfin l'éternité le change [Such as into Himself eternity finally changes him]." In the achieved eternity of his death, the poet is freed from the taints and imperfections of life, and transformed into "Himself." By a final change, he is freed from change, able at last to repose securely and truthfully within himself. The "désastre obscur [obscure disaster]" of his writing, or of his miserable life and death, leaves behind it only a tombstone, a "calme bloc [calm block]" of granite serving as a limit to the "sortilège [spell, or charm]" of future metamorphoses. At least, such is Mallarmé's fervent wish: "Que ce granit du moins montre à jamais sa borne / Aux noirs vols du Blasphème épars dans le futur [That this granite at least may forever show its boundary / To the black flights of Blasphemy scattered in the future]."

But doesn't the glorification of Poe bespeak a more fundamental defensiveness? Mallarmé writes this funeral poem in order to keep Poe in his tomb, to prevent him from returning from out of the grave. Is the Blasphemy which the sonnet—and the actual tomb—seeks to exclude merely the calumny which darkened Poe's life? Such at least is the tenor of Mallarmé's own deceptively naive commentary on the poem: "Blasphemy means against poets, such as the charge of Poe being drunk" (see Robert Greer Cohn, *Toward the Poems of Mallarmé*, 153–57). But more disturbingly, Blasphemy is also the inner movement of poetry itself, the transgression of the boundaries between life and death, the horror recounted so often in Poe's own stories. The "obscure disaster" is less what interrupts Poe's writing than what actually speaks in that writing. And this is the paradox of Mallarmé's aesthetics of idealization. All of Mallarmé's poetry, culminating in "Un coup de dés," can be read as a meditation on the "désastre obscur," on its unrepresentability and its randomness. And even in the sonnet on Poe, Mallarmé approaches Blanchot's sense that the disaster can never be spoken in the present tense (*L'écriture du désastre; The Writing of the Disaster*). But in erecting Poe's "Tombeau," Mallarmé nonetheless seems concerned to give the disaster a fixed identity, and thereby to abolish it. Its fragmentary trace becomes an all-too-solid and all-too-visible funerary monument, a memorial of what cannot be remembered, a fetish protecting against the repetition of the event that produced it. The residue of transgression marks a boundary against transgression. Poe's death leaves behind the ideal forms of his works; idealization proceeds from death. Yet those very works recount, with monotonous insistence, the inconclusiveness or outright failure of this idealization, this death.

Thus in "Ligeia": "But why shall I minutely detail the unspeakable horrors of that night? Why shall I pause to relate how, time after time, until near the period of the gray dawn, this hideous drama of revivification was repeated; how each terrific relapse was only into a sterner and apparently more irredeemable death; how each agony wore the aspect of a struggle with some invisible foe; and how each struggle was succeeded by I know not what of wild change in the personal appearance of the corpse?" (Poe, *Complete Tales and Poems*, 665). This obsessive repetition of the death agony absolutely resists idealization. The continual "wild change in the personal appearance of the corpse" endlessly defers any hope for a decent burial. And the story can do nothing but "minutely detail" what it denounces as futility and superfluity. The event of death does not occur once and for all, but must be passed through again and again. Death, in its horror, always precedes itself. This failure of death to be pacified even in death is the worst—the most obscure—disaster.

But on the other hand, even if we were to assume that death *has* at last taken place, that is not the end of it. A similar resistance to idealization may be noted on the side of the hysterical insistence of the remains. Even when there finally is a corpse, its sheer *physicality* is an embarrassment which gets in the way of the aesthetic ritual or funeral rites. Poe's finished works cannot be divorced from the impure and indeed nauseating circumstances in which his detractors claim they were produced: "le flot sans honneur de quelque noir mélange [the flood without honor of some black mixture]." Such viscous materiality is supposed to congeal into the solidity of granite. But Poe's works embody, or give voice to, precisely the disgust that Mallarmé wishes to foreclose: "As I rapidly made the mesmeric passes, amid ejaculations of 'dead! dead!' absolutely *bursting* from the tongue and not from the lips of the sufferer, his whole frame at once—within the space of a single minute, or less, shrunk—crumbled—absolutely *rotted* away beneath my hands. Upon the bed, before that whole company, there lay a nearly liquid mass of loathsome—of detestable putrescence" ("The Facts in the Case of M. Valdemar," 103).

Death as obsessive "revivification," or death as hysterical "ejaculation": either of these instances gives a bizarre twist to Mallarmé's claim "Que la mort triomphait dans cette voix étrange! [that death triumphed in this strange voice!]." For what triumphs is not the ideality of absence, but the messiness of convulsions and of "putrefaction," or what the poem characterizes as a "vil sursaut d'hydre [vile starting up of a hydra]." The movement of dying precedes and survives itself, anticipates and recollects itself, but in any case never coincides with itself. It is never pure, and its hollow, uncanny discourse, "from the tongue and not from the lips of the sufferer," impossibly referring to its own inability to speak, ruins in advance any project for purifying speech. The "obscure disaster," the *event* of death, in its ungraspable, repetitive insistence, prevents the Poet from ever achieving the ultimate, eternal form of "Himself."

Mallarmé's poetics of idealization is crucial for the later developments of modernism; although (as I have been suggesting) the actual interest of his poetry comes from the ways in which such a project is continually (if ambiguously) thwarted. Dickinson, in contrast, rejects outright the perfection of an achieved death, in order to affirm the impurity and inconclusiveness of the event. Her position is also that of Stevens, for whom "speech is not dirty silence / Clarified. It is silence made still dirtier" ("The Creations of Sound," in *The Palm at the End of the Mind*, 251). If there is no absolute silence, there can also be no purification of speech. If there is no finality of death, there can also be no idealization. As Blanchot's narrator ironically remarks, speaking from the space between life and death, between pure silence and purified speech, "souvent je mourais sans rien dire [often I lay dying without saying anything]" (*FJ*, 22; *MD*, 11). No suspension of time, no "ditties of no tone," can put an end to what Hegel would call the "bad infinity" of "breathing human passion." So long as the death agony, or the liminal journey, continues, there is no room for a self-sufficing and self-reflecting subject to contemplate a perfect, disincarnated, eternal object. Death implies not so much the final alteration of the object, or the apotheosis of the subject, as a continuing alteration *within* the subject, which is no longer able simply to register changes in objects from a stable and unchanging point. "Consciousness," in Dickinson's poetry, is at once exacerbated and attenuated, as it finds itself continually "traversing the interval" between the multiplicity of "experience" and the singularity of "experiment" (#822).

If Poe is the narrator of the blasphemous intermingling of death with life, then Dickinson is the poet of the infinite extendability of the very instant of death as separation. She makes the startling claim that "Eternity" is not a terminus, but only an arbitrary "Term" in the course of an interminable journey, an "odd Fork in Being's Road—" (#615). "Oneself" is therefore never an ultimate and perfected state, but rather an interval, a point of metamorphosis, a middle term in a series without termination: "Behind Me—dips Eternity— / Before Me—Immortality— / Myself—the Term between—" (#721). In such an infinite series, the "Soul" can neither shed itself of its experiences in life, nor be identified once and for all in death, but is instead "condemned to be— / Attended by a single Hound / Its own identity" (#822). In these lines, the hiatus after "be" is of extreme importance. The Soul is "condemned to be," sentenced to a continuing singular existence, without outlet, without possibility of escape, even in the death that defines its solitude, and of which it is so obsessively aware. But at the same time, the Soul is also "condemned to be attended by"—that is to say accompanied by, but never able to coincide with— "its own identity": its defining characteristic of subjectivity is bound to, yet separated from, itself. In this powerfully eccentric image of consciousness without a subject, Dickinson nevertheless sees, not deprivation, but an ongoing "adventure." Again and again in her poems, aesthetic disinterest collapses into a "Maelstrom" (#721) of passions and desires.

II

There is one obvious objection to everything I have been saying so far. In speaking of death, I have been forgetting that I am merely *speaking* of death. I am confusing the sign with its referent, ignoring the fact that language is not the same as simple presence, that signification is already a kind of idealization. The death which I find resisting idealization, in Poe, Dickinson, or Blanchot, is not a real death, but death as represented in language. Insofar as it is represented, the resistance to idealization has already been idealized. I have been confusing death as represented *in* language with the death which *is* language. For there is no more fundamental axiom of recent critical discourse than the one stating that language is founded upon absence, and therefore upon death. The signifier is always the death of the thing. Or, more precisely, as Jacques Lacan puts it, "The symbol manifests itself first of all as the murder of the thing, and this death constitutes in the subject the eternalization of its desire" (*Ecrits*, 104).

In enunciating this basic proposition of modernism, Lacan is following Mallarmé, and ultimately (via Kojève) Hegel. The attack on notions of immediacy and presence is not a contemporary invention. Long before structuralism, Hegel defines the movement of the dialectic as the disqualification of identity and simple presence. From the beginning of the *Phenomenology of Spirit*, death or absence is at work. Even at the moment of "Sense-Certainty," I destroy the immediacy of the present instant in the very act of saying "now," of referring to "*this* instant.*" It is only a step from the *Phenomenology* to Mallarmé's more aestheticized version of language as a power of negation: "Je dis: une fleur! et, hors de l'oubli où ma voix relègue aucun contour, en tant que quelque chose d'autre que les calices sus, musicalement se lève, idée même et suave, l'absente de tous bouquets [I say: a flower! and, out of the oblivion where my voice relegates any contour, insofar as [it is] something other than known calyxes, musically arises, idea itself and exquisite, the one absent from all bouquets]" ("Crise de vers," in *Œuvres complètes*, 368).

This flower of language, symbol or trope, is (like Poe's tomb) the ideality or "pure notion" which arises when we are able to forget or put at a distance the "embarrassment" of concrete existence: "pour qu'en émane, sans la gêne d'un proche ou concret rappel, la notion pure [so that the pure notion may issue from it, without the embarrassment of a near or concrete recall]" (368). With his emphasis on oblivion, on musicality, on the exquisiteness or "suavity" of the idea, Mallarmé endeavors to suppress the *violence* of this separation from the real. But Blanchot, summarizing the common argument of Hegel, Kojève, and Mallarmé, explains why idealization, if a necessary condition of all speech, is also a kind of murder:

> Je dis: cette femme. . . . Le mot me donne ce qu'il signifie, mais d'abord il le supprime. Pour que je puisse dire: cette femme, il faut que d'une manière ou d'une autre je lui retire sa réalité d'os et de chair, la rende absente et l'anéantisse. Le mot me donne l'être, mais il me le donne privé d'être. Il est l'absence de cet être, son néant, ce qui demeure de lui lorsqu'il a perdu l'être,

c'est-à-dire le seul fait qu'il n'est pas. . . . Mon langage ne tue personne. Mais, si cette femme n'était pas réellement capable de mourir, si elle n'était pas à chaque moment de sa vie menacée de la mort, liée et unie à elle par un lien d'essence, je ne pourrais pas accomplir cette négation idéale, cet assassinat différé qu'est mon langage. ("La littérature et le droit à la mort," in *La part du feu*, 312–13)

> I say, 'This woman'. . . . A word may give me its meaning, but first it suppresses it. For me to be able to say, 'This woman,' I must somehow take her flesh and blood reality away from her, cause her to be absent, annihilate her. The word gives me the being, but it gives it to me deprived of being. The word is the absence of that being, its nothingness, what is left of it when it has lost being—the very fact that it does not exist. . . . My language does not kill anyone. But if this woman were not really capable of dying, if she were not threatened by death at every moment of her life, bound and joined to death by an essential bond, I would not be able to carry out that ideal negation, that deferred assassination which is what my language is. (*GO*, 41–43)

The "eternalization" provided by discourse is not only a consequence of the inevitable fact of our mortality, but the active result of a violent negativity, of a project of aggression and domination. By changing Mallarmé's "flower" into a "woman," Blanchot subtly underscores the actual price of aesthetic idealization. Recent feminist theorists have amply demonstrated the extent to which the allegedly neutral speaking subject of dialectics is implicitly male. A woman can be interpellated by this male discourse, recognized within it, only to the extent that she is first an object of male aggression, "threatened by death at every moment of her life." As Blanchot says elsewhere, "Lorsque je parle, toujours j'excerce un rapport de puissance, j'appartiens, que je le sache ou non, à un réseau de pouvoirs dont je me sers. . . . Toute parole est violence [When I speak, I am always exercising a relationship of power, I belong, whether I know it or not, to a network of powers of which I make use. . . . Every word is violence]" (*EI*, 60). Significa-tion is never neutral; it always bears the marks of particular relations of power. Herbert Marcuse, commenting on this same conjunction of Hegel, Mallarmé, and Blanchot, asserts the necessity of a "language of negation": "the absent must be made present because the greater part of the truth is in that which is absent" (*Reason and Revolution*, x). Blanchot suggests, rather, that the aesthete's or dialectician's claim to universality is always founded on the violence of an exclusion. The one thing that is forever omitted from the totality, never represented in the dialectical process of linguistic symbolization, is precisely—that which is being represented. Literally speaking, "My language does not kill anyone." But the power of death inherent in the word insures that speech is never merely literal. Thus, for instance, a "deferred assassination," a making-absent of women, is necessary in order that (as psychoanalysis, among other institutions of discourse, claims) the "truth" of "woman" be revealed as "lack."

Truth in language is always a consequence of this violent making-absent, of domination enforced by the threat of murder. Such a relation of power, such violence, is present in any discourse of knowledge or of truth, as in any attempt to assign identities or names. As Foucault puts it, every *savoir* (knowledge) implies a correlative articulation of *pouvoir* (power). And the violent suppression of the body (for example) *from* discourse is accomplished, not by a suppression *of* its discourse, but precisely by a continual "incitement to discourse" (*History of Sexuality*, 1:17–35), by inducing or compelling it to enter the space of regular discourse. For Blanchot, similarly, the roll call in the Nazi death camps (*Le pas au-delà*, 56–57) and torture as the infliction of pain in order to extort "true" speech (*EI*, 60–61) are only the most extreme examples of a relation which is inherent in every social practice of linguistic identification or idealization. Theorists of language tend either to elide or to sanitize such violence, in order to arrive at the simple conclusion that language equals absence. Once this is granted, it is of little consequence whether we are promised (as with Marcuse) that through further negation and idealization the repressed will be recovered, the absent made present; or whether (as is more the contemporary fashion) we are told that absence or alienation in language is our permanent condition.

What is missing from all such idealist accounts of language is Foucault's sense of discourse as an event. But in his radical, obsessive concern with the obscurity and inauthenticity of dying, Blanchot is no longer merely reiterating the cliché that language is founded upon absence or death. What is in question for him is not the truth of language as absence, but the continuing insistence of that which is always absent *from* the truth. The *event* of death is neither the motor of truth in language, nor the repressed truth of language, but rather that which language must first foreclose in order for there to be such a thing as truth at all. It is only by idealizing death itself that we are able to make death into a *power* of idealization. Blanchot reminds us again and again that "en cette dénaturation idéalisante, c'est l'obscurité même et la noire réalité de l'événement indescriptible qui s'est perdue [in this idealizing denaturation, it is the very obscurity and the dark reality of the indescribable event which is lost]" (*EI*, 49). Idealization brings everything into the light. But thereby it loses the event, the unknowable and undescribable, "l'inconnu au neutre [qui] appartient à une 'region' étrangère à cette découverte qui s'accomplit dans et par la lumière [the unknown in the neuter, belonging to a 'region' foreign to that discovery which is accomplished in and through the light]" (*EI*, 443).

When death is idealized, it never confronts, and for that very reason can never murder or abolish, the inauthenticity of the *event* of dying. The event is that excessive part of the experience of death that cannot be stated in the present, because it does not coincide with its concept, or with any concept. Its obscure otherness cannot be adequated to any subject; it is a residue or surplus in relation to any possible meaning. Isn't the harshest reality of death precisely its incommensurability, its *démesure*? "La mort, nous n'y sommes pas habitués [Death: we are not accustomed to it]" (*Le pas au-delà*, 7). Even though I know that I am going to die, it is impossible for me to assimilate my death within the horizon of my expectations. We are unable to conceive death, unable to anticipate or master it, ultimately therefore unable to *accomplish* it. The irreparable and irrecuperable *impropriety* of dying is our most shocking and most radical experience of its movement, that which makes it "non pas le terme, mais l'interminable, non pas la mort propre, mais la mort quelconque, non pas la mort vraie, mais, comme dit Kafka, 'le ricanement de son erreur capitale' [not the term, but the interminable, not death proper (or: not a proper death), but any death whatever, and not true death, but, as Kafka says, 'the sneer of its capital error']" (*EL*, 205; *SL*, 155). This "error" is what we abstract from, and try vainly to suppress, when we find the truth of infinite possibility, or even the truth of human finitude, in death: "et peut-être, en effet, est-ce la vraie mort, la mort devenue le mouvement de la vérité, mais comment ne pas pressentir qu'en cette mort véritable s'est bel et bien dérobée la mort sans vérité, ce qui en elle est irréductible au vrai, à tout dévoilement, ce qui jamais ne se révèle ni ne se cache ni n'apparaît? [and perhaps, in fact, this is the true death, death become the movement of the truth, but how can we not have the foreboding that in this true death there is hidden a death without truth, that which in death is irreducible to the truth, to any unveiling, that which never reveals itself, never conceals itself, never appears?]" (*EI*, 50).

It is now possible to respond to the objection I raised earlier. Signification, like any other form of idealization, is never total or conclusive. The signifier has no special privileges. The idealization that *is* language is no less troubled by ambiguities than the idealization that is merely recounted in language. The ideality of the signifying order is always *also* traversed by the event that it can never acknowledge, include, or represent, but that it is equally unable to expel or render absent. In a certain sense, there are no limits to idealization. We can always move self-reflexively to a higher level, take our own limits and presuppositions into account, create a metalanguage. Anything repressed can be recovered, anything hidden can be revealed, anything excluded can be reclaimed. "Admirable puissance [What wonderful power]," says Blanchot, with more than a touch of sarcasm (*La part du feu*, 316; *GO*, 46). For such victories ring hollow. When death is made into the truth of the spirit or of the signifier, it marks everything with the tautological "law" of its own limits. The self-reflecting spirit has the power of transforming everything into itself, but at the price of never being able to encounter anything other than itself. An event can always be recorded, signified, narrated, idealized; but once we have done so, what we have taken hold of is no longer an event. Everything can be explained, but what is explained is no longer what happened. "Je leur racontai l'histoire tout entière qu'ils écoutaient, me semble-t-il, avec intérêt, du moins au début. Mais la fin fut pour nous une commune surprise. 'Après ce commencement, disaient-ils, vous en viendrez aux faits.' Comment cela! Le récit était terminé [I told them the whole story and they listened, it seems to me, with interest, at least in the beginning. But the end was a surprise to all of us. 'That was the beginning,' they said. 'Now get down to the facts.' How so? The story was over!]" (*FJ*, 36; *MD*, 18).

Precisely because the idealizing process is unlimited, it can also never come to a conclusion. Everything is subsumed, murdered, dissected, reduced to nothing. One analyzes more and more, one reflects further and further, one kills again and again. Final clarity, pure visibility, is the goal. But this obsessive drive toward illumination is itself mad, excessive, a blindness. Nothing can be revealed, because nothing has been hidden. But language continues to be haunted by "ce moment qui la précède. . . . ce qui est le fondement de la parole et que la parole exclut pour parler, l'abîme, le Lazare du tombeau et non le Lazare rendu au jour, celui qui déjà sent mauvais, qui est le Mal, le Lazare perdu et non le Lazare sauvé et ressuscité [this moment which precedes it. . . . what is the foundation of speech and what speech excludes in speaking, the abyss, Lazarus in the tomb and not Lazarus brought back into the daylight, the one who already smells bad, who is Evil, Lazarus lost and not Lazarus saved and brought back to life]" (*PF*, 316; *GO*, 46). Language cannot bring back the Lazarus who is still lost; but in the process of reviving him language itself becomes lost. Symbolization does not create enough of a void. Idealization fails, not so much by any default of presence, as by a default of absence. Even when it destroys its objects, it cannot void itself of the simulacral obscurity it is pledged to overcome. This failure of negativity prompts the sardonic remark: "le vide m'a bien déçu [the void certainly disappointed me]" (*FJ*, 15; *MD*, 8). Or as the narrative voice of *Le dernier homme* similarly states, "il semble que le vide ne soit jamais assez vide [it seems that emptiness is never empty enough]" (145). It is within language itself, and not by recourse to ineffable mysteries, that we encounter the limits of signification. Like Dickinson's "Loaded Gun," the word has "but the power to kill, / Without—the power to die—" (#754).

The obscurity or "dissimulation" (*EL*, 359; *GO*, 89, *SL*, 263) of death as an event is irreducible alike to truth and falsehood, to assertion and negation, to presence and absence. And yet, the insistence of dying's inauthenticity and nontruth can be described as an *affirmation*, an affirmation which affirms nothing, which cannot even maintain itself, but which continues to affirm (*EI*, 310–11). And this affirmation corresponds to a radical materialism, what Bataille calls a "bas matérialisme [base materialism]" (*OC*, 1:220; *VE*, 45). This *neuter* movement, neither positive nor negative, is yet an affirmation of the exteriority of matter, of its irreducibility to thought. It is a materialism, not of objects as "things in themselves," but of the simulacra or images which precede any constitution of the world into objects: "Dans l'image, l'objet effleure à nouveau quelque chose qu'il avait maîtrisé pour être objet, contre quoi il s'était édifié et défini [In the image, the object again touches something it had mastered in order to be an object, something against which it had built and defined itself]" (*EL*, 347; *GO*, 81, *SL*, 256). We like to insist on the ideality of language and of the image, in order to forget their "ressemblance cadavérique [cadaverous resemblance]" (*EL*, 350; *SL*, 257, *GO*, 82). But in every idealization, the

uncanny duplicity of death continually returns; "l'apparente spiritua-
lité, la pure virginité formelle de l'image est originellement liée à l'étrangeté élémentaire et à l'informe lourdeur de l'être présent dans l'absence
[the apparent spirituality, the pure formal virginity of the image is
fundamentally linked to the elemental strangeness and to the shapeless
heaviness of the being that is present in absence]" (*EL*, 351; *GO*, 83,
SL, 258).

In every absence, there remains a certain nonideality, not only of
things, but even of language itself. This nonideality evades identity,
refuses definition in two ways: it *insists* in the indefiniteness of the
simulacrum (of the image which does not refer back to an original),
and it *subsists* as a viscous or ponderous materiality. This materiality
is what one aspect of modernist writing strives to affirm, *against* the
idealizing exigencies of the "world," of aesthetics, of religious and humanistic culture: "Elle n'est pas au-delà du monde, mais elle n'est pas
non plus le monde: elle est la présence des choses, avant que le *monde*
ne soit, leur persévérance après que le monde a disparu, l'entêtement
de ce qui subsiste quand tout s'efface et l'hébétude de ce qui apparaît
quand il n'y a rien [It is not beyond the world, but neither is it the
world itself: it is the presence of things before the *world* exists, their
perseverance after the world has disappeared, the stubbornness of what
remains when everything vanishes and the dumbfoundedness of what
appears when nothing exists]" (*La part du feu*, 317; *GO*, 47).

Idealization can never break free of the event, although the event
itself always evades idealization. It is in this sense that *La folie du jour*
continually narrates its own unnarratability. The authorities tirelessly
demand the truth behind the event, its cause or origin: "Qui vous
a jeté du verre à la face? Cette question revenait dans toutes les questions [Who threw glass in your face? That question would reappear
in all the other questions]" (*FJ*, 35; *MD*, 17). And the narrator, out
of a perverse sense of humor—or out of his profound sense that his
experience has not given him any special privileges, that he is no different from anybody else—is only all too eager to help them. But the
more the story turns back upon itself, accounts for its own lapses,
places itself ever more firmly under the interpreters' inquisitorial gaze,
the more baffling and frustrating does it become:

> Ils interpellaient mon histoire: Parle, et elle se mettait à leur
> service. En hâte, je me dépouillais de moi-même. Je leur distri-
> buais mon sang, mon intimité, je leur prêtais l'univers, je leur

donnais le jour. Sous leurs yeux en rien étonnés, je devenais une goutte d'eau, une tache d'encre. Je me réduisais à eux-mêmes, je passais tout entier sous leur vue, et quand enfin, n'ayant plus présente que ma parfaite nullité et n'ayant plus rien à voir, ils cessaient aussi de me voir, très irrités, ils se levaient en criant: Eh bien, où êtes-vous? Où vous cachez-vous? Se cacher est interdit, c'est une faute, etc. (*FJ*, 28–29)

They would challenge my story: 'Talk,' and my story would put itself at their service. In haste, I would rid myself of myself. I distributed my blood, my innermost being among them, lent them the universe, gave them the day. Right before their eyes, though they were not at all startled, I became a drop of water, a spot of ink. I reduced myself to them. The whole of me passed in full view before them, and when at last nothing was present but my perfect nothingness and there was nothing more to see, they ceased to see me too. Very irritated, they stood up and cried out, 'All right, where are you? Where are you hiding? Hiding is forbidden, it is an offense,' etc. (*MD*, 14)

As Foucault suggests, for the very reason that "power is every-where," it is also never total and all-encompassing. It diffuses and mul-tiplies, proliferates and at the same time loses itself: "Qui était inter-rogé? Qui répondait? L'un devenait l'autre. Les mots parlaient seuls. Le silence entrait en eux, refuge excellent, car personne que moi ne s'en apercevait [Who was being questioned? Who was answering? One became the other. The words spoke by themselves. The silence entered them, an excellent refuge, since I was the only one who noticed it]" (*FJ*, 36; *MD*, 17–18). Power itself never notices, but the one thing it cannot regulate or pacify is its own violent arbitrariness, its own quality as an event. Power is never firmly in place, but always continu-ally *happening*: "It is produced from one moment to the next, at every point, or rather in every relation from one point to another" (Foucault, *History of Sexuality*, 1:93). Power seeks to regularize and immobilize the delirious movement or vain agitation which alone makes it possible, and which continually escapes its grasp. The *chance* of resistance is already inscribed within, and against, every imposition of power; just as death repeatedly resists its own idealization. The *event* of death is also the infinitely extended point or moment at which death fails to be established once and for all: "Elle n'est pas non plus la mort, car en elle se montre l'existence sans l'être, l'existence qui demeure sous l'existence, comme une affirmation inexorable, sans commencement et sans terme, la mort comme impossibilité de mourir [And it is not death either, because it manifests existence without being, existence which remains below existence, like an inexorable affirmation, without beginning or end—death as the impossibility of dying]" (*La part du feu*, 317; *GO*, 47).

III

Why do we so carefully, so resolutely, deny this "inexorable affirmation"? Why do we prefer the certainty of death to the "impossibility of dying"? Aesthetic idealization is perhaps best defined as a will-to-death, a refusal at once of living and of dying: "Les hommes voudraient échapper à la mort, bizarre espèce. Et quelques-uns crient, mourir, mourir, parce qu'ils voudraient échapper à la vie. 'Quelle vie, je me tue, je me rends.' Cela est pitoyable et étrange, c'est une erreur [Men want to escape from death, strange beings that they are. And some of them cry out, 'Die, die' because they want to escape from life. 'What a life. I'll kill myself. I'll give in.' This is lamentable and strange; it is a mistake]" (*FJ*, 12–13; *MD*, 7). But what Blanchot's narrator finds so bizarre is precisely our culture's "common sense." The desire of aesthetics is a desire to lay everything to rest, to put things in their proper places, in their tombs, once and for all. And this will-to-death is not merely a psychological quirk or an existential condition. "Rendre à la mort une sorte de pureté a toujours été la tâche de la culture: la rendre authentique, personelle, propre ou encore la rendre possible [The task of culture has always been to give a kind of purity to death: to make it authentic, personal, proper, or even to render it possible]" (*EI*, 269–70). The will-to-death has an immense presence in our social life: in the political form of techniques and practices of domination, and the cultural form of a nihilistic cultivation of the death instinct. In Heidegger's words, "death reveals itself as that *possibility which is one's ownmost, which is non-relational, and which is not to be outstripped*" (*Being and Time*, 294). That is to say, it is by idealizing and investing my own death that I both preserve meaning in the world, and create a firm sense of myself. I imagine that my death can be "proper," that somehow it can *belong* to me. Which comes down to saying that I belong to it. The correlate of a life filled with care (*Sorge*) is the suicidal narcissism of such a being-towards-death. The culmination of aesthetic idealism is the state in which one feels, as Stevens puts it, "that one's desire / Is too difficult to tell from despair" ("Esthétique du Mal," in *Palm*, 262).

In short, we seek to ward off catastrophe by imagining its accomplishment, and appropriating to ourselves the achieved perfection of an "authentic" death. "Les hommes, la terreur les assiège, la nuit les perce, ils voient leurs projets anéantis, leur travail réduit en poussière, ils sont stupéfaits, eux si importants qui voulaient faire le monde, tout s'écroule [Men are assaulted by terror, the night breaks through them, they see their plans annihilated, their work turned to dust. They who were so important, who wanted to create the world, are dumbfounded; everything crumbles]" (*FJ*, 13; *MD*, 7). This terror, this male anxiety over the loss of potency, leads to an abject clinging to truths and values. The best terms for describing these processes are still, as I have already suggested, those of Nietzsche in the *Genealogy of Morals*. Idealization is a kind of asceticism, and aesthetic ideals are ascetic ideals. In order that there be some meaning, some stability, we worship, and will into existence, the very values which debase and oppress us: "Lieber will noch der Mensch *das Nichts* wollen, als *nicht* wollen . . . [Man would rather will *nothingness*, than *not* will . . .]" (*Genealogy of Morals*, 3:28, 163). We convince ourselves that the function of art is, and ought to be, to pacify ourselves through disinterest (the beautiful), to chasten and subdue ourselves by the purgation of pity and terror (the tragic), or finally to achieve transcendence by first humiliating ourselves before higher powers (the sublime).

The problem that I am trying to approach is that of getting away from our ascetic/aesthetic ideals, in order to "[voir] face à face la folie du jour [see face to face the madness of the day]," to approach the blinding brightness or palpable obscurity of the event. Not the worship of death and death's monuments, and certainly not the moral prejudice that suffering ennobles; but (as Nietzsche puts it) "an overflowing feeling of life and energy within which even pain acts as a stimulus. . . . Affirmation of life [*Das Jasagen zum Leben*] even in its strangest and sternest problems, the will to life rejoicing in its own inexhaustibility through the *sacrifice* of its highest types" (*Twilight of the Idols*, 110). If the flower's "Beauty," as Dickinson suggests, is an "Affliction" which "Bereaves the Mind," this is because it brings us a heightened affectivity, an intensification of life and death even to the point of excess: a moment of experience before or beyond experience, one which aesthetic "Tradition" will never know (#1456). Similarly, Blanchot parodies and inverts Mallarmé in order to evoke that flower whose interminable insistence no poetic voice can "relegate" to nothingness, and which therefore cannot become an aesthetic ideal:

> *Je dis une fleur!* Mais, dans l'absence où je la cite, par l'oubli où je relègue l'image qu'elle me donne, au fond de ce mot lourd, surgissant lui-même comme une chose inconnue, je convoque passionnément l'obscurité de cette fleur, ce parfum qui me traverse et que je ne respire pas, cette poussière qui m'imprègne mais que je ne vois pas, cette couleur qui est trace et non lumière. (*La part du feu*, 316)

> *I say a flower!* But in the absence where I cite it, through the oblivion to which I relegate the image it gives me, in the depths of this heavy word, itself looming up like an unknown thing, I passionately summon the darkness of this flower, I summon this perfume that passes through me though I do not breathe it, this dust that impregnates me though I do not see it, this color which is a trace and not light. (*GO*, 46)

Even as a word, this "flower" is "not ideas about the thing, but the thing itself" (Stevens, *Palm*, 387): an intensity of *sensation* which subsists (like Proust's madeleine) even in the midst of oblivion and absence. And the voice of the poet, correspondingly, no longer performs an act of magisterial incantation, but rather incarnates a *passion*, a passive alteration bringing the subject into a "contact atroce," a direct and "agonizing contact" with the day (*FJ*, 23; *MD*, 12). The subject is brought face to face with, forced to confront, an "outside" which it can never claim as its "ownmost possibility," which it cannot refer back to itself. Sensation and passion are two dimensions of an unidealizable, nonsubjective, and acultural *affectivity*: the brilliance and obscurity, the singularity and multiplicity, of the event. We are no longer in the realm of truth and values, of care and the project, of disinterest and self-recognition, of the reverent investiture of language as the voice of Being or as the Symbolic order. It is rather a question of what Blanchot sometimes calls *l'imaginaire* (the imaginary) or *le neutre* (the neuter), and which corresponds to what Lacan calls the Real; we have come "d'avoir affaire directement au jour [to be dealing directly with the day]" (*FJ*, 23; *MD*, 12).

According to Lacan's famous formula, the Real is "impossible," because it refuses all signification. It cannot be conceived or comprehended, and yet it continues violently to insist: "The Real, or that which is perceived as such, is that which absolutely resists symbolization. Doesn't the sentiment of the Real finally present itself at its maximum in the scorching [*brûlante*] manifestation of an irreal, hallucinatory reality?" (*Le séminaire*, 1:80). Elsewhere, Lacan defines "the encounter with the Real" as a trauma, as the shattering intrusion of that which is "unassimilable" to the analytic or Symbolic order (*Four Fundamental Concepts*, 53–55).

In thus invoking the Lacanian Real, I am assuming the need to re-situate some of Lacan's terms, and to dismantle his hierarchy. Lacan's supreme reference remains linguistic; his insistence on the supremacy of the Symbolic makes him an exponent of aesthetic idealization, in the sense which I have been trying to define. Language, or the Symbolic, is said to be the place of the Other, that of a nonidentity which precedes, interpellates, constitutes, and subverts any particular subject. Yet the very notion of a Symbolic, as a closed, structural order, as a force of universal mediation, as a regulator of social exchange, and as a manifestation of patriarchal Law, confines and limits the play of otherness and difference. Even though the signifier cannot itself be reduced to a fixed meaning, it produces, defines, and "anticipates" (*Ecrits*, 153) the continued *possibility* of meaning. In such a context, Lacan presents the "impossibility" of the Real only negatively, as a limit to the cure, and as the locus of a foreclosure from the Symbolic.

But in the evocation of the Real as "scorching manifestation" and as traumatic encounter, it may be that the limits of idealization are (for once) breached. For the violent irruption of the Real marks the intrusion of an alterity far more radical than any imposed by the Symbolic. The "unassimilable" arrival of the event—madness of the day, palpable obscurity of the night, ecstatic nullity of the erotic, inexhaustibility of dying—ruins any project of pacifying difference, of reducing it to possibility, of recuperating otherness in terms of dialectics or structure. The arrival of the event is at once unthinkably distant (since I cannot grasp or contain it) and impossibly immediate (since it is closer to me than I myself am): "C'est l'intimité comme Dehors, l'extérieur devenu l'intrusion qui étouffe et le renversement de l'un et de l'autre [It is intimacy as Outside, the exterior become suffocating intrusion and the reversal of each into the other]" (*EI*, 65–66). This is not the negativity of language as a great Other, but the "interval" or "interruption" of a radical discontinuity that unsettles both language and the subject, both the Symbolic and the Imaginary, both the social and the individual. Exteriority: neither a transcendental condition that would ground and anticipate possibility, nor an ultimate, transcendent term that would triumphantly establish a higher possibility beyond all possibility, but the uncanny affirmation of "impossibility."

For Blanchot, this "impossibility" of the Real is not the negation or privation of experience, but rather "cette *autre* expérience qui toujours précède [l'être] et qui est toujours plus initiale que l'affirmation qui nomme l'être [this *other* experience which always precedes Being and which is always more initial than the affirmation which names Being]" (*EI*, 67). Impossibility is even experience at its most vital, at its most extreme point: "L'impossibilité n'est rien de plus que le trait de ce que nous nommons si facilement l'expérience, car il n'y a expérience au sens stricte que là où quelque chose de radicalement *autre* est en jeu [Impossibility is nothing more than the mark of what we so facilely call experience, since there is experience in the strict sense only when something radically *other* is at stake]" (*EI*, 66). Impossibility as experience is as unavoidable as it is unassimilable, "ce qui échappe en ceci même qu'il n'y a pas à lui échapper, l'*insaisissable* dont *on ne se dessaisit pas* [that which escapes precisely in this, that it cannot be escaped, the *ungraspable* which *one does not relinquish*]" (*EI*, 65); or again, "l'inaccessible que je ne puis cesser d'atteindre, ce que je ne puis prendre, mais seulement reprendre—et jamais lâcher [the inaccessible that I cannot cease attaining, what I cannot take but only take back—and never give up]" (*EL*, 23; *GO*, 73, *SL*, 31). We have come back to the experience of Thomas, whose vision consists in his inability to see, and yet still greater inability not to see.

This impossible contact, which I am unable to accomplish but equally unable to escape, is that aspect of "experience" (of seeing and sensing, of living and dying) that remains irreducible to idealization. Blanchot describes it variously as *attirance* (attraction), *attente* (waiting), *rencontre* (encounter), and desire. For in the Real, "Le désir est précisément ce rapport à l'impossibilité . . . il est l'impossibilité qui se fait rapport, la *séparation* elle-même, en son absolu, qui se fait attirante et prend corps [Desire is precisely this relation to impossibility . . . it is impossibility which becomes relation, absolute *separation* itself, which becomes attractive and takes shape (body)]" (*EI*, 67–68). Separation is not overcome, impossibility is not transformed into the possibility which is linguistic articulation or which is personal initiative. In impossibility, there is no power, no sense of desire as the *power* of the negative. And yet, on the other hand, "Ce non-pouvoir . . .

ne serait pas la simple négation du pouvoir [This non-power . . . would not be the simple negation of power]" (*EI*, 62; cf. *EI*, 310). Desire is not fulfilled or satisfied, but neither can it be defined by "un manque qui attend d'être comblé [a lack which waits to be filled]." For desire as impossibility "est désir de ce qui ne nous manque pas, désir qui ne peut être satisfait et ne désire pas s'unir avec le désiré [is desire of that which is not lacking, desire which cannot be satisfied and which does not desire to unite itself with what it desires]" (*EI*, 76). Such a desire is not constituted by, and cannot be referred to, an ideal or patriarchal Law of interdiction and prohibition. The narrator of *La folie du jour* encounters a strange figure of the law: "non pas la loi qu'on connaît, qui est rigoureuse et peu agréable: celle-ci était autre [not the law which everyone knows, which is severe and hardly very agreeable; this law was different]" (*FJ*, 29; *MD*, 14). Desire defined by this *other* law loves and desires its own impossibility. It is neither negation *as* power, nor the negation *of* power. But rather, separation itself takes on a body, becomes desirable and attractive, becomes a relation.

In this context, the affectivity of the event is indeed "impossible" in the primary sense that it is cannot be experienced by a fully constituted phenomenological or psychoanalytic subject. The event is first of all a literally blinding, violent excess of sensation: "La lumière devenait folle, la clarté avait perdu tout bon sens; elle m'assaillait déraisonnablement, sans règle, sans but [The light was going mad, the brightness had lost all reason; it assailed me irrationally, without control, without purpose]." Such a perception is not spontaneity or immediacy, but something "prior" even to these, which affects us *before* being "given" to us in phenomenological intuition, which "fills the being before the mind can think" (Stevens, "Saint John and the Back-Ache," in *Palm*, 328). It "me traverse [passes through me]," and "m'imprègne [impregnates me]," but "I" as a subject do not see or feel it, and cannot comprehend it as *my* experience. "Présent en quoi toutes choses présentes et le moi qui y est présent sont suspendus . . . [A present in which all things present, and the ego present to them, are suspended . . .]" (*EI*, 65). Or as Deleuze describes the "insistence" and "interminable presence" of sensation in hysteria: "the identity of an already-there and of an always-late, in excessive presence. Everywhere a presence acts directly on the nervous system, and makes impossible the putting-in-place or putting-at-a-distance of a representation" (*Francis Bacon: Logique de la sensation*, 36). Everything is too close, too immediate, to admit of idealization: "J'eus l'impression de rentrer dans le mur, de divaguer dans un buisson de silex [I had the feeling I was going back into the wall, or straying into a thicket of flint]."

We are approaching a strange point, that of a nonperceptible which infects perception, an exceeding of the sensible which yet is not supersensible. As Wittgenstein says of pain or any other nonlinguistic sensation, "Sie ist kein Etwas, aber auch nicht ein Nichts! [It is not a *something*, but not a *nothing* either!]" (*Philosophical Investigations*, #304). It is equally mistaken, Wittgenstein argues, to deny the existence of an experience of pain apart from its linguistic expression, and to assert anything positive, within language, about such an experience. It is equally misleading to imagine a pure interiority of sensation prior to its expression (the idealist position denounced alike by Wittgenstein and by Derrida), and to imagine that sensation is therefore *nothing but* its expression in language and behavior (the position shared, oddly enough, by neo-behaviorists and neo-pragmatists like Richard Rorty, and by literary deconstructionists like Paul de Man and his followers). Wittgenstein, like Blanchot and Bataille, rather indicates sensation as a paradoxical "expérience de la non-expérience [experience of non-experience]" (*EI*, 311). It is an experience without categories and without unity, "où l'*autre* ne revient jamais au même [where the *other* never comes back to the same]" (*EI*, 65), which has no positive content, but which for this very reason is "pure affirmation, elle ne fait qu'affirmer [pure affirmation, it only affirms]" (*EI*, 310).

This radical affectivity is indeed "without a concept," but in a very different sense than that intended by Kantian aesthetics. The difference may be indicated briefly. If the imagination operates without concepts, then the work of synthesis in the imagination takes place without fitting into the form of the transcendental unity of apperception in the ego. The synthesis is asubjective and nonspontaneous, or what Deleuze calls a "passive synthesis" (*Différence et répétition*, 97–115), which also defines a desire not founded in negativity (*Anti-Oedipus*, 25–29). There is no freedom in the sense of unconstrained free play of the faculties (as beauty is defined by Kant); but rather the constraint that an immediate, more-than-spontaneous sensation exerts on the sensibility. And passion, as we shall see, alters the subject, rather than molding itself in spontaneous harmony with a pregiven form of unity in the understanding. The insistence of the "impossible" event reintroduces the materiality of sensation (as a compulsion or interest) into the notion of the beautiful, and the singularity of passion (as an impersonal, but nonnegative and nonuniversalizable, form of desire) into the notion of the sublime.

What can be said, then, of an "*other* experience," one which eludes linguistic, aesthetic, logical, and ontological definition? What of the movement of "separation," the "impossible" relation of the subject in the Real, a relation which is not one of comprehension or representation? A second aspect of the event is the ex-centric movement of passion: "J'avais à tenir tête à la lumière de sept jours: un bel embrasement! Oui, sept jours ensemble, les sept clartés capitales devenues la vivacité d'un seul instant me demandaient des comptes. Qui aurait imaginé cela? [I had to hold my own against the light of seven days—a fine conflagration! Yes, seven days at once, the seven deadly lights, become the spark of a single moment, were calling me to account. Who would have imagined that?]" (*FJ*, 22; *MD*, 11). The subject is "called to account" by an instance it cannot comprehend or even possibly imagine; it "responds" only to the extent that it is irrevocably altered by the multiplicities it encounters. The more-than-passivity of a subject that cannot endure or sustain it is the mark of passion at its most intense and most pure: "l'impossibilité est le rapport avec le Dehors et, puisque ce rapport sans rapport est la passion qui ne se laisse pas maîtriser en patience, l'impossibilité est la passion du Dehors même [impossibility is relation with the Outside; and since this relation without relation is passion which does not let itself be mastered into patience, impossibility is the passion of the Outside itself]" (*EI*, 66).

This splendid and terrible "conflagration," or hysterical condensation of light into a "single moment," is also what Dickinson calls a journey, a traversal, "a transport one cannot contain" (#184). A double movement of displacement and intensification is always in process, neither beginning nor ending at any fixed point. Passion is transition, a repeated Nietzschean *Untergang* (going-under), absolute displacement: "Affliction cannot stay / In Acres—Its Location / Is Illocality—" (Dickinson, #963). The impassioned subject is the site of this "Illocality," an undeterminable point of metamorphosis. In the midst of its journey, the subject neither enacts nor suffers its passions, so much as it finds itself already affected by them. The passion most proper to the subject approaches it only from outside and marks within it only a perpetual disjunction: "En outre, j'entendais des cris d'hyène qui me mettaient sous la menace d'une bête sauvage (ces cris, je crois, étaient les miens) [What was more, I heard hyena cries that exposed me to the threat of a wild animal (I think these cries were my own)]"

(*FJ*, 21; *MD*, 11). The narrator is nakedly exposed to the "menace" of passion in these cries, which traverse him, alter him, and leave him behind. Yet it is only when he is no longer shaken by them, no longer the one who utters them, that he can claim such cries as his own.

Passion, in Dickinson's terms, is "Acute Degree" (#1072), a degree or level of intensity which nevertheless is not a degree *of* something in particular. Passion does not inhere in a subject or substance, it does not qualify anything; its specificity is that of an adjective without a noun, an accident or modification not attached to any substrate. "Acute Degree" is literally oxymoronic; it is transport and pain, "Title divine" and dispossession, affliction and *jouissance*, all at the same moment. As Deleuze and Guattari describe it: "there is a schizophrenic experience of intensive quantities in their pure state, to a point that is almost unbearable—a celibate misery and glory experienced to the fullest, like a cry suspended between life and death, an intense feeling of transition, states of pure, naked intensity stripped of all shape and form" (*Anti-Oedipus*, 18).

However unbearable, however impossible, however ambiguous, this passion, this "Acute Degree," this agony of "a Soul *at the White Heat*" (Dickinson, #365) marks a radical break from the morbidity of a tradition that knows only care, abjection, and despair. For, again and again, such an experience of "pure intensity" is finally and (as Blanchot says) inexorably *affirmative*: "Je vis que même aux pires jours, quand je me croyais parfaitement et entièrement malheureux, j'étais cependant, et presque tout le temps, extrêmement heureux [I saw that even on the worst days, when I thought I was utterly and completely miserable, I was nevertheless, and nearly all the time, extremely happy]" (*FJ*, 12; *MD*, 7).

The narrator adds that "cette découverte n'était pas agréable [This discovery was not a pleasant one]" (*FJ*, 12; *MD*, 7). And indeed, I am never equal to it. It is this excessive happiness and affliction, this affirmation, this unbearable extremity of desire, which provokes the defensive anxieties of aesthetic idealization. The event, sensation and passion, admits of no fixity, no determination. Unlimited modification, continual metamorphosis, it always involves violence and destruction. But these permanent revolutions of desire could not be further removed from the will-to-death of critical negativity and nihilistic *ressentiment*. The event's violence is rather that "approbation de la vie jusque dans la mort [approbation of life up to the point of death]" (*OC*, 10: 17; *Erotism*, 11) by which Bataille defines eroticism. Its destructivity is rather that performed by the joyous music at the end of Marguerite Duras's *Détruire dit-elle* [*Destroy She Said*], "fracassant les arbres, foudroyant les murs [felling trees, knocking down walls]" in the movement of Alissa's "rire absolu [absolute, or pure, laughter]" (136–37; 85). The ground is not solid; when things seem most "still," when power appears most firmly entrenched, the earth is traversed and undermined by the obscure, yet overwhelming, irruption of "A quiet— Earthquake Style." Like Dickinson's sexual "Volcano," which is not to be separated from "Life" itself, the event may be "too subtle" for the eyes of power to "detect," or even "suspect"; yet its "hissing Corals part—and shut— / And Cities—ooze away" (#601).

The event is absolutely ambiguous, because it is at once impossible and inescapable, unapproachable and insurmountable, invisible and all too visible. Blinding, or "erasing sight—" if looked at directly, the event is therefore all too easily *over*looked. Various strategies are available for such overlooking. There are the positivist and sociological reductions, which simply declare the event inexistent, because unrepresentable. Complementary to this position is its idealizing opposite, which seeks precisely to represent the event, to render it visible, to fix it in the final form of "itself." There are phenomenological approaches, which attempt to master the excess of sensation by referring it back to a transcendental subject; and negative-theological ones, which recuperate the displacements of desire by reading the very insufficiencies of representation as signs of absolute transcendence. Either we flee the event in terror; or else we are lulled with assurances that it is something to which we are already "appropriated," that it is already our own.

The absolute ambiguity of the event, its gratuitousness, its not having any proper "truth" of its own, makes possible all these exclusions and recuperations, disavowals and recognitions. Anything is possible, when the event as such, as the Real, is "impossible." Yet if we never stop making sense, never stop erecting tombstones or aesthetic monuments, we *also* never succeed in freeing ourselves from the obsession, the madness, what Blanchot calls the *fascination* (*EL*, 22–27; *GO*, 72–76, *SL*, 30–33) of the event itself: "Je ne pouvais ni regarder ni ne pas regarder; voir c'était l'épouvante, et cesser de voir me déchirait . . . [I could not look, but I could not help looking. To see was terrifying, and to stop seeing tore me apart]." The event is traumatic, make no mistake; but we need more such traumas, to upset the fatal equilibrium of power, to disrupt the complacencies of culture. "La beauté sera CONVULSIVE ou ne sera pas [Beauty will be CONVULSIVE or not at all]" (Breton, *Nadja*). This trauma and convulsion is not a master-trope or a hidden meaning. It is "untimely" (*unzeitgemäss*), its effect "posthumous," in Nietzsche's peculiar sense of these words. For perhaps the event is always going to be buried under the dual weight of Imaginary denial and Symbolic idealization. Belief in a "true world," what Nietzsche calls the long "history of an error," is not going to vanish overnight (*Twilight of the Idols*, 40). And yet the error which we call truth is not self-sufficing and all-inclusive. The moment comes when the security it offers is not enough: "Je voulais voir quelque chose en plein jour; j'étais rassasié de l'agrément et du confort de la pénombre. . . . Et si voir c'était le feu, j'exigeais la plénitude du feu, et si voir c'était la contagion de la folie, je désirais follement cette folie [I wanted to see something in full daylight; I was sated with the pleasure and comfort of the half light. . . . And if seeing was fire, I required the plenitude of fire, and if seeing would infect me with madness, I madly wanted that madness]" (*FJ*, 23–24; *MD*, 12).

*Ecrire en ce sens . . . suppose une changement radicale
d'époque—la mort même, l'interruption—ou, pour parler hyperboliquement, "la fin de l'histoire," et, par là,
passe par l'avènement du communisme, reconnu comme
l'affirmation ultime, le communisme étant toujours
encore au-delà du communisme.*
—Maurice Blanchot, *L'entretien infini*

CHAPTER   2

Reckless Calculations

Bataille and the Political Economy of Expenditure

Car ce qui est tombé dans un vide sans fond est l'*assise* des choses. Et ce qui est proposé à une conquête impavide—non plus à un duel où se joue la mort du héros contre celle du monstre, en échange d'une durée indifférente—ce n'est pas une créature isolée, c'est le vide même et la chute vertigineuse, c'est le TEMPS. Car le mouvement de toute la vie place maintenant l'être humain dans l'alternative de cette conquête ou d'un désastreux recul. L'être humain arrive au seuil: là il est nécessaire de se précipiter vivant dans ce qui n'a plus d'assise ni de tête. (*OC*, 1:513)

For it is the *foundation* of things that has fallen into a bottomless void. And what is fearlessly conquered—no longer in a duel where the death of the hero is risked against that of the monster, in exchange for an indifferent duration—is not an isolated creature; it is the very void and the vertiginous fall, it is TIME. The movement of all life now places the human being before the alternatives of either this conquest or a disastrous retreat. The human being arrives at the threshold: there he must throw himself headlong into that which has no foundation and no head. (*VE*, 222)

Few modern writers confront the violence of the *event* as directly and as urgently as does Georges Bataille. Few insist with such passion on the necessity of sacrifice, the splendor of the "vertiginous fall." Yet if the intensity of Bataille's involvement is clear, the details of its expression are not. Does the passage which I have just quoted function as description or as exhortation? On what sort of threshold are we standing, and what is the nature of the "void" which lies beyond it? At such a point, what kind of "alternative" is at stake? What further disaster could be entailed by a "retreat"? And is it even possible to retreat? Since the foundations have already crumbled, is not a fall inevitable? But what sort of courage is available in such a situation? What kind of "conquest" is it which is no longer played out according to the dialectic of master and slave, with the risk of heroic death as ultimate stake? What experience of TIME is realized by this leap into the void?

The only way to answer such questions may be to alter the way in which they are posed. For the peculiar effect of Bataille's work is that it offers no satisfying conclusions, no points of repose. Not even the satisfaction of absolute destruction. His obsessive meditations concern—and participate in—a catastrophe all the more obscure and unsettling in that it refuses apocalyptic closure. "Ce qui seul demeure est l'agitation circulaire—qui ne s'épuise pas dans l'extase et recommence à partir d'elle [What alone remains is circular agitation—which does not exhaust itself in ecstasy and begins again from it]" (*OC*, 5:130; *IE*, 111). The "vertiginous fall" takes place in a "bottomless void," and consequently never hits bottom. The privileged act of sacrifice serves no end, leads to no appeasement. And despite Bataille's frequent sexual stereotyping and invocations of virility, his "interior experience" does not culminate in any display of phallic mastery. Pure loss, expenditure without recompense, it issues only in an absurd compulsion to repeat, to approach the threshold of disaster again and again. The "summit" of ecstasy cannot be extricated from a concomitant "decline": "De même que le sommet n'est à la fin que l'inaccessible, le déclin dès l'abord est l'inévitable [Just as the summit is finally only the inaccessible, so the decline, from the very first, is inevitable]" (*OC*, 6:57). The exuberant violence of Bataille's texts is matched only by the pointless dissipation of the energies they invoke. Fractured temporality, terrifying affirmation of the Eternal Return: "L'acte d'audace qui représente le 'retour,' au sommet de ce déchirement, ne fait qu'arracher à Dieu mort sa puissance *totale* pour la donner à l'absurdité délétère du TEMPS [The audacious act that represents the 'return' at the summit of this rending agony only wrests from the dead God his *total* strength, in order to give it to the deleterious absurdity of TIME]" (*OC*, 1:510; *VE*, 220).

But how can such an affirmation of TIME take place within ordinary time? The "vertiginous fall" marks a radical rupture of linear temporality. It is a "present" that no longer assures the homogeneous passage from past to future, and that refuses subordination to any teleology. Yet for this very reason, it cannot be posited outside time and history, as if it were static and eternal. "Le temps extatique ne peut se trouver que dans la vision des choses que le hasard puéril fait brusquement survenir: cadavres, nudités, explosions, sang répandu, abîmes, éclat du soleil et du tonnerre [Ecstatic time can only find itself in the vision of things that puerile chance causes brusquely to appear: cadavers, nudity, explosions, spilled blood, abysses, sunbursts, and thunder]" (*OC*, 1:471; *VE*, 200). The accidents that violently extricate us from historical context and linear order are themselves arbitrary waste products of the most massively overdetermined historical movements. The event remains embedded within the chain of causes whose continuity it randomly disrupts. Bataille's affirmation of the event as "chance" implies both its insurpassable historicity (it is radically contingent, and could not have occurred in any other way, or at any other time than just now), and its gratuitousness or lack of necessity (it is so radically contingent that it cannot be predicted or determined as a function of the historical situation out of which it "brusquely" and unexpectedly emerges).

The "deleterious absurdity" of the event must thus be approached by way of its specific social and political context, even if its whole import is to disrupt that context. "The movement of all life" which compels a "conquest" of the abyss is that of the rise of fascism in Europe in the years just before World War II. Progressivist historicism was unable to account for or respond to this situation. The forces of social conflict—which Hegelian Marxism was accustomed to view in terms of an unfolding of rational necessity—had instead gone disastrously astray. In the crisis-ridden economic climate of the 1930s, bourgeois society indeed seemed on the verge of total collapse. But the Soviet Union, under Stalin, no longer offered any prospects of revolutionary transformation. And the fascist states of Germany and Italy could not be explained away as merely momentary aberrations. Their "solutions" to the antinomies of bourgeois social life were all too brutally effective. Putting negativity to work as never before, fascism increasingly appeared as a terrifying, ironic realization of the Hegelian dream of "the end of history."

Such was the situation that Bataille confronted in his early essay (1933–34) "La structure psychologique du fascisme" ["The Psychological Structure of Fascism"] (*OC*, 1:339–71; *VE*, 137–60). The very magnitude of the fascist threat, its success in mobilizing the masses, cast traditional notions of meaningful political activity into doubt. On one hand, the weakness of reformist or social-democratic approaches to the problems of capitalism was evident as never before. But on the other hand, revolutionary action seemed equally lacking in efficacy. For the radical convulsions traversing Western bourgeois society showed a fatal tendency to issue more in imperative (fascist, totalitarian) than in subversive (communist, revolutionary) forms. The Left was faced, according to Bataille, with the horrible irony of a radical disjunction between the so-called objective and subjective conditions for revolution: "à mesure que les possibilités révolutionnaires s'affirment, disparaissent les chances de la révolution ouvrière, les chances d'une subversion libératrice de la société [the chances for a working class revolution, a liberating subversion of society, disappear to the extent that revolutionary possibilities are affirmed]" (*OC*, 1:370; *VE*, 159). In such a situation, revolutionary action seems doomed in advance, defeated more effectively by co-optation than it ever could be by outright suppression.

Clearly a new approach was needed to the task of forging "la destinée humaine libre, l'arrachant à l'asservissement rationnel de la production comme à l'asservissement irrationnel au passé [a free human destiny, tearing it away from the rational enslavement of production, as well as from the irrational enslavement to the past]" (*OC*, 1:465; *VE*, 194). In the rituals of Acéphale, the "secret society" or "conspiracy" which absorbed most of his efforts between 1936 and 1939, Bataille sought to articulate a sufficiently violent libertarian response to fascism's sinister sublimation of violence and binding of social energies. From a position of willed marginality, the Acéphale group attempted at once to make a decisive political intervention, and to transgress the limits which circumscribe any definition of the "political." "Il est nécessaire de produire et de manger: beaucoup de choses sont nécessaires qui ne sont encore rien et il en est également ainsi de l'agitation politique [It is necessary to produce and to eat: many things are necessary that are still nothing, and so it is with political agitation]" (*OC*, 1:442; *VE*, 179). Political necessity is a matter of survival and may not be belittled or denied. But it must be fused with "interior experience" in the sacrificial violence of "nonproductive expenditure." Such a movement finds its highest, most violent expression in the simultaneous ascent (of the scaffold) and fall (into the abyss) of the act of decapitation. Making a bloody sacrifice of all coherence and all order: for it seemed that only the most intense movement of decomposition could have sufficient explosive force to disrupt the rigidity of fascist organization.

Bataille was not alone at this time in being driven to what might seem to be "metaphysical" extremes. Walter Benjamin—whose relation with Bataille and with Bataille's colleagues in the Collège de Sociologie has still not been adequately explored—was also obsessed with the role of catastrophe (in Benjamin's terms, "shock") as a crucial experience of modern capitalist culture. Shock, for Benjamin, is an overdetermined, intensely ambiguous, and inescapable moment of violent condensation. Abolishing traditional structures of subjectivity, it is a dominating instance of both actual oppression and possible liberation. Both the psychological devastation caused by the worker's enslavement to the assembly line and the unleashing of subversive energies as a result of unchecked processes of mechanical reproduction may be seen (like the experience of the urban crowd) as repercussions of "the disintegration of the aura in the experience of shock" (*Illuminations*, 194). And the traumatic, double-bind structure of "shock," the simultaneous necessity and impossibility of mastering it or finding some adequate response to it, leads to an extreme polarization of political alternatives. The most obvious and frightening reaction is the fascist aestheticization of politics, its apotheosis of violence in the shape of spectacle. But in the face of such a reality, Benjamin can posit liberation only in a form equally marked by the trauma of shock. In the "Theses on the Philosophy of History," he proposes a Messianic vision of revolution as a violent explosion of heterogeneity, rupturing linear, progressive time.

The extremism of Benjamin's and Bataille's formulations makes it difficult to see how they can be applied to concrete situations of social struggle. It is easy to point out the absurdity of Acéphale's projects of voluntary self-sacrifice and communal ecstasy. But this is an "absurdity" on which Bataille himself was the first to insist. Absurdity, for Bataille, is not the negative condition it is regarded as by teleological thinkers and existentialists. It is an affirmation that opposes the capitalist logic of putting all productive forces to work. "[L'homme] est libre de ressembler à tout ce qui n'est pas lui dans l'univers. Il peut écarter la pensée que c'est lui ou Dieu qui empêche le reste des choses d'être absurde [(Man) is free to resemble everything that is not himself in the universe. He can set aside the thought that it is he or God who keeps the rest of things from being absurd]" (*OC*, 1:445; *VE*, 180). The problem, then, is not how to give meaning and force to otherwise absurd and inefficacious acts. It is rather how to prevent sacrifice and expenditure from becoming (as is the case in fascism) new grounds of power or signification.

The crucial point is the relation of gratuitous expenditure to actual configurations of power (processes of exploitation and domination). Bataille, like Benjamin, points to the role of violent excess within capitalism. The ideological premise of bourgeois society is its ability to "keep the rest of the universe from being absurd," by means of an infinite process of rationalization and calculation. But in times of extreme political tension, like the 1930s, it becomes less and less possible to rationalize the political and economic realms, to keep them separate from the blinding exigencies of "l'immense travail d'abandon, d'écoulement et d'orage qui constitue [la vie] [the immense travail of recklessness, discharge and upheaval that constitutes life]" (*OC*, 1:318; *VE*, 128).

The convulsions of a period like the 1930s only make more evident the violence which always subtends bourgeois culture. Most obviously, violence on a massive scale is required (under the cloak of political legitimacy) first to accomplish primitive accumulation, and then to continue to enforce capitalist property relations. But beyond this, an ever-present possibility of catastrophic dislocation haunts the sphere of market equivalences itself. The "psychological" notions of shock in Benjamin and expenditure in Bataille find their economic counterpart in Marx's fundamental insight that disequilibrium—repeated economic crisis—is a "normal" condition, immanent to the functioning of capitalism as a system. Marx's matchless irony is never more in evidence than when he discusses the simple and expanded reproduction schemes in volume 2, and the transformation of values into prices in volume 3, of *Capital*. In both cases, the derivation of equilibrium conditions has the force of a *reductio ad absurdum*—so many unwarranted or unlikely assumptions are necessary in order to achieve the homeostatic balance which bourgeois political economists consider a "natural" outcome of the free market. The machine of capitalist production and circulation operates only "by continually breaking down" (as Deleuze and Guattari paraphrase Marx, *Anti-Oedipus*, 8).

For Bataille as for Marx, such breakdown is the inescapable horizon of bourgeois property relations. The imminence of crisis or catastrophe at once permits and limits those relations. This is because the universal equivalence defined by exchange values, although ubiquitous, is not exhaustive. Capitalism defines a totality (a "restricted economy"), but at the same time unleashes forces which exceed and disrupt that totality. According to Marx, the perpetual threat of economic crisis is inscribed within the capitalist system at precisely that point around which the system as a whole is articulated: that of the extraction, without an equivalent, of surplus value. Disequilibrium is endemic to the system because it is the condition under which commodity production, and the concomitant establishment of money as universal equivalent, is alone possible.

The same point can be made in more specifically Bataillean terms. Exchange value is the capitalist form of what Bataille, in the essay on fascism, calls *homogeneity*, and all capitalist relations are inscribed in the utilitarian or *homogeneous* sphere. "*Homogénéité* signifie ici commensurabilité des éléments et conscience de cette commensurabilité. . . . La base de l'*homogénéité* sociale est la production. . . . La commune mesure, fondement de l'*homogénéité* sociale et de l'activité qui en relève, est l'argent [*Homogeneity* signifies here the commensurability of elements and the awareness of this commensurability. . . . Production is the basis of social *homogeneity*. . . . The common denominator, the foundation of social *homogeneity* and of the activity arising from it, is money]" (*OC*, 1:340; *VE*, 137–38). And in the capitalist world of abstract labor and generalized commodity production, nothing escapes reduction to homogeneity (everything is a commodity, everything has its price). Even (or especially) human subjectivity is commodified and reproduced, in the form of labor power.

But although no element of society escapes being coded by the abstract possibility of homogeneous exchange, this process of universal coding is not self-sufficient and self-perpetuating. "En principe, l'*homogénéité* sociale est une forme précaire, à la merci de la violence et même de tout dissentiment interne [As a rule, social *homogeneity* is a precarious form, at the mercy of violence and even of internal dissent]" (*OC*, 1:341; *VE*, 139). The reduction to homogeneity always also involves a certain reference to processes which *at the same time* cannot be adequated to or included within this reduction. Social existence also entails the play of what Bataille calls *heterogeneous* elements, in themselves "éléments impossibles à assimiler [elements that are impossible to assimilate]" (*OC*, 1:344; *VE*, 140), but whose "imperative" force makes reduction and assimilation possible.

Bataille makes the same point in another way in his major essays on economics, "La notion de dépense" ["The Notion of Expenditure"] (*OC*, 1:302–20; *VE*, 116–29) and *La part maudite* (*OC*, 7:17–179). He insists that the violent excess and sheer waste of "dépense improductive [unproductive expenditure]" is inherent in all social formations. Although capitalism attempts to perform precisely such a reduction, "l'activité humaine n'est pas entièrement réductible à des processus de production et de conservation [human activity is not entirely reducible to processes of production and conservation]" (*OC*, 1:305; *VE*, 118). Given "le caractère secondaire de la production et de l'acquisition par rapport à la dépense [the secondary character of production and acquisition in relation to expenditure]" (*OC*, 1:308; *VE*, 121), the logic of accumulation governing capitalist economic relations leads only to a hypocritical dissimulation of primary expenditure, not to its abolition.

Heterogeneous existence, and unproductive expenditure, are therefore crucially, and irreducibly, ambiguous. They have a peculiar status, at once inside and outside the circuit of production, acquisition, and exchange. They seem in one way to participate in homogeneous reduction, and in another way to refuse such participation. They exceed the limits of the economic, but can only be represented within those limits. They escape power and subordination, and yet provide the basis for all impositions of power. For its part, the capitalist economy is founded simultaneously upon their rejection and their incorporation. Bataille is in accord with Marx in insisting at once on the insurpassability and the inadequacy of political economy, or (as Gayatri Spivak puts it with regard to Marx) in rejecting "economic reductionism" and "the disavowal of the economic" alike (*In Other Worlds*, 169).

To the extent that they are posited as objectively real, heterogeneous elements do not escape the adequation in terms of exchange value that ontologically as well as economically defines the objective social world. Heterogeneity is not a separate realm of privileged entities or superior values that somehow escape reification and commodification. Rather, its elements are unassimilable only insofar as they are not entities, and do not possess value or meaning in the manner usually understood. Mobile and evanescent, they cannot be posited, fixed, or located.

> La réalité des éléments *hétérogènes* n'est pas du même ordre que celle des éléments *homogènes*. La réalité *homogène* se présente avec

l'aspect abstrait et neutre des objets strictement définis et identifiés (elle est, à la base, réalité spécifique des objets solides). La réalité *hétérogène* est celle de la force ou du choc. Elle se présente comme une charge, comme une valeur, passant d'un objet à l'autre d'une façon plus ou moins arbitraire. (*OC*, 1:347)

The reality of *heterogeneous* elements is not of the same order as that of *homogeneous* elements. *Homogeneous* reality presents itself with the abstract and neutral aspect of strictly defined and identified objects (basically, it is the specific reality of solid objects). *Heterogeneous* reality is that of a force or shock. It presents itself as a charge, as a value, passing from one object to another in a more or less arbitrary fashion. (*VE*, 143)

The paradoxical tensions which define the relation of heterogeneous to homogeneous elements, and of unproductive expenditure to utility and conservation, cannot be called "contradictions," because they are not susceptible to teleological unfolding or dialectical resolution. As Joseph Libertson, Bataille's most attentive and insightful reader, puts it, Bataille's logic "consists of two terms which oppose each other violently, and simultaneously condition each other so intimately as to compromise the univocity of their opposition" ("Bataille and Communication," 679). It is within the same movement that heterogeneity or expenditure is a catastrophic, unassimilable nonpower, that it is a power which enforces assimilation, and that it is itself subordinated or assimilated.

In the first place, "L'existence *hétérogène* peut être représentée par rapport à la vie courante (quotidienne) comme *tout autre*, comme *incommensurable*, en chargeant ces mots de la valeur *positive* qu'ils ont dans l'expérience vécue *affective* [Compared to everyday life, *heterogeneous* existence can be represented as *entirely other*, as *incommensurate*, by charging these words with the *positive* value they have in *affective* lived experience]" (*OC*, 1:348; *VE*, 143). If definition, like expression in terms of exchange value, is what makes disparate objects or concepts interchangeable, then heterogeneous elements necessarily escape definition. Their radical alterity means that they can be characterized only by their "*différence non logique* [nonlogical difference]" (*OC*, 1:319; *VE*, 129) from commodities, or from objects possessing an intelligible signification and susceptible to pragmatic manipulation. They are *exceptions* to the values and constraints of a rationalized social existence, which is to say that they are in a radical sense meaningless and useless. For from the point of view of utility, they are nothing more than irreducible remainders, embodying a certain quantity of loss or waste which is inevitable in every closed system. Expenditure, therefore, cannot be given any substantial expression or assigned any mode of presence. It is not reducible to conceptual formulation for the same reason, and to the same extent, that it is not recuperable within social production. For to capture, exploit, or express it in any way is ipso facto to place it within the horizon of utility, hence to misconstrue it. Recognized or put to work, it is no longer free and unproductive.

The only positive "reality" attributable to heterogeneous elements is that of a sort of random violence unleashed when boundaries break down, when the isolation of determinate subjects and objects is ecstatically or brutally ruptured. "Il n'y a plus sujet=objet, mais 'brèche béante' entre l'un et l'autre et, dans la brèche, le sujet, l'objet sont dissous, il y a passage, communication, mais non de l'un à l'autre: *l'un* et *l'autre* ont perdu l'existence distincte [There is no longer subject=object, but a 'gaping breach' between the one and the other and, in the breach, the subject and object are dissolved, there is passage, communication, but not from one to the other: *the one* and *the other* have lost their separate existence]" (*OC*, 5:74; *IE*, 59). Unproductive expenditure is nothing other than the "force" or "shock" of such a breach or rupture. In the violence of this movement, there is neither fusional identity between subject and object, nor separation of one from, and possession of one by, the other. The "discontinuity" of the isolated entity is broken, but it is not replaced by participation in some higher unity. Nothing remains constant except for the impossibility of limiting or specifying this process. "Le mouvement est la figure de l'amour incapable de s'arrêter sur un être en particulier et passant rapidement de l'un à l'autre [Movement is the figure of love, incapable of stopping at a particular being, and rapidly passing from one to another]" (*OC*, 1:83; *VE*, 7).

Bataille insists upon the "valeur *positive* [*positive* value]," the affirmative quality of this movement of unproductive expenditure. He enacts a Nietzschean "reversal of perspectives" in order to approach utilitarian closure from the point of view of the "énergie excédente [exceeding energy]" (*OC*, 7:31), which it is unable to contain. It is only by homogeneous reduction that heterogeneous elements appear as remainders and exceptions. From the point of view of "l'économie à la mesure de l'univers [economy on a universal scale]" (*OC*, 7:9–23), the action of heterogeneity is not exhausted by the impossibility of possessing or representing it. The *excess* which is deducted or excluded from useful and comprehensible activity nonetheless positively invests that activity. Far from being merely instances of loss and waste, these orgies of heterogeneous expenditure—sacred or obscene moments of affective fascination—define the "possibilités *excessives* [*excessive* possibilities]" of life lived to its fullest (*OC*, 3:381).

The hierarchy of utility must therefore be inverted: it is only the need to expend energy on a massive scale which makes production and conservation possible and necessary. From the perspective of excess, "il devient possible, toute réserve abandonée, d'assigner à l'utilité une valeur *relative*. Les hommes assurent leur subsistance ou évitent la souffrance, non parce que ces fonctions engagent par elles-mêmes un résultat suffisant, mais pour accéder à la fonction insubordonée de la dépense libre [it becomes possible, having abandoned all reserves, to assign a *relative* value to utility. Men assure their own subsistence, or avoid suffering, not because these functions themselves lead to a sufficient result, but in order to accede to the insubordinate function of free expenditure]" (*OC*, 1:320; *VE*, 129). Stability and internal cohesion are secondary functions of the very processes which disrupt them, and which they are unable to include or take into account. No representation, no ordering of power relations, is thinkable without reference to an unthinkable and irreducible *outside*. Even subjectivity is generated only by the "contagion" of outside elements: "Ce sont des contagions d'énergie, de mouvement, de chaleur ou des transferts d'éléments, qui constituent intérieurement la vie de ton être organique [These are contagions of energy, of movement, of heat, or transfers of elements, which internally constitute the life of your organic being]" (*OC*, 5:111; *IE*, 94).

As an affirmative force, expenditure remains outside the "totality" or closed economic system which it nonetheless affects by "contagion." The contaminating influence of heterogeneity on the homogeneous world can be summarized under three rubrics: it is simultaneously evasive, constitutive, and disruptive. In the first place, the "exceeding energy" of pure loss cannot be conceptualized, captured or (re)presented. But in the second place, it is only the investment of this energy which makes the limited economy of representation and homogeneous reduction possible. Any system of calculation and regulation is finally dependent upon forces and movements which cannot themselves be calculated and regulated, or represented within it. Yet in the third place, this investment is not the ultimate horizon of heterogeneity. The effect of "exceeding energy" on a limited system is ultimately catastrophic. Radical expenditure continually haunts and threatens to disrupt, even as it escapes from, the various modes of social organization and regulation.

The ambiguity of expenditure suggests that the simple distinction between heterogeneity and homogeneity is less important than "le dualisme fondamental du monde *hétérogène* [the fundamental dualism of the *heterogeneous* world]" (*OC*, 1:349; *VE*, 144) itself, its division into subversive (affirmative or catastrophic) and imperative (reactive or conservative) forms. For heterogeneity as such cannot be voluntarily accepted or refused; it will affect or invest homogeneity in any case. The important question is what form this intervention will take. If expenditure is not actively affirmed, it will still insist reactively. If it is dialectically recognized and reduced, "taken into account" rather than allowed free discharge, it will nonetheless incalculably insinuate itself. "Tant que les hommes oublieront la véritable nature de la vie terrestre, qui exige l'ivresse extatique et l'éclat, cette nature ne pourra se rappeler à l'attention des comptables et des économistes de tout parti qu'en les abandonnant aux résultats les plus achevés de leur comptabilité et de leur économie [As long as men forget the true nature of terrestrial life, which demands ecstatic drunkenness and splendor, nature can only come to the attention of the accountants and economists of all parties by abandoning them to the most complete results of their accounting and economics]" (*OC*, 1:472; *VE*, 201).

Expenditure is primarily affirmative, subversive, and catastrophic. It is a positive expression of the "principe d'insuffisance [principle of insufficiency]" which, Bataille says, "existe à la base de la vie humaine [exists at the basis of human life]" (*OC*, 5:97; *IE*, 81). Blanchot rightly insists on the importance of this notion for Bataille, and on the impossibility of deriving it from a previously established concept of completion or sufficiency (*CI*, 15–20; *UC*, 5–8). Neither an individual subject nor a community can escape the radical and incessant putting into question of its internal coherence, its hierarchical organization, and its claim to totality or closure. This putting-into-question is what Marx calls class struggle, and what Bataille describes as an infinite process of "contestation." The social totality, like the individual organism, is traversed by a potential for catastrophe, an irreducible "outside" inscribed within its very being.

It is in this sense that the "most complete result" of bourgeois economic calculation is ironically its own decomposition. In and of itself, utilitarian or productive activity lacks finality; as a practice of universal subordination, it "constitue une existence *pour autre chose que soi* [constitutes an existence *for something other than itself*]" (*OC*, 1:340; *VE*, 138). Everything is a means, and the *otherness* of the end is infinitely deferred. But in the absence of any teleology, the internal regulation of a system of endless economic activity becomes increasingly problematic. The more homogeneous a society becomes, the more its hierarchies of power and value tend to be leveled, and the less capable that society is of enforcing the homogeneous reduction on which it is predicated. This is why capitalism is characterized by "une dissociation tendancielle [a tendential dissociation]" (*OC*, 1:343; *VE*, 140), an intrinsic movement that opens it to multiplicity and conflict. For Bataille as for Marx, "tendential" processes are not extrinsic influences or negative determinations, but positive movements inherent in the very structures they seem to disrupt (see Etienne Balibar's discussion of Marx's notion of "tendency" in Althusser et al., *Reading Capital*, 286–93). *Heterogeneity* is affirmative or subversive to the extent that it is already immanent, as a tendency, within the homogeneous economic world.

This leads to a more general point. A social formation should be defined not by its banal and oppressive modes of cohesion, but by the possibilities, immanent within it, that something will escape from it, or that the system as a whole will explode. Deleuze and Guattari are very close to Bataille here when they claim that a society is determined by its "lines of flight" rather than by its contradictions (*A Thousand Plateaus*, 216). There is no liberation without violent destruction. But destruction can be revolutionary and creative only when it is directly affirmative, rather than the reactive consequence of a need to assert authority, of fear and *ressentiment*. (This point is made repeatedly by Nietzsche and Deleuze.) For Bataille, "la souveraineté est révolte, ce n'est pas l'exercice de pouvoir [sovereignty is revolt, it is not the exercise of power]" (*OC*, 5:221). Catastrophic expenditure is the most radical putting-into-question, "la pratique aveugle de la perte personnelle ou sociale [the blind practice of personal or social loss]" (*OC*, 1:319; *VE*, 129). It is the immanent affirmation of "insufficiency," and therefore of contingency, openness, and change. As such, it must be distinguished from the various forms of putting-to-work, of destruction for the sake of power and acquisition, of the labor of the negative, which are hegemonic in modern capitalist society: increasing militarization, to be sure, but also the drive to continual innovation in production which is essential to the reproduction and accumulation of capital (and which is also enshrined in bourgeois ideology in the form of the myth of the "creative" entrepreneur).

This is not to deny that Bataille himself sometimes fails to make this distinction. There are points in the course of his arguments when he falls into what can only be called metaphysical formulations. This is the naturalistic and dialecticizing error for which Jean Baudrillard, in an otherwise laudatory passage, sharply criticizes him (*L'échange symbolique et la mort*, 236–42). At such moments, Bataille repeats what he has elsewhere so well diagnosed as the Christian mistake of *substantializing* the sacred (*OC*, 1:562; *VE*, 242). He seems to present excess as a superabundance of being, rather than as a nonpresence, a positive insufficiency formally irreducible to being. Energy is grasped, in an entirely Hegelian manner (as in "Force and the Understanding," *Phenomenology of Spirit*, 79–103), as the inner essence of phenomena. It becomes a cosmic principle, a gift of nature, a magical animating force. Correlatively, the "insufficiency" of the individual entity is coded as dialectical negativity, and "transgression" is identified with the *Aufhebung*. The rupturing of the individual's boundaries is seen anthropologically as a moment of mass identification and social cohesion.

These confusions are not merely accidental. But for this very reason, we should not be overly hasty to seize upon them in order to limit or "deconstruct" Bataille's affirmations. It will not do to say, as does Baudrillard, that the movement of expenditure is "symbolic" and not "real" (240), and that Bataille goes wrong by forgetting this difference. It is rather the possibility of maintaining such an opposition as that between symbolic and real that this movement throws into doubt. Instead of criticizing Bataille's supposed investment of metaphysics, it is preferable, as Derrida suggests in his important article on Bataille, to "interpret Bataille against Bataille, or rather, interpret one stratum of his work from another stratum" (*Writing and Difference*, 275). It is necessary, in other words, to situate, rather than reject, Bataille's metaphysical language. For its presence in his argument is not merely a result of the problematic status of language and representation.

Metaphysical ambiguity haunts Bataille's discourse precisely to the extent that it insinuates itself within the social reality which that discourse describes. Bataille cannot avoid a metaphysics of energy and its determinate negations, since the concrete practice of that metaphysics—the recuperation and realization of death as negativity— is all too massive a social phenomenon. In the very instance of "shock" by which it escapes presentation, and disrupts all closed entities and fixed values, expenditure *also* "presents itself" as a "charge" or (new source of) "value." The rupture of the integrity of individual beings, for example, is what allows them to be coded in the new forms of abstract labor and ubiquitous exchange value. It may no longer be possible to posit "objects" as self-sufficient entities, but they can equally well be circumscribed when they are represented in terms of the intrinsic energies that constitute or invest them. This is the sense in which the homogeneous world (whether it be that of capitalism, fascism, or Stalinism) is not disrupted by heterogeneity, but defined and stabilized by it. The dissimulation of radical expenditure is already a function of that expenditure. And this dissimulation and stabilization are crucial to the constitution of power relations (exploitation and domination). Bataille's metaphysical language corresponds to this secondary, representational moment of expenditure, in which heterogeneity is reactive, imperative, and conservative.

Expenditure can "present itself" reactively because its primary movement of dissociation is merely virtual or tendential, and not necessarily actual. It implies only a *potential* for catastrophe. Revolutionary heterogeneity is a "spectre" that haunts capitalism, its insurpassable limit. Yet if it cannot be exorcised once and for all, it also cannot avoid being limited in turn by the processes which it unsettles, but within which it remains inscribed. A "tendency" is not a dialectical contradiction, but rather—as Balibar puts it—a process that need never attain its limits, since it carries them along with it and continually reproduces them (*Reading Capital*, 291). It cannot be divorced from the "counteracting factors" (as Marx calls them in his discussion of the falling rate of profit) which are themselves intrinsic to the "tendential" movement. Catastrophic violence can be indefinitely recuperated or deferred. The major problem of radical politics is how to exceed the limits of capitalist reproduction, how to liberate this potential for catastrophe, how to actualize bourgeois society's "lines of flight." In Marxist terms, this is the question of how a situation of crisis (endemic to capitalism) can be intensified, transformed into one of revolution.

From the point of view of capitalist society itself, of course, the problem is the opposite one: how to *manage* crisis, to maintain maximum homogeneity, to recuperate expenditure and ward off catastrophe. The "counteracting factors" opposing dissolution must themselves be mobilized. Unproductive activity cannot be altogether eliminated, but to the extent that it is given a transcendent and regularized form, instead of an immanent and unpredictable one, it is no longer a threat. Moreover, such reference to stable transcendent elements can provide a logic and a finality for the homogeneous realm which otherwise—insofar as it denies heterogeneity and transcendence—would lack them. It is therefore ironically necessary for bourgeois society to have recourse to heterogeneity itself, in an idealized form, in order to avert the danger of dissociation which that heterogeneity most immediately represents.

The genesis of reactive or imperative heterogeneity can thus be traced back to capitalism's need to find a way of validating and regulating itself. In analyzing this process of idealization and equilibration, Bataille gives social application to some of Nietzsche's fundamental psychological insights. Reactive or ascetic morality, according to Nietzsche, "is an expression of the basic fact of the human will, its *horror vacui: it needs a goal* . . ." (*Genealogy of Morals*, 3:1, 97). Such a goal—an *end* answering to capitalism's reduction of everything to mere *means*—is established by a kind of projection, a *"moral-optical* illusion" (*Twilight of the Idols*, 39). The needs, and "necessary errors" or limitations of perspective, which are immanent expressions of one particular form of life, are removed from their immediate field of application. They are abstracted and generalized, in order to be posited as universal values. Such values judge life from the outside, assigning it an extrinsic goal to which it is required to conform, and in reference to which it can be praised or condemned. And not only are these values separated from the concrete conditions that determine them, but by an "error of mistaking cause for consequence" (*Twilight of the Idols*, 47) they are retroactively regarded as the causes of the very states of affairs of which they are in fact the expressions. A particular form of life (a particular social class, we might say, with its own particular interests and desires) can in this way assert its social hegemony. The hierarchy of values thus established is at once an actual set of power relations, and an ideological or metaphysical justification for those relations.

"*We* invented the concept 'purpose' [*Zweck*]; in reality purpose is lacking" (*Twilight of the Idols*, 54). The nonfinality of the homogeneous world is reactive or nihilistic, in that it is defined by a hypostasized Lack, or centered around an "end" which is nonetheless perpetually absent (and which for that very reason must be posited as transcendent). The nonfinality of subversive heterogeneity is by contrast purely affirmative, a liberation not only from ends but from the need to impose them. Expenditure cannot be an end in itself, for the same reason that it cannot be a means: in either case, its link to some notion of purposiveness (be it that of an aesthetic "purposiveness without purpose") would entail its subordination. Bataille indeed sometimes writes of heterogeneity as if it were—in contrast to merely utilitarian activity—"une activité *pour soi*" or "*valable en soi*" ("activity *for itself*" or "*valid in itself*") (*OC*, 1:340; *VE*, 138). But he is always quick to add that "l'opération souveraine, *qui ne tient que d'elle-même l'autorité—expie en même temps cette autorité* [the sovereign operation, *which gains authority only from itself, at the same time expiates this authority*]" (*OC*, 5:223). Expenditure as such continually exempts itself from the teleology which, by virtue of its insubordination, it seems to authorize or make possible. Or to put this another way: expenditure is never a function of power, even though the sublimation, recuperation, or redirection of its "exceeding energy" is a necessary condition for any exertion of power.

Bataille develops a typology of social formations by classifying the various ways in which hegemony is established by the projection of heterogeneity as an end or cause. In particular—although this concern is not always foregrounded in his texts—he traces a tendential "becoming-reactive" of social forces (to borrow a term from Deleuze: *Nietzsche and Philosophy*, 64). Heterogeneity becomes imperative rather than subversive when expenditure is reduced to a mere social function, at the same time that it is enshrined as the source of all value and power.

> La société *homogène* utilise en fait contre les éléments qui lui sont les plus incompatibles les forces impératives libres. . . . C'est l'incapacité de la société homogène de trouver en soi-même une raison d'être et d'agir qui la place dans la dépendance des forces impératives, de même que c'est l'hostilité sadique des souverains contre la population misérable qui les rapproche de toute formation cherchant à maintenir cette dernière dans l'oppression. (*OC*, 1:353)

> To combat the elements most incompatible with it, *homogeneous* society uses free-floating imperative forces. . . . The inability of *homogeneous* society to find in itself a reason for being and acting is what makes it dependent upon imperative forces, just as the sadistic hostility of sovereigns toward the impoverished population is what allies them with any formation seeking to maintain the latter in a state of oppression. (*VE*, 146–47)

La part maudite (written after the war) describes some of the ways in which different societies capture and employ expenditure in order to assure social solidarity and maintain a rigid class structure. In precapitalist societies, expenditure is a religious obligation or a source of prestige, the privilege and responsibility of a ruling class. The sovereign possibility of loss and destruction becomes the property of one class, and thereby an instrument of class domination. The relative prestige of rival chiefs is at stake in the potlatch ceremony. The war machine of early Islam, the monasticism of Tibet, and the building of cathedrals in medieval Christendom serve to consolidate the class structures of those societies by providing a safe outlet both for intra-ruling-class rivalries and for the anger and potential resistance of the exploited classes. That which is pure loss from a strictly economic point of view is politically recuperated and "put to work" on a different (noneconomic) level. One might say (using, and perhaps abusing, one of Althusser's crucial concepts) that this deployment of expenditure is the manner in which noneconomic factors are "determined" to be "dominant" in the various precapitalist social formations.

The situation under capitalism is rather different, and a great deal more complicated. Of course, ostentatious expenditure is still evident in such phenomena as conspicuous consumption among the rich and the enormous defense budgets of the Cold War. But the paradox of capitalism is that of a system in which, for the most part, heterogeneous expenditure is banished. "Aujourd'hui, les formes sociales, grandes et libres, de la dépense improductive ont disparu. Toutefois, il ne faut pas en conclure que le principe même de la dépense a cessé d'être situé au terme de l'activité économique [Today, the great and free forms of unproductive social expenditure have disappeared. One must not conclude from this, however, that the very principle of expenditure is no longer the end of economic activity]" (*OC*, 1:312; *VE*, 124). Expenditure is rather dissimulated, turned hypocritically back upon itself. "La haine de la dépense est la raison d'être et la justification de la bourgeoisie: elle est en même temps le principe de son effroyable hypocrisie [The hatred of expenditure is the *raison d'être* and the justification for the bourgeoisie; it is at the same time the principle of its horrifying hypocrisy]" (*OC*, 1:314; *VE*, 124–25). The general economy of expenditure takes on other forms, more sinister and more shadowy, in a situation in which the (restricted) economic level itself is "determined" to be "dominant."

The dissimulation of heterogeneous expenditure is concomitant with the processes traced by Marx in *Capital*: the generalization of money and of the circulation of commodities. There is no room for *gloire* (glory) and *déchéance* (degradation), or in general for "la création de valeurs improductives [the creation of unproductive values]" (*OC*, 1:319; *VE*, 128), in a society which reduces everything to a single quantitative standard of value. All the possibilities of consumption are rendered interchangeable through the mediation of money in the infinitely extendable process of circulation. Henceforth, there is no field of social activity which escapes the pressures of homogenization. In this context, Marx's protest against money is not (as Jean-François Lyotard claims in his confrontation of Marx and Bataille: *Economie libidinale*, 167–74, and 117–88 passim) the frustration of a metaphysician at an instance of irrecuperable alienation and radical impropriety. It is rather (as Spivak forcefully argues) the passion of a materialist confronting the effacement of multiplicity and difference. Marx deploys all his irony and sarcasm against the workings of a restricted economy which finds its "innermost principle of life" in the self-renewing self-identity of money. "Just as in money every qualitative difference between commodities is extinguished, so too for its part, as a radical leveller, [circulation] extinguishes all distinctions" (*Capital*, 1:229–30).

Of course, the ubiquity of money and of the commodity form is itself a development of the capitalist mode of production. Bourgeois society does not merely strive to regulate, reduce, and privatize the expenditures of consumption. Its major imperative is one of incessant productivity and ever greater valorization: the accumulation of capital, and its reproduction on an expanded scale. "Capital has one sole driving force, the drive to valorize itself, to create surplus-value, to make its constant part, the means of production, absorb the greatest possible amount of surplus labour" (*Capital*, 1:342). The appropriation of surplus value corresponds to an unparalleled absorption and reinvestment of energy. Heterogeneity is absorbed, coded as negativity, and "put to work" as never before. In contrast to the merely transitory function of economic activity in precapitalist societies, "the circulation of money as capital is an end in itself, for the valorization of value takes place only within this constantly renewed movement. The movement of capital is therefore limitless" (*Capital*, 1:253). Nothing is allowed to escape the circuit of reproduction. Waste, or unreserved and nonreciprocal expenditure, is the one possibility that remains absolutely unthinkable.

Capital can reproduce itself on an expanded scale only by means of a calculated reduction of excess. It must capture and incorporate external sources of wealth and energy. But to appropriate an excess is to efface its status *as* excess, to reduce it to the dimensions of *homogeneous* existence, to reinscribe it in the horizon of definite value. Appropriation thus involves a crucial ambiguity. Expansion must take place at the same time that the strict equivalencies of a restricted economy are maintained. It is here that Marx introduces the paradoxes of the notion of surplus value. In the extraction of surplus value, "every condition of the problem is satisfied, while the laws governing the exchange of commodities have not been violated in any way. Equivalent has been exchanged for equivalent. . . . Yet for all that [the capitalist] withdraws . . . more from circulation than he originally threw into it" (*Capital*, 1:301–2).

How is this possible? In every social system human beings "se trouvent constamment engagés dans des processus de dépense [find themselves constantly engaged in processes of expenditure]" (*OC*, 1:319; *VE*, 128). But under capitalism, even "loss" is quantified and given a definite magnitude. "Labor," or the free discharge of human energy, is captured and turned to account in the form of the commodity of labor power. Expenditure, one might say, is "lost" in the profound sense of no longer being permitted to lose itself. It is transformed into a measurable capacity, a source of productive potential energy. Surplus value is then the *trace* of indefinite expenditure, the mark of heterogeneity subsisting even within the movement of appropriation. "The value of labour-power, and the value which that labour-power valorizes in the labour-process, are two entirely different magnitudes; and this difference was what the capitalist had in mind when he was purchasing the labour-power" (*Capital*, 1:300). It is therefore only the operation of extorting surplus value which allows the capitalist to realize a profit. The capitalist literally makes this profit by measuring and purchasing an incommensurability. He harnesses an "exceeding energy" which has no presence of its own, which can come into play only insofar as it is irretrievably lost. Lost to the worker, that is, but not in this case to the capitalist. "All wasteful consumption of raw material or instruments of labour is strictly forbidden, because what is wasted in this way represents a superfluous expenditure of quantities of objectified labour, labour that does not count in the product or enter into its value" (*Capital*, 1:303). The economy of capitalism remains haunted by the possibility of loss, the extravagance which it cannot do without but also cannot afford to recognize. It needs both to kill the possibility of expenditure and to keep it alive. It is nourished only by that which it is compelled to exclude. This is why, in Marx's famous phrase, "capital is dead labour which, vampire-like, lives only by sucking living labour, and lives the more, the more labour it sucks" (*Capital*, 1:342).

In this manner, expenditure is reduced, and all forms of individual and social practice are subordinated to the exigencies of expanded reproduction. But "the circuit of reproductive consumption," insofar as it becomes an end in itself, carries even to excess this process of subordination. Accumulation implies an infinite deferral. The logic of ownership and of the reinvestment of profits works against any "taking profit," any *jouissance* (a word which refers both to the expenditure of orgasm and to the unproductive consumption of the profits deriving from private ownership). When the servile principle of value and calculation is rendered absolute, it is divorced from the merely relative considerations of use or need. "Use-value is certainly not *la chose qu'on aime pour lui-même* in the production of commodities. Use-values are produced by capitalists only because and insofar as they form the material substratum of exchange-value, are the bearers of exchange-value" (*Capital*, 1:293). In an economy of universal subordination, nothing can have value without having use, and yet the supremacy of value makes "use" (in any naturalistic or pre-economic sense) irrelevant. There is no end to accumulation, no ulterior goal for the sake of which useful activities must be performed. The triumph of the capitalist mode of production radically abolishes all hierarchies of means and ends, and hence all teleologies. But this means that the frenzy of expanded reproduction uncannily comes to resemble the violence of free expenditure. Excess cannot be altogether abolished; it continues to operate, rechanneled into obsessive movements of production and valorization. The dissimulation of expenditure, the abolition of any autonomous realm for the display of heterogeneity, has the effect of making waste and unproductive activity coextensive with the entire field of homogeneous economy.

In such an inherently unstable situation, the reactive recuperation of heterogeneity is all the more necessary to preserve the system; but it can only occur in a schizophrenically dissimulated fashion. As homogeneity increasingly imposes itself as the immanent law of production under capitalism, it threatens to become more and more disorderly, to run more and more out of control. In compensation, the imperative to order must be projected in an ever more transcendent and absolute form. "The real world, unattainable, undemonstrable, cannot be promised, but even when merely thought of [is] a consolation, a duty, an imperative" (Nietzsche, *Twilight of the Idols*, 40). Imperative heterogeneity becomes on one hand more and more distant and unthinkable, and on the other hand more and more demanding and oppressive. Society appears increasingly anarchic and "dissociated," while at the same time the imperative agency (since it is no longer embodied in any real social elements) takes on the internalized psychological forms of the indeterminable categorical imperative and the stern superego. It is on this psychological and "superstructural" level that Bataille is able to explain what traditional Marxist theory could not: the appeal of fascism in advanced capitalist society, and the failure (increasingly evident in the 1930s) of the revolutionary alternative.

When social power is not directly linked to a representation of transcendence, but instead coded by ubiquitous exchange value, "l'instance impérative *hétérogène* . . . est réduite à une existence atrophiée et tout changement possible n'apparaît plus nécessairement lié à sa destruction [the *heterogeneous* imperative agency . . . is reduced to an atrophied existence, so that its destruction no longer appears to be a necessary condition of change]" (*OC*, 1:369; *VE*, 158). Capital is everywhere and nowhere, omnipotent and omnipresent, but for that very reason impersonal and largely invisible. Since an imperative agency cannot be easily identified and targeted, it cannot be easily overthrown. It becomes ever more difficult to give a psychological focus to revolutionary energy. Indeed, such a focus is provided more readily by the fascism that galvanizes capitalism in order to save it than by the subversive goals of the movements that seek to overthrow it. The energy of rebellion need not be opposed to social regulation, and may even be used to support it. "Et lorsque la société *homogène* subit une désintégration critique, les éléments dissociés n'entrent plus nécessairement dans l'orbite de l'attraction subversive: il se forme en outre, au sommet, une attraction impérative qui ne voue plus ceux qui la subissent a l'immobilité [And when *homogeneous* society undergoes a critical disintegration, the dissociated elements no longer necessarily enter the orbit of subversive attraction: in addition there forms at the top an imperative attraction that no longer immobilizes those who are subject to it]" (*OC*, 1:369; *VE*, 158).

There is in this sense a profound complicity between fascism, on the one hand, and the "atrophied," decentered forms of liberal democracy on the other. This is evident today to an even greater extent than could have been foreseen by Bataille in the 1930s. Subversive expenditure is foreclosed, and its energy diverted to the purposes of exploitation and domination, class oppression and social control, alternatively by fascism and other imperative formations, and by the hypercommodification and normalizing regulation characterizing late capitalist culture. These seemingly opposed modes of organization of bourgeois society serve the same requirements of capital accumulation and crisis management. They both mobilize reactive, negative, and imperative heterogeneity on a scale previously unknown in order to reconstitute homogeneous closure.

In the terms of contemporary theoretical debates, we may say that the logic of simulation that Baudrillard identifies as a crucial feature of postmodern society does not (as he claims) supersede the more traditional logic of production and negativity that Marx saw as the primary feature of classical capitalism. Rather these two processes are closely coordinated. And not only because (although this is extremely important) Western prosperity rests on hyperexploitation in the Third World. But also because these logics are neither incompatible nor mutually independent. Real commodity production and hyperreal simulation are alike forms under which heterogeneity is rendered "present" and active. They are deployed in turn as strategies for averting catastrophic expenditure and reducing social life to universal necessity and servility. That is to say, in both of these modes capitalism rationalizes society and nature by assigning them a *head*. "La vie humaine est excédée de servir de tête et de raison à l'univers. Dans la mesure où elle devient cette tête et cette raison, dans la mesure où elle devient nécessaire à l'univers, elle accepte un servage [Human life is exhausted from serving as the head of, or the reason for, the universe. To the extent that it becomes this head and this reason, to the extent that it becomes necessary to the universe, it accepts servitude]" (*OC*, 1:445; *VE*, 180).

For its part, fascism provides an almost ideal synthesis of reactive forces. It combines the rationalizing exigencies of capitalist production with a massive appeal to the irrationality of a mythical past. It captures and sublimates a potentially disruptive—but tendentially vanishing—heterogeneity, assuring the cohesion and stability that capitalism traditionally finds so difficult to provide. At the same time, it integrates this imperative agency with the homogeneity of money-capital and of the requirements of utility. Far from marking an inexplicable crisis in bourgeois social relations, fascism preserves those relations. It reduces excess by giving transcendent sanction to the logic of subordination and negativity. Its violence is not an explosion of catastrophic expenditure; it is all the more sinister for being a massive, nihilistic recuperation of the forces of catastrophe. Fascism might be called the *religion* implicit in modern capitalism. Nietzsche observes that "nihilism as a psychological state is reached . . . [when] a soul that longs to admire and revere has wallowed in the idea of some supreme form of domination and administration" (*The Will to Power*, 12). God, or a fascist dictator (who is God's modern equivalent), is quite literally the *head*: an instance of imperative *heterogeneity* which, by concentrating all the forces of society within itself, all the more surely establishes a rigidly repressive, intensely *homogeneous* social order. "Le fascisme qui recompose la société à partir d'éléments existants est la forme la plus fermée de l'organization, c'est-à-dire l'existence humaine la plus proche du Dieu éternel [The fascism that recomposes society on the basis of existing elements is the most closed form of *organization*; in other words, the form of human existence closest to the eternal God]" (*OC*, 1:467; *VE*, 197).

On the other hand, the recuperation of unproductive energies, which fascism endeavors to accomplish in such spectacular form, is performed much more efficiently today by the cynicism of multinational capital. Periodic economic crisis seems less an opportunity to overthrow capitalism than an already planned part of its cycle, an excuse for it to modernize and renew itself. Late capitalist society tends toward what is in one sense a "headless" state, best described in Foucault's terms as a regime of "sex without the law and power without the king" (*History of Sexuality*, 1:91). Yet such a regime only refuses difference and enforces homogeneous order all the more rigidly. One might say that in such a society God is not dead, so much as he is entirely immanent. The principle of servitude and organization is (in Kantian terms) transcendental and regulative instead of transcendent and constitutive. With the ubiquity of exchange value, and the inescapability of multiple technologies of power and surveillance, everything is assigned its place within the parameters of utility. Bourgeois democracy "repose sur une neutralisation d'antagonismes relativement faibles et libres; elle exclut toute condensation explosive [rests on a neutralization of relatively free and weak antagonisms; it excludes all explosive condensation]." There is no longer a separate head only because everything is now the head, "car le principe même de la tête est réduction à l'unité, *réduction* du monde à Dieu [because the very principle of the head is the reduction to unity, the *reduction* of the world to God]" (*OC*, 1:469; *VE*, 199).

Bataille's anarchic political vision is directed against, and situated in the interstices between, these contrasting but coordinated structures of servitude. At the opposite extreme from fascism, "dans la révolution sociale (mais non dans le stalinisme actuel), la décomposition atteint au contraire son point extrême [in social revolution (but not in Stalinism as it exists today) decomposition conversely reaches its extreme point]" (*OC*, 1:468; *VE*, 198). And in opposition to the uniformities of late capitalism and bureaucratic state socialism, "la seule société pleine de vie et de force, la seule société libre est la société *bi ou polycéphale* qui donne aux antagonismes fondamentaux de la vie une issue explosive constante mais limitée aux formes les plus riches. La dualité ou la multiplicité des têtes tend à réaliser dans un même mouvement le caractère *acéphale* de l'existence [the only society full of life and force, the only free society, *is the bi- or polycephalic* society that gives the fundamental antagonisms of life a constant explosive outlet, but one limited to the richest forms. The duality or multiplicity of heads tends to achieve in the same movement the *acephalic* character of existence]" (*OC*, 1:469; *VE*, 199). Against fascism's idealized closure, Bataille calls for a kind of perpetual revolution. He affirms the possibilities of "une désintégration constante [a constant disintegration]" (*OC*, 1:468; *VE*, 198) in opposition alike to totalitarian visions of perfection and to the hypocrisy (or cynicism) of conservative defenses of the inevitable imperfections of the status quo.

Expenditure is not in itself either revolutionary or reactionary, because it has no proper essence "in itself." But the freeing of expenditure from the recuperations of class society is nevertheless a major condition of revolutionary activity. In capitalist and precapitalist social formations, expenditure is restricted to the privileged experience of a ruling class, and recuperated for the purposes of that class. "La lutte de classes devient au contraire la forme la plus grandiose de la dépense sociale lorsqu'elle est reprise et dévelopée, cette fois au compte des ouvriers, avec une ampleur qui menace l'existence même des maîtres [Class struggle, on the contrary, becomes the grandest form of social expenditure when it is taken up again and developed, this time on the part of the workers, and on such a scale that it threatens the very existence of the masters]" (*OC*, 1:316; *VE*, 126). Class struggle, abolishing the privileges of class, is the form in which expenditure, or *acephalic* existence, becomes available to all.

The most powerful expression of *acephalic* existence is the revolutionary act of decapitation. Such an act is approached—as Bataille suggests in *"L'obélisque"* ["The Obelisk"] (*OC*, 1:501–13; *VE*, 213–22)—in the symbolic violence of regicide during the French revolution, and on a larger scale in Nietzsche's parable of the madman, the "mystery" of the death of God (*The Gay Science*, 181–82, §125). The violence of decapitation marks the abasement and overthrow of the elevated or "erect" imperative function. It is a disturbance all the more troubling because it arises unforeseeably in a situation of absolute order and deathly calm.

> La place de la Concorde est le lieu où la mort de Dieu doit être annoncée et criée précisément parce que l'obélisque en est la négation la plus calme. . . . L'obélisque est sans doute l'image la plus pure du chef et du ciel . . . l'obstacle le plus sár et le plus durable à l'écoulement mouvementé de toutes choses. (*OC*, 1:503–4)

> The Place de la Concorde is the space where the death of God must be announced and shouted precisely because the obelisk is its calmest negation. . . . The obelisk is without a doubt the purest image of the head and of the heavens . . . the surest and most durable obstacle to the drifting away of all things. (*VE*, 215)

The obelisk is the assertion, the symbol, and the reminder of absolute power. It marks the arrest and completion of time, the denial of contingency and change. The "head" is an enormous fetish, a phallus perpetually maintaining its own erection. As the extreme modern form of imperial domination, fascism is at once a hysterical expression of male sexual panic (the need to preserve sperm, to regulate discharge, to maintain mastery and patriarchal privilege in the sexual act) and the ultimate Hegelian movement of realization of Absolute Spirit. Bataille ironically proposes to undo this movement, to overthrow this structure of mastery, in a parodic inversion of the Hegelian slave's gesture of recognition: "Dans la mesure où l'obélisque est maintenant, avec toute cette grandeur morte, *reconnu*, il ne facilite plus le glissement de la conscience, il fixe l'attention sur l'échafaud [To the extent that the obelisk is now, with all this dead grandeur, *recognized*, it no longer facilitates the flight of consciousness; it focuses the attention on the guillotine]" (*OC*, 1: 512; *VE*, 221). Once the forces of decomposition are put in motion, the imposing size of this sexual and metaphysical edifice only helps to provoke and intensify its collapse. The phallic monuments of unity and domination have been raised only to be pulverized in the acephalic (and a-phallic) moment of catastrophe and sacrifice.

If the construction of imperative structures, culminating in fascism, marks a tendential becoming-reactive of social forces, then the act of decapitation, of expenditure without reserve, reverses the direction of this evolution. In the course of a long "history of an error" (like that recounted by Nietzsche in *Twilight of the Idols*), a sinister history of idealization and sublimation, "l'univers moqueur était lentement livré à la sévère *éternité* de son Père Tout-Puissant, garant de la stabilité profonde [the mocking universe was slowly given over to the severe *eternity* of the Almighty Father, guarantor of profound stability]" (*OC*, 1:505; *VE*, 216). Decapitation, in contrast to this patriarchal recuperation, affirms the free discharge of forces that have been not so much pent up or repressed as they have been recognized, worshipped, and thereby *employed*. "La tête, autorité consciente ou Dieu, représente celle des *fonctions serviles* qui se donne et se prend elle-même pour une fin, en conséquence celle qui doit être l'objet de l'aversion la plus vivace [The head, conscious authority or God, represents one of the servile functions that gives itself as, and takes itself to be, an end; consequently, it must be the object of the most inveterate aversion]" (*OC*, 1:470; *VE*, 199). Or as Nietzsche puts it: "The concept 'God' has hitherto been the greatest *objection* to existence. . . . We deny God; in denying God, we deny accountability; only by doing *that* do we redeem the world" (*Twilight of the Idols*, 54).

La transgression ne transgresse pas la loi, elle l'emporte avec elle. . . . Ne plus pouvoir, en sorte qu'après ces mots on ne puisse non plus savoir ce qui ne se peut plus.
—Maurice Blanchot, *Le pas au-delà*

CHAPTER 3

Transgression, Interdiction, Affirmation

Bataille and Contemporary Theory

The vision of a frenzied moment of decapitation marks the *summit* of Bataille's thought and action. But every *summit*, as Bataille insists repeatedly, entails its own decline: "le déclin est l'inévitable et le sommet lui-même l'indique; si le sommet n'est pas la mort, il laisse après lui la nécéssité de descendre [Decline is inevitable and the summit itself indicates it; if the summit is not death, it leaves behind it the necessity to descend]" (*OC*, 6:57). The impulsion of expenditure outlives its own affirmation and must therefore be reinscribed in secondary (reactive or negative) forms. The *decline* is the long process in which sovereignty is lost, in which the attainment of the summit is forgotten—inescapably so, since sovereignty itself is loss, and the summit is never something to be attained. It is the movement in which power is consolidated, in which expenditure is transformed, appropriated, and reabsorbed. And the decline is also the movement in which *theory* gets written. Theory can point toward the experience of the summit—it can propose the summit as its goal—but it cannot reach or participate in the summit. "En vérité, le sommet proposé pour fin n'est plus le sommet: je le réduis à la recherche d'un profit *puisque j'en parle* [In truth, the summit proposed as an end is no longer the summit: I reduce it to the search for a profit *because I speak of it*]" (*OC*, 6:57). Theory is always recuperative; it cannot avoid subordinating its objects, since such a subordination is precisely its function as discourse.

The discursive or theoretical moment is an insurpassable one; the *mistake* of theory is only to deny, or on the other hand to confound itself with, the expenditure which it reduces, and to which it reactively responds. The forgetting of free expenditure is one with its being accounted for, explained or represented. And this misconception is the very process of conceptualization itself; the mistake made by theory is its positive function, that which constitutes it *as* a science.

> La science a pour objet de fonder l'*homogénéité* des phénomènes; elle est, en un certain sens, une des fonctions éminentes de l'*homogénénité*. Ainsi, les éléments *hétérogènes* qui sont exclus par cette dernière se trouvent également exclus du champ de l'attention scientifique: par principe même, la science ne peut pas connaître d'éléments *hétérogènes* en tant que tels. (*OC*, 1:344)

> The object of science is to establish the *homogeneity* of phenomena; that is, in a sense, one of the eminent functions of *homogeneity*. Thus, the *heterogeneous* elements excluded from the latter are excluded as well from the field of scientific considerations; as a rule, science cannot know *heterogeneous* elements as such. (*VE*, 141)

The impossibility of knowing, or in any way of capturing, *heterogeneity* as such, is the impasse in which every would-be "scientific" discourse is caught. This problem, dissimulated in most theoretical writing, is Bataille's explicit concern. "J'échoue, quoi que j'écrive, en ceci que je devrais lier, à la précision du sens, la richesse infinie—insensée—des possibles [I fail, no matter what I write, in this, that I should be linking the infinite—insane—richness of 'possibles' to the precision of meaning]" (*OC*, 5:51; *IE*, 38). Bataille's writing is literally torn apart by the double bind of these contradictory requirements. His fiction, his short texts of the 1930s, and above all the *Somme athéologique* (written during the War) attempt to testify, by means of an aggressive stylistic fragmentation, to the delirium—and the futility—of free expenditure. "Le désordre est la mésure de mon intention [Disorder is the measure of my intention]" (*OC*, 3:381). But in some of his later writing—in works such as *L'érotisme*, *La part maudite*, and *Théorie de la religion*—Bataille retreats into a more detached, more discursive, more objective and scientific mode of discourse. He seems to be trying to systematize his thought, to present an organized theoretical account of sacrifice and transgression. His language becomes enmeshed in the recuperative qualifications of dialectics. These later books achieve a certain coherence and conviction, but at the price of submerging their own most radical and most audacious insights. These texts often seem disappointing in comparison to Bataille's earlier writing. They are the works in which Bataille needs to be read, most guardedly, against himself. But in so strangely simulating traditional philosophical discourse, and in emphasizing the reactive, recuperative side of transgression (the manner in which it *founds* the interdiction against which it is directed), these texts also call attention to, and in their own writing participate in, the process of *decline* of which they endeavor to speak.

Bataille's writing thus fluctuates between ecstatic fragmentation and discursive continuity, between the richness of infinite possibility and the precision of meaning. Theory is a matter, not of rigor and formalization, but of *economy* and *strategy*. This "logic" of Bataille's discourse is best described by Derrida: "The writing of sovereignty places discourse *in relation* to absolute non-discourse. Like general economy, it is not the loss of meaning, but, as we have just read, the 'relation to this loss of meaning'. . . . The known is related to the unknown, meaning to nonmeaning" (*Writing and Difference*, 270–71). The crucial question is one not of the content, but of the *direction* of theoretical discourse. Bataille's actual writing remains (as it cannot help doing) within the confines of *homogeneous* representation and understanding. But it is *oriented* away from meaning, away from recuperation, away from the project that informs it.

Bataille is ultimately less a theorist than a parodist of theory, or a writer of anti-theory. The lucidity with which he remains always aware of his continuing implication within the reactive processes by which meaning is established and maintained is the necessary precondition for his abandoning himself to the nonlucidity and absurdity of free, heterogeneous expenditure. Bataille is oppressively aware that "l'existence ne peut être à la fois autonome et viable [existence cannot be at once autonomous and viable]" (*OC*, 6:63). But "inviability" is the defining characteristic, and not the limiting condition, of sovereignty. It marks the direction in which expenditure continues to be active rather than reactive, purely and irreducibly affirmative. Bataille's catastrophic vision of decapitation affirms *excess* in a very precise sense. Expenditure has no proper essence, and no place within Being. It exceeds the formulations of metaphysics and ontology no less than the circuits of capitalist economy. It remains external to representation even as representation becomes a privileged expression of its inevitable decline. In contrast to the centrifugal direction of Bataille's writing, the attempt made by philosophy and theory to enclose expenditure within various restricted conceptual horizons appears as abusive as is the social and economic attempt to put it to work in the service of particular class and power relations.

In this chapter, I am attempting to repeat and reaffirm the strategic gestures of Bataille's thought, in order to differentiate it from, and to criticize, varieties of contemporary theoretical discourse that move in the opposite direction. There are three forms of conceptual reduction and recuperation which I would like in particular to consider, because of their prominence in philosophical and critical thought today: those associated with anthropology, with psychoanalysis, and with pragmatism.

It is disingenuously reductive, in the first place, to see the discharge of energy in expenditure as a defensive or substitutive gesture, a turning away of that energy from initially dangerous consequences. Bataille's formulations have little to do with René Girard's anthropology or with the psychology of the scapegoat. Decapitation cannnot be subsumed within a dialectic of narcissism, dualistic conflict, and transcendent mediation. Sacrifice, in Bataille's terms, is not the secondary dissipation of a violence which would otherwise fuel fascism and repression, or mimetic rivalry and resentment. Rather, it is the very process of warding off catastrophe by reconstituting the head which generates both mimetic desire and its fascist or theological resolution. The displacement of the former by the latter in Girard's system, the ritual transference of aggression onto a "surrogate victim," serves only to dissimulate a more fundamental reactive process: the ruling class appropriation, and concomitant transcendent representation, of expenditure.

The mimetic violence which, according to Girard, it is the task of myth and ritual to dispel cannot be identified with Bataille's sense of radical subversion. For mimetic violence is already a recuperation of expenditure, taking the form of petty intra-ruling-class rivalry: "Autour des banques modernes comme autour des mâts totémiques des Kwakiutl, le même désir d'offusquer anime les individus et les entraîne dans un système de petites parades qui les aveugle les uns contre les autres comme s'ils étaient devant une lumière trop forte [Around modern banks, as around the totem poles of the Kwakiutl, the same desire to dazzle animates individuals and leads them into a system of petty displays that blinds them to each other, as if they were staring into a blinding light]" (*OC*, 1:313; *VE*, 124). This struggle for recognition that ends only in blindness, this movement of Imaginary misrecognition and conflict (to use Lacan's terms for the same process), is not altogether futile and empty. For the ability to engage in such "petty displays" is always the exclusive privilege of a dominant group. Mimetic rivalry is not free expenditure, since it has social use value as a signifier of power and prestige. It is founded upon, and serves the purpose of diverting attention away from, a more fundamental exclusion. For example, rivalry among males is predicated upon a previous subordination of females. Or again, the members of a ruling class can hazard the stakes by means of which they compete among themselves only insofar as they commonly exploit the labor of other sectors of society. This suggests that Girard's warnings against the dangers of mimetic violence conceal a more basic reactive fear: a fear of base heterogeneity, of class struggle, and of revolution.

The nihilism of mimetic violence is thus dangerous only in a particular, restricted sense. Its function is to provide the *appearance* of a threat to society, in order to establish an alibi for the perpetuation of social hierarchy. Girard describes the substitution of a "surrogate victim" in myth and ritual as "that mechanism which, in a single decisive movement, curtails reciprocal violence and imposes structure on the community" (*Violence and the Sacred*, 317). But Bataille—like Nietzsche—is above all suspicious of this imposition of structure, all the more so in that it involves a surplus gratification derived from the substitutive sacrifice of another. "Dans les formes rituelles de sacrifice commune, une bête est lâchement substituée au sacrifiant [in ritual forms of communal sacrifice an animal is substituted for the one performing the sacrifice—a cowardly gesture]," so that the one performing the sacrifice escapes unscathed (*OC*, 1:268; *VE*, 69). The moment of substitution is the quintessentially fascist moment in which the destructive impulses—instead of leading to self-transformation and revolutionary ferment—are mobilized against multiplicity and change. There is only a difference of degree between this movement in "primitive" forms of sacrifice and its massive amplification in the sadistic structure of Christianity, in which bliss is derived from contemplation of the torture of Christ and of the eternal torments of the damned (see Nietzsche's continual polemic, and especially *Genealogy of Morals*, 1:15, 48–52).

The crucial point, for Bataille, is that the transcendent mediation of mimetic rivalry does not break with a reactive logic of recuperating expenditure for the sake of expanded domination, but merely repeats that logic on a larger scale. If we were to follow things out from the perspective of expenditure, "l'utilisation du mécanisme sacrificiel à diverses fins telles que la propriation ou l'expiation serait regardée comme secondaire et l'on ne retiendrait que le fait élémentaire de l'*alteration* radicale [the use of sacrificial mechanisms for various ends, such as propriation or expiation, would be seen as secondary, and one would only retain the elementary fact of radical *alteration*]" (*OC*, 1:269; *VE*, 70). Substitution can be defined as a secondary utilization—which is to say a primary denial—of expenditure: a way of avoiding alteration, or better of allowing it to be appropriated by a fixed subject. The subject experiences change vicariously, and thereby itself remains unaltered. Imaginary conflict already presupposes substitution in this sense, on the part of all the parties involved. The resolution of that conflict by appeal to a neutral or Symbolic third term accomplishes the same reduction on a social level. Reactive violence is all the more gratified in that it now serves to guarantee the unity of the self and the xenophobic closure of society. Girardian substitution thus solidifies ruling class hegemony by simultaneously internalizing (in the form of guilt and bad conscience) and projecting outwards (in the form of torture and aggression) the resentment which that hegemony has itself incited. The cure is only an intensification of the disease: a nihilistic spiral of petty self-aggrandizement accompanied by fear, servitude, and abjection. "C'était DIEU et déjà la pesanteur chrétienne qui dominait la tragédie de la *passion* de la hauteur du ciel et réduisait la 'mort de Dieu' à l'abjection des hommes, au péché, le TEMPS au MAL [It was GOD, and already the heaviness of Christianity, which dominated the tragedy of the *passion* of the heavens and reduced 'the death of God' to the debasement of men and to sin, and turned TIME into EVIL]" (*OC*, 1:508; *VE*, 218).

A second form of reduction, the psychoanalytic—intersecting in some ways with Girard's—treats decapitation as a form of castration. Such an interpretation reinscribes, a priori, the very conceptual framework Bataille wishes to contest. It assumes, as Lacanian theory so massively does, the priority of a Symbolic structure over those forces which at once disrupt and invest it. The totalizing logic of such a structure denies any possibility of escape. For the Symbolic order not only provides an infinitely extendable matrix of representations, it also self-reflexively posits mechanisms whose specific task is to account for whatever resists incorporation within that matrix (repression and negation), and even for the radical exteriority that was never part of it in the first place (Lacan's notion of foreclosure). As Deleuze and Guattari put it, phallocentrism "overcodes" the elements of the unconscious, subjecting them to the law of a "despotic signifier" (see especially the discussion of "imperial representation," *Anti-Oedipus*, 200–217). Since the phallic metaphor is taken as given in advance, the destruction of the father is seen as an oedipal gesture, a reactive movement which acknowledges and reasserts, by reversal, the Law of the Father. Decapitation is identified with castration, because the disruption of presence which it entails is regarded only as "lack," or as a "barring" which refuses to satisfy, and thereby perpetuates, teleological desire. "Transgression" is conceived only negatively and dialectically, as a kind of adolescent rebellion, or as an infraction that, by its very insistence, confirms the interdiction that it oversteps.

Psychoanalysis discovers the forms of radical heterogeneity, whose reality, Bataille says, "est identique à la structure de l'*inconscient* [is identical to the structure of the *unconscious*]" (*OC*, 1:347; *VE*, 143). But psychoanalysis misconstructs this structure, to the extent that it aspires to be a "science of the unconscious." Such an aspiration is unavoidable: it corresponds to the actual functioning of psychoanalysis, both in theory and in practice. Like any science, psychoanalysis is not limited to the passive role of presenting phenomena from the perspective of an already existing homogeneity. More crucially, it has the active, "eminent function" of directly constituting that homogeneity. It *founds* the commensurability of different forms of experience and discourse, by enforcing their common subjection to the laws of signification. It does not misrepresent unconscious experience (which would imply that a correct representation is somehow possible), so much as it *misencounters* that experience by appropriating it to a dialectic of representation. Everything is required to pass through the signifier. "For the signifier, by its very nature, always anticipates meaning by unfolding its dimension before it" (Lacan, *Ecrits*, 153). Freud's concern with dreams and symptoms as ideational presentations (*Vorstellungen*) and Lacan's dictum that "the unconscious is structured like a language" indicate the inability of psychoanalysis to approach *heterogeneity* in other than representational terms. Instead, the non-presence of the unconscious is fetishized as its fundamental *linguistic* characteristic. Expenditure as a nonconceptualizable "experience" of excess is replaced by the easily formalizable "overabundance of the signifier." And in therapeutic practice, the interminability of analysis, or the impossibility of definitively grasping the unconscious relation, is only—as Foucault points out—a continual "incitement to discourse" (*History of Sexuality*, 1:17–35).

Psychoanalysis produces, through its emphasis on reconstituting discourse, an inverted representation of the unconscious which serves the purpose of reducing intensity, of containing and regulating heterogeneous elements or drives. It achieves this by channeling these drives into the restricted form of a "split" (the Freudian or Lacanian *Spaltung*) between *Vorstellung* and affect, Symbolic and Real, representation and the inaccessible realm of that which is represented. The division that "subverts" the subject simultaneously ratifies the oppressive order in which that subject is inscribed, and on the basis of which it can alone be thought. On one side of the *Spaltung*, the site of representation is one of negativity and prohibition. On the other side, whatever is not exhausted by representation acquires the shadowy status of a "thing in itself" (the unknowable Real as limit), or else is dismissed as an Imaginary delusion (the apparent spontaneity and self-presence of the ego, actually founded on an alienating identification). Insofar as it comprehends the unconscious by positing a primal complicity between desire and the law, or desire and repression, psychoanalysis is *even in theory* only able to account for reactive forces. Indeed, any force is already necessarily reactive, to the extent that it has been theoretically explained or accounted for. And in practice, the psychoanalytic cure itself involves a presentation or recognition, which is to say a "becoming-reactive," of unconscious forces.

Psychoanalysis denies the possibility of establishing any adequate correspondence between signifier and signified, even as it shows that the subject's coincidence with itself is impossible. It thereby asserts its radical break with the metaphysics of subjectivity and self-identity. But a more fundamental metaphysical gesture has already been made: that which consists in problematizing representation in the first place, in restating all questions in a representational framework. The primacy of representation is not overthrown merely by insisting on the arbitrariness of the signifier. If anything, such an insistence reinforces a metaphysical sense of entrapment within a linguistic prison from which we can never escape. Lacan all too fully confirms Nietzsche's suspicion: "I fear we are not getting rid of God because we still believe in grammar" (*Twilight of the Idols*, 38). Psychoanalysis remains unable to *affirm* nonidentity and nonadequacy; it continues to represent them only as negative conditions. Lacan's theory of desire unwittingly perpetuates, as its support, the metaphysical notion it is intended to criticize: that of a primary, even if always frustrated, narcissistic quest for identity and totality.

For Bataille, "ne plus se vouloir tout est tout mettre en cause. N'importe qui, sournoisement, voulant éviter de souffrir se confond avec le tout de l'univers, juge de chaque chose comme s'il l'était, de la même façon qu'il imagine, au fond, ne jamais mourir [to no longer wish oneself to be everything is to put everything into question. Anyone wanting slyly to avoid suffering, identifies with the entirety of the universe, judges each thing as if he were it, in the same way that he imagines, at bottom, that he will never die]" (*OC*, 5:10; *IE*, xxxii). Psychoanalysis parallels Bataille in its critique of such illusions of immortality. But it fails to put things radically into question, because it only chronicles the impasses of our need to be everything, without ever abandoning that need itself. In positing the insurpassability of narcissism, it regards multiplicity and change only from the restricted viewpoint of a static representation which is unable to encompass them. Hence follows the inexorability of the Law standing at the limits of representation. The paranoid logic of such a restricted or transcendental economy is well delineated by Deleuze, in terms that apply to Freud and Lacan as well as to Kant: "*The Law*, as defined by its pure form, without substance or object or any determination whatsoever, is such that no one knows nor can know what it is. It operates without making itself known. It defines a realm of transgression where one is already guilty, and where one oversteps the limits without knowing what they are, as in the case of Oedipus" (*Masochism*, 73).

Now Bataille, like Kafka and Proust, is obviously deeply concerned with this structure of unconscious guilt as a major determinant of modern bourgeois society. Such a psychological structure is a crucial focus of the endless process of "putting into question." And as Foucault suggests, this "contestation" must be linked in turn to Bataille's continued exploration of "that opening made by Kant in Western philosophy when he articulated, in a manner which is still enigmatic, metaphysical discourse and reflection on the limits of reason" ("Preface to Transgression," 38). But it is precisely here that the radicality of Bataille's Nietzscheanism makes itself felt, in contrast to the recuperative gestures of psychoanalysis (which in this respect perpetuates the responses of Kant, Hegel, and Heidegger). Foucault notes that in the main tradition of Western thought the Kantian "opening" is immediately closed again, by Kant himself in the form of an "anthropological" reduction, and yet more decisively when "dialectics substituted for the questioning of being and limits the play of contradiction and totality" (38).

Bataille strives to widen the "brèche béante [gaping breach]" which psychoanalysis endeavors to thematize, and thereby to a certain extent to master. The crucial difference is in the *direction* of thought, toward or away from the servilities and power relations of the homogeneous social world. Bataille is all too aware that the point of opening which he seeks is the very point from which (as is the case with Hegel, with Heidegger, and subsequently with Lacan) subordination and closure can be most effectively derived. This is why he continues to insist on a "communication" that paradoxically requires "silence" rather than any form of discourse. An impossible, contestatory silence, to be sure, since it does not refer to any region 'beyond' discourse any more than it can be contained within discourse. But silence nonetheless, as the experience of a nondialectical play of limits, or of what Foucault calls a "philosophy of nonpositive affirmation" rather than one of contradiction: "This does not imply a generalized negation, but an affirmation that affirms nothing, a radical rupture of transitivity" ("Preface to Transgression," 36). The continual affirmation of this rupture, the unending struggle for silence, is necessary in order to avoid hypostasizing the experience of the limit in the form of a transcendental condition.

Bataille insists, then, on a rupture in, or a disruption of, the very possibility of language, rather than on a "gap" that would be constitutive of language. He refuses to privilege discourse and signification as approaches to the unconscious. He regards language, like other utilitarian social practices, as a mode of reduction and assimilation. The "interior experience" must be affirmed against language, all the more so in that its ineffability cannot be posited as a higher, extra-linguistic mode of thought or of presence. Language can only mislead, even (or especially) when it calls attention to its own propensity to mislead.

Bien que les mots drainent en nous presque toute la vie . . . il subsiste en nous une part muette, dérobée, insaisissable. . . . Ce sont des mouvements intérieurs vagues, qui ne dépendent d'aucun objet et n'ont pas d'intention . . . si bien que le langage . . . est dépossédé, ne peut rien dire, se borne à dérober ces états à l'attention. . . . Si nous vivons sans contester sous la loi du langage, ces états sont en nous comme s'ils n'étaient pas. . . . Mais la difficulté est qu'on n'arrive facilement ni tout à fait à se taire, qu'il faut lutter contre soi-même. (*OC*, 5:27)

Although words drain almost all life from within us . . . there subsists in us a silent, elusive, ungraspable part. . . . They are the vague inner movements, which depend on no object and have no intention . . . so that language . . . is dispossessed, can say nothing, is limited to drawing our attention away from these states. . . . If we live under the law of language without contesting it, these states are within us as if they didn't exist. . . . But the difficulty is that one does not succeed easily nor completely in silencing oneself, that one must fight against oneself. (*IE*, 14–15)

It is extremely difficult for us to escape this colonization of the unconscious by language. But it is equally difficult to enforce this colonization: the unconscious resists linguistic determination as much, and in the same way, as any other form of determination. Our conception of the unconscious needs to be undone by silence rather than defined through language, rhetoric, or speech. And one cannot get around this difficulty by referring to the effects of the *Spaltung*, or differentiating between a first-level reality and its discursive, or scientific, representation. Any attempted reduction to utility—and any resistance to this reduction—takes place simultaneously on both planes: "Cette impossibilité qui touche à la base l'assimilation sociale touche en même temps l'assimilation scientifique. Ces deux sortes d'assimilations ont une seule structure [This impossibility, which has a fundamental impact on social assimilation, likewise has an impact on scientific assimilation. These two types of assimilation have a single structure]" (*OC*, 1:344; *VE*, 140–41). Neither the disruptive effect of the unconscious, nor its reduction and regulation, can be particularly or exclusively attributed to, or located within, language.

Bataille, like the later Wittgenstein, therefore affirms the multiple and heterogeneous interpenetration of language and other "forms of life" or aspects of social reality, prior to the point at which the question of their representational adequacy to one another, or lack of it, can even arise. Discourse is implicated within, and itself implies, other social practices, to a degree that renders any hierarchy of representations, or metalinguistic "theory of types," entirely arbitrary. As Jean-François Lyotard points out—commenting on Luce Irigaray's rejection of the Lacanian distinction between the phallus as Symbolic operator and the penis as actual organ—the elevation of such a hierarchy by the assertion of the primacy of the signifier (and of the phallus as ultimate signifier) rests on a logically ungrounded "decision" which in fact constitutes a brutal imposition of power ("One of the Things at Stake in Women's Struggles"). The Symbolic model of the unconscious is an essentially theological category, whose imposition has the obvious consequence of reconfirming, rather than upsetting, power relations (or worse, of mystifying power in the form of an insurpassable "authority"). The phallus as transcendental signifier, like the Kantian categorical imperative, functions all the more tyrannically insofar as it is absent and inaccessible, and insofar as its representative, the analyst, disclaims responsibility for its commands since he cannot, on his own account, be "supposed to know."

Decapitation as an affirmative gesture ruptures the self-validating logic of this transcendental structure; in this sense, it cannot be identified with castration. It is only in a secondary movement that the Symbolic hierarchy (and the castration threat which supports it) is reconstituted, when in the wake of violent metamorphosis, or of revolutionary upheaval, "la structure sociale détruite se recompose en développant lentement en elle une aversion pour la décomposition initiale [the destroyed social structure recomposes itself by slowly developing an aversion for the initial decomposition]" (*OC*, 1:468; *VE*, 198). This defensive "aversion," this hysterical refusal of instability and metamorphosis, marks the "becoming-reactive" of desire. In a secondary, reactive process of reconstitution by nihilistic projection, society transforms "nonpositive affirmation" into the Christian and psychoanalytic "esthetics of transgression" anatomized and criticized by Baudrillard (*L'échange symbolique et la mort*, 242). It is the reduction of expenditure, its being assigned a socially "useful" role, which makes possible the impasses of narcissism, the imperialism of language, and the worship of "lack" and castration denounced by Deleuze and Guattari as constitutive features at once of psychoanalysis as a doctrine and of modern bourgeois society in its actual functioning.

I will deal more briefly with a third kind of reduction, one which is American rather than European, and which relies on a certain pragmatic and quasi-historical argument. It may be said that the violent, excessively dramatic tone of Bataille's writing is understandable in the face of the horrors of the thirties and forties; but it seems far less appropriate now. So radical and uncompromising a vision is out of place in an age of postmodern irony. We have long since fallen into the "void" which Bataille contemplated with fascination in 1938. Recent American philosophers—Richard Rorty is a prime example— decry the puerility and sensationalism of that post-structuralist thought that is so deeply indebted to Bataille. Such thought, they argue, makes too big a fuss over the collapse of moral and epistemological absolutes, a collapse that Anglo-American philosophy has long since taken for granted. One hundred years after Nietzsche announced the death of God, there is no longer any need to lament or celebrate the fall of the foundations into a bottomless void. On this view, Bataille's meditations would be at best the ironic or anguished expression of a regressive metaphysical nostalgia. His writings would be marked by his inability to give up the totalizing and theological explanations in which he no longer believes, but which he feels compelled to perpetuate in negative form.

To respond to such arguments it is necessary, once again, to shift the terms of the discussion. For Bataille, traditional philosophical discourse, as much as that of any other discipline, remains situated within the horizon of utility. Philosophy, whether prescriptive or descriptive, is an imposition of closure, a setting of things in place. It denies contingency (either by excluding it or by recuperating it), and imposes conceptual (and often more than just conceptual) law and order. It conforms itself to, and exists only to serve, the goals of stability and preservation. It establishes knowledge as its primary concern, regardless of whether it claims to set limits to knowledge (as in skeptical and critical thought) or conversely to extend the possibilities of knowledge beyond previously established limits. In either case it subordinates experience to comprehension, and thereby fails to be sufficiently extreme: "Aller au bout signifie tout au moins ceci: que la limite qu'est la connaissance comme fin soit franchie [Going to the end signifies at least this: that the limit, which is knowledge as a goal, be crossed]" (*OC*, 5:20; *IE*, 8). Philosophy remains essentially contemplative, confirming the order of things as they are, or rationalizing the processes by which they change. And one cannot escape these constraints by creating a better, more accurate, or less mystified philosophy, but only by reaching the point where philosophy as such ceases. "Plus loin la tête éclate: l'homme n'est pas contemplation (il n'a la paix qu'en fuyant), il est supplication, guerre, angoisse, folie [Further on one's head bursts: man is not contemplation (he only has peace by fleeing); he is supplication, war, anguish, madness]" (*OC*, 5:49; *IE*, 36–37).

Bataille's discourse is radically a-philosophical, in that its violent agitations exclude any moment of contemplative resolution: "Oubli de tout. Profonde descente dans la nuit de l'existence. Supplication infinie de l'ignorance, se noyer d'angoisse [Forgetting of everything. Deep descent into the night of existence. Infinite supplication of ignorance, drowning oneself in anguish]" (*OC*, 5:49: *IE*, 36). Such a procedure does not pose uncertainty or the absence of God as a metaphysical (ontological, existential, or epistemological) problem. It rather abandons any claim regarding the possibility *or* impossibility of knowledge. What is at stake is not the determination of concepts, nor the elucidation of pragmatic distinctions. Bataille does not seek to establish ideal conditions of possibility, any more than he remains content with actual circumstances of use. His method is transgressive and subversive, and not evaluative or descriptive. Where philosophy seeks to define or delimit a given notion (or use of language), to found, legitimate, or circumscribe it, Bataille's continual effort is to de-define it, to un-ground it. He asks how to break out of the constraints of value, purpose, and meaning, how to escape those already socially given conditions. He seeks not to state a doctrine, but to affirm a process involving continual "contestation d'elle-même et non-savoir [contestation of itself and non-knowledge]" (*OC*, 5:120; *IE*, 102). And he necessarily approaches this dilemma in the "absurd," exacerbated form of a paradoxical effort—one whose implications are simultaneously political and personal—"sortir par un projet du domaine du projet [to leave the realm of the project by means of a project]" (*OC*, 5:60; *IE*, 46).

The question, then, is not one of accepting or rejecting "metaphysics" on a conceptual level. It is rather one of preserving or contesting a society that reduces the other to the same and defines all activity in terms of projects and goals. From the point of view of utility and social function, contemporary American pragmatism and "postanalytic" philosophy remains in continuity with the metaphysics it rejects. For example, Rorty's commitment to holism and "solidarity" and his vision of philosophy as an ongoing, edifying "conversation" reduce difference by confining it within the framework of an allegedly common participation in a homogeneous cultural heritage. The effect is to neutralize and normalize even the most extreme demands, to manage conflict by enforcing a consensus. After all, no matter what you say, it is all part of the same polite discussion. Even in the absence of grounds, everything must be tidily accounted for: "Our community— the community of the liberal intellectuals of the secular modern West— want to be able to give a *post factum* account of any change of view. We want to be able, so to speak, to justify ourselves to our earlier selves" ("Solidarity or Objectivity?" 12). The culture of utility cannot be contested, because differing positions can be recognized only insofar as they are articulated from *within* that culture and its continuities. Rorty's facile pluralism thus forecloses conflict, heterogeneity, and non-utility just as effectively as does any appeal to a priori principles or to the supremacy of Reason.

All the reductive interpretations that I have been considering take as primary phenomena the reactive movements described by Bataille at various points in his argument. These reactive instances—solidified into "positions"—are then "put to work" in order to redefine Bataille's affirmative gestures in their own negative terms. Now the point is that such readings are in a certain sense unavoidable. Not only can they be accounted for according to the logic of Bataille's text, but in economic terms they arise precisely to the extent that that text itself tries to "account for" anything. The very ambiguities upon which Bataille most strongly insists draw his discourse in directions that can only contradict his polemical intent. Since his writing makes strategic use of philosophical notions it does not finally accept, he cannot preserve his argument from various tendentious dismissals and appropriations. This is why, for example, he finds it so difficult to defend himself from the misconstructions of phenomenologically oriented critics such as Sartre. (See Sartre's notorious review of *L'expérience intérieure*, "Un nouveau mystique," *Critiques littéraires*, 174–229; and Bataille's "Réponse à Jean-Paul Sartre," *OC*, 6:195–202).

In the "Discussion sur le péché [Discussion on Sin]" (*OC*, 6:315–59) which followed Bataille's presentation of his theses on "Le sommet et le déclin [The Summit and the Decline]," Sartre and Hyppolite make much of the ambiguities surrounding the use of the word or concept *néant* (nothingness). They seek to show that Bataille cannot avoid defining desire dialectically, as a form of negativity that seeks plenitude or repletion outside of itself. For Sartre, the alternative is clear: "Ou nous sommes des plénitudes et ce que nous recherchons, c'est le néant, ou nous sommes vides et ce que nous recherchons, c'est l'être [Either we are plenitudes, and we seek nothingness; or we are empty, and we seek being]" (*OC*, 6:339). Sartre's position, the Hegelian and existentialist one, is the latter; he attributes the former to Bataille. And on a certain level of discursive argument Bataille finds it impossible to reject Sartre's strictures, or to deny that his own "onto-logical" definition of *néant* (*OC*, 6:337) has been contaminated by the dialectical definition that would identify it with the power of the negative. Nonetheless, it should be clear by this point that expenditure is a movement that is precisely irreducible to any conception of the labor of the negative, and that Bataille's non-negative definition of desire is not simply an inversion of the negative, Hegelian one. In Bataille's schema, we are not plenitudes (the excess which defines us is an affirmation, but it is irreducible to presence); and the nothingness which we would seek is in principle, as well as in fact, unrealizable (hence the necessity of the decline). The "insufficiency" which, according to Bataille, haunts both being and nothingness, prevents any realization of the negative no less than any positive closure. But this "insufficiency" is also, in the "general economy" by which it functions, unable to exclude those very notions which endeavor to deny, reduce, or recuperate it.

Bataille's discourse is therefore incessantly contaminated by the very metaphysical notions it is directed most powerfully against. In particular (as I have already suggested), *transgression* is a deeply compromised word or notion, in that it implies a primary reference to the order being transgressed. Bataille is never more ambiguous than when he asserts that "la transgression n'est pas la négation de l'interdit, mais elle le dépasse et le complète [transgression does not negate the prohibition, but surpasses and completes it]" (*OC*, 10:66; *Erotism*, 63). This is one of the points where, as Derrida points out, Bataille needs to be read most carefully against himself. For if "surpass and complete" are understood in a Hegelian or Freudian sense (as *Aufhebung*, or as repression followed by a return of the repressed), then Bataille is still presenting transgression as a source of social harmony and solidarity, a movement which confirms the Law in the very act of violating it. And according to Bataille's argument, such a process does in fact take place in all known human societies: it is precisely in this way that power (exploitation or domination) is generated. The mistake—or more accurately, the "becoming-reactive"—of various critical, philosophical, religious, psychoanalytic, and scientific discourses occurs when they ratify, identify with, or participate in this process, when they themselves become instruments of utility, domination, and abstract contemplation.

It is in order to avoid such a recuperative notion of transgression that the most radical contemporary French thought has turned toward "a generalized anti-Hegelianism: difference and repetition have taken the place of the identical and the negative, of identity and contradiction" (Deleuze, *Différence et répétition*, 1). The rejection of transgression is part of a more general attack on the logic of negation. Such an anti-Hegelian move is of course the basic premise of Althusser's Marxism, with its notions of overdetermination and structural causality. But an even more fundamental break with any logic of the negative characterizes Foucault's nondialectical and nonrepresentational analytics of power. And Deleuze and Guattari are altogether explicit in their rejection of the concomitant notions of Law, and of desire as lack. All these theorists suggest that dialectical negativity is neither capable of explaining actual conditions of oppression (since it is compelled to resort to such dubious notions as existential alienation and psychological repression) nor helpful in articulating a possible revolutionary alternative to existing power relations (since the negative remains implicated with the totality which it is supposed to alter or abolish).

The notion of transgression can easily be assimilated to other forms of generalized negation. (Such is certainly the case in Bakhtin's analyses of the carnivalesque, as well as in the anthropological studies, by Mauss, Caillois, and others, that most directly influenced Bataille.) For this reason the theorists just mentioned take their distance with regard to Bataille. Thus Foucault's later work seems founded on a recantation of his earlier interest in Bataillean transgression, in the experience of limits and of infinite contestation. In his account of the "repressive hypothesis" and of the inadequacies of a certain rhetoric of sexual liberation, he disparagingly remarks that "to conceive the category of the sexual in terms of the law, death, blood, and sovereignty—whatever the references to Sade and Bataille, and however one might gauge their 'subversive' influence—is in the last analysis a historical 'retroversion'" (*History of Sexuality*, 1:150).

Yet obviously I have been trying to suggest that a rejection of the dialectical logic of Law and negativity is already—in its very ambiguity—the most crucial feature of Bataille's own text. Transgression is not, finally, a negation; it is an affirmative movement that by its mobility and excess both generates and disintegrates social and individual "arrangements" (what Deleuze and Guattari call *agencements*) of power. It is therefore in a still profoundly Bataillean inspiration that Foucault is able to describe a "power" that is multiple, immanent, and affirmative, and attack the restrictive logic that would represent power in "juridico-discursive" terms (*History of Sexuality*, 1:81–102). When Bataille affirms transgression, he is recalling that the logic of utility and negativity is not exhaustive, even though the movement of transgression itself is most frequently, and with horrible effectivity, captured for the purposes of utility, negativity, and power. He is insisting that "la déchirure est l'expression de la richesse [laceration is the expression of richness]" (*OC*, 5:95; *IE*, 80), in contrast to an entire tradition that sees nonpresence and nonidentity only as the effects of prohibition and restriction. In Bataille's logic of excess, it is not the transgression which confirms the priority of the interdiction, so much as the interdiction that is a bizarre secondary recuperation—or conceptualization—of the impossibility put into play by transgression. As Blanchot explains it in one of his commentaries on Bataille:

> *L'interdit marque le point où cesse le pouvoir.* La transgression n'est pas un acte dont, dans certains conditions, la puissance de certains hommes et leur maîtrise se montreraient encore capables. Elle désigne ce qui est radicalement hors de portée: l'atteinte de l'inaccessible, le franchissement de l'infranchissable. (*EI*, 308)

> *The interdiction marks the point where power ceases.* Transgression is not an act of which, in certain conditions, the power and mastery of certain men would still be capable. It designates that which is radically out of reach: the attainment of the inaccessible, the crossing of the uncrossable.

Transgression and sacrifice, for Bataille, do not confirm the solidity, the power relations, of this world or of any world. Rather than maintaining my existence at the cost of my nullification, for the benefit of Law and hierarchy, I rupture that Law and that hierarchy in the same movement by which I lose myself: "Ce sacrifice *que nous consommons* se distingue des autres en ceci: le sacrificateur lui-même est touché par le coup qu'il frappe, il succombe et se perd avec sa victime [This sacrifice *which we consummate* is distinguished from others in this way: the one who performs the sacrifice is himself touched by the blow which he strikes, he succumbs and loses himself with his victim]" (*OC*, 5:176; *IE*, 153). Such is the radical, affirmative force of Bataille's notion of sacrifice. It contests power not by opposing another power to it (which would serve merely to reinstate the Law or the order of power), but by *losing* it, *forgetting* it. Or as Blanchot so beautifully puts it, "La transgression ne transgresse pas la loi, elle l'emporte avec elle [Transgression does not transgress the law, but carries the law away with it]" (*Le pas au-delà*, 139).

Le vif de la vie, ce serait l'avivement qui ne se contente
pas de la présence vivante, qui consume ce qui est présent
jusqu'à l'exemption, l'exemplarité sans exemple de la
non-présence ou de la non-vie, l'absence en sa vivacité,
toujours revenant sans venue.
—Maurice Blanchot, *L'écriture du désastre*

CHAPTER 4

Decapitations

Affect and Exteriority
in Bataille

Bataille struggles to mobilize, within his own discourse, those forces of dispersion and conflict that discourse is never able to encompass or represent. Contesting rationality and utility in the name of passion, he is nonetheless impelled to have recourse to conceptual language—if only to turn this language against itself. In one sense, this is a necessary detour. As Blanchot puts it, "En définitive, pour se taire, il faut parler. Mais de quelle sorte de paroles? [Finally, in order to be silent, it is necessary to speak. But with what sort of words?]" (*CI*, 92; *UC*, 56). If Bataille must use words in order to become silent, then he will insist on unstable "mot[s] glissant[s] [slipping words]" such as, in particular, the word "silence":

> "Du mot il est déjà, je l'ai dit, l'abolition du bruit qu'est le mot; entre tous les mots c'est le plus pervers, ou le plus poétique: il est lui-même gage de sa mort. . . . Le silence est un mot qui n'est pas un mot. (*OC*, 5:28–29)

> It is already, as I have said, the abolition of the sound which the word is; among all words it is the most perverse, or the most poetic: it is the token of its own death. . . . Silence is a word which is not a word. (*IE*, 16)

It may be that when we invoke silence we are still, for all that, within the "prison-house of language," still being compelled to speak. But perhaps it is rather our speech which, in the very moment in which it proclaims its victories, meets its death, as it is traversed and undone—subtly and imperceptibly, or violently and outlandishly—by the perversity of silence.

Such silence is not a purity before or beyond speech. It does not indicate calm or appeasement. It is rather a violent convulsion, a catastrophe that overwhelms all sound and all speaking. "Joie inerte de mourant, de désert, chute dans l'impossible, cri sans résonance, silence d'accident mortel [Inert joy of someone dying, of the desert, fall into the impossible, cry without resonance, silence of a fatal accident]" (*OC*, 5:65; *IE*, 51). A silence that cannot be contained, cannot be designated, by the orders of rationality and of language, even though it is only within those orders that it is found. After all the explaining, one must have done with explanations. And if one exhausts all the reasons and all the languages, and reaches, impossibly, "l'extrême du possible [the extreme limit of the possible]" (*OC*, 5:51; *IE*, 38), how shall one continue to speak of one's experiences? "Les bruits de toutes sortes, cris, bavardages, rires, il faut que tout se perde en lui, se vide de sens dans son désespoir [Noises of all sorts, cries, chatter, laughter—it is necessary that everything be lost within him, become empty of meaning in his despair]" (*OC*, 5:51; *IE*, 39).

It is not silence which must be spoken or understood, so much as it is speaking and understanding which contain their own deaths within them, which are unable to manifest themselves apart from silence. Just as, similarly, all vision is implicated with, and articulated upon, darkness.

> Il est dans l'entendement une tache aveugle: qui rappelle la structure de l'oeil. . . . Dans la mesure où l'entendement est auxiliaire de l'action, la tache y est aussi négligable qu'elle est dans l'oeil. Mais dans la mesure où l'on envisage dans l'entendement l'homme lui-même, je veux dire une exploration du possible de l'être, la tache absorbe l'attention: ce n'est plus la tache qui se perd dans la connaissance, mais la connaissance en elle. L'existence de cette façon ferme le cercle, mais elle ne l'a pu sans inclure la nuit d'où elle ne sort que pour y rentrer. (*OC*, 5:129)

There is in understanding a blind spot: which is reminiscent of the structure of the eye. . . . To the extent that understanding is auxiliary to action, the spot within it is as negligible as it is within the eye. But to the extent that one views in understanding man himself, by that I mean an exploration of the possibilities of being, the spot absorbs one's attention: it is no longer the spot which loses itself in knowledge, but knowledge which loses itself in it. In this way existence closes the circle, but it couldn't do this without including the night from which it proceeds only in order to enter it again. (*IE*, 110–11)

In this movement of pure loss, there is no veiling and no unveiling, no hiddenness and no revelation. Just as silence interrupts speech and yet cannot be recovered as a hidden essence behind speech, so darkness interrupts the light of comprehension and yet must not be hypostasized as a secret truth beyond comprehension. In this darkness and this silence, there can be no ontology and no hermeneutics, no semantic or semiotic analysis. "Il est vain d'envisager uniquement dans l'aspect des choses les signes intelligibles qui permettent de distinguer divers éléments les uns des autres [It is vain to consider, in the appearances of things, only the intelligible signs that allow the various elements to be distinguished from each other]" (*OC*, 1:173; *VE*, 10). In the night, it is no longer possible to differentiate signs. Given this experience of radical unintelligibility, the ocular and the linguistic are equally unacceptable as models of thought. Or rather, they are necessarily insufficient insofar as they are only *models* or *metaphors* of thought: models of a thinking which has no model, metaphors of a movement which can be similar to nothing. This is why, insofar as Bataille must speak, the preferred terms in his vocabulary are words like "silence," or like "informe [formless]": "*informe* n'est pas seulement un adjectif ayant tel sens mais un terme servant à déclasser. . . . Ce qu'il désigne n'a ses droits dans aucun sens et se fait écraser partout" ["*formless* is not only an adjective having a given meaning, but a term that serves to bring things down in the world. . . . What it designates has no rights in any sense and gets itself squashed everywhere]" (*OC*, 1:217; *VE*, 31).

Bataille's writing neither designates objects, nor signifies ideas, nor manifests a hidden order of reality. Rather it charts the *expérience-limite* (*limit-experience*), as Blanchot puts it, of a "détour de tout visible et

de tout invisible [turning away from every visible and every invisible]"
(*EI*, 311). Thought, at the limit, is uncategorizable, because it is entirely visceral: *literally* spasmodic and excremental. "Comme si des im-
pulsions explosives devaient jaillir directement du corps par la bouche
sous forme de vociférations [As if explosive impulses were to spurt
directly out of the body through the mouth, in the form of screams]"
(*OC*, 1:237; *VE*, 59). The screaming human mouth is little different
from "les fesses obscènes et brenneuses de certains singes . . . ces impu-
diques protubérances, sortes de crânes excrémentiels aux couleurs
éblouissantes, parfois diaprées, allant du rose vif à un violet nacré extra-
ordinairement horrible [the shit-smeared and obscene anuses of certain
apes . . . these filthy protuberances, dazzlingly colored excremental
skulls, sometimes dappled, going from shocking pink to an extraordi-
narily horrible, pearly violet]" (*OC*, 2:16; *VE*, 75). In the case of both
orifices, expression begins as excretion, a movement at once glorious
and degraded: "un certain potentiel d'éclat et d'éblouissement propre
à la nature animale [a certain potential for brilliance and dazzle proper
to animal nature]" (*OC*, 2:16; *VE*, 75), realized in the wastefulness
of display, in the screams of orgasm or of agony, and in the ambivalent
fascination with shit. Bataille suggests that "la séduction extrême est
probablement à la limite de l'horreur [extreme seductiveness is probably
at the boundary of horror]" (*OC*, 1:187; *VE*, 17); in any case, seduction and horror are the oldest forms of expression, and this expression
takes place first of all in the involuntary movements of the body.

Expression, then, precedes intention, precedes the existence of any
content to be expressed. Thought and language emerge out of vocifera-
tions and physical contortions, and not from Symbolic articulation.
Bataille's theory of language is as far removed from structural linguis-
tics, or from various theories of the autonomy of the signifier, as it
is from idealist notions of the transparency of speech. It is closer, perhaps, to Jean-Pierre Brisset's schizophrenic insistence on the multiplicity and materiality of discourse, as described by Foucault: "Phonetic
repetition does not mark the total liberation of language with respect
to things, thoughts, and bodies; it does not reveal in discourse a state
of absolute weightlessness; to the contrary, it thrusts syllables into the
body, it gives them back the functions of cries and gestures; it rediscov-
ers the great plastic power which vociferates and gesticulates; it puts
words back in the mouth and around the sexual organs; in a time
faster than any thought it gives birth to and effaces a whirlwind of

frantic, savage, or exultant scenes, from which words arise and which words call forth" (*Sept propos sur le septième ange,* 42–43).

It is in a similar sense that, for Bataille, "le *copule* des termes [the *copula* of terms]" cannot be separated from "celui [le *copule*/la *copulation*] des corps [the *copulation* of bodies]" (*OC,* 1:81; *VE,* 5). Thought must not be posed abstractly, as if cognition were something apart from the passions that constitute and impel it. Thought *is* affect, and not the expression or substitutive representation of affect. And affect in turn is not a fixed state, but the immediacy of a passage or an alteration. The incessant *circulation* of meanings and phrases is an effect, not of laws of signification, but of the multiple affections and interchanges that traverse and disarrange actual bodies. "La vie n'est jamais située en un point particulier: elle passe rapidement d'un point à l'autre (ou de multiples points à d'autres points), comme un courant ou comme une sorte de ruissellement électrique [Life is never situated at a particular point; it passes rapidly from one point to another (or from multiple points to other points) like a current or like a sort of streaming of electricity]" (*OC,* 5:111; *IE,* 94).

All this is to say that the passion of the "interior experience" does not originate, and does not conclude, either in myself as subject or in the self-referring systems of Being and language. "Plus loin, ta vie ne se borne pas à cet insaisissable ruissellement intérieur; elle ruisselle aussi au-dehors et s'ouvre incessamment à ce qui s'écoule ou jaillit vers elle [Further on, your life is not limited to that ungraspable inner streaming; it streams to the outside as well and opens itself incessantly to what flows out or surges forth towards it]" (*OC,* 5:111; *IE,* 94). Thought or passion, in its very immediacy, is at the same time absolute exteriority. Not my reaction to, or alienation from, a world of external objects, but the irreducible insistence of an unconceptualizable materiality that has already formed and deformed me. This affirmation is the basis of Bataille's materialism, of "un matérialisme n'impliquant pas d'ontologie, n'impliquant pas que la matière est la chose en soi. . . . La matière basse est extérieure et étrangère aux aspirations idéales humaines et refuse de se laisser réduire aux grandes machines ontologiques résultant de ces aspirations [a materialism not implying an ontology, not implying that matter is the thing-in-itself. . . . Base matter is external and foreign to ideal human aspirations, and it refuses to allow itself to be reduced to the great ontological machines resulting from these aspirations]" (*OC,* 1:225; *VE,* 49–51).

It is not that I *have* an experience *of* exteriority. There is no primary intentionality, no phenomenological consciousness-of-something. Nor do I need consciously to register or represent the changes of which I am already composed. Indeed, the "blind spot" in discursive comprehension reduces to absurdity any attempt at originary apperception, or subsequent self-reflection. The exteriority of "base matter" is itself the pathos of my thought, the "experience" that Bataille defines as "interior." This excrementality, this sheer physicality, positively invests—even as it invades and disrupts—my being. In this sense, my thought is both immediate and unstable, neither opposed to the world nor forming some sort of unity in or with the world. All I can apprehend is a certain *douleur* (pain), *inquiétude* (disquiet), or *angoisse* (anxiety), experience of the manner in which "l'obstacle que tu es doit se nier lui-même et se vouloir détruit, du fait qu'il est partie des forces qui le brisent [the obstacle which you are must negate itself and wish itself destroyed, given that it has set out from the forces which break it]" (*OC*, 5:113; *IE*, 96). My existential isolation, which is to say my self-consciousness, is only a temporary effect, a relative viscosity or partial coagulation, of the very movement which renders it impossible. "Les fragiles parois de ton isolement où se composaient les multiples arrêts, les obstacles de la conscience, n'auront servi qu'à réfléchir un instant l'éclat de ces univers au sein desquels tu ne cessas jamais d'être perdu [The fragile walls of your isolation, which comprised the multiple halts and obstacles of consciousness, will have served only to reflect for an instant the brilliance of those universes in whose bosom you have never ceased to be lost]" (*OC*, 5:112; *IE*, 95).

Thought is passion, and not representation: "*changement pur* [pure change]" (*OC*, 5:89; *IE*, 74), a continual being-affected. It is only to the extent that thought actually *suffers* these violent agitations that it is then able to "reflect" them. "Tu ne pourrais devenir le miroir d'une réalité déchirante si tu ne devais *te briser* . . . [You could not become the mirror of a heart-rending reality if you were not compelled to *shatter yourself* . . .]" (*OC*, 5:113; *IE*, 96). At the very point of annihilation, experiencing its own "déchirure [laceration]" (*OC*, 5:113; *IE*, 96), thought directly affirms the real. All the categories of language and consciousness, all the structures of subjectivity and objectivity, of intuition and comprehension, have collapsed, and yet an indefinable violence, a sense of pain or ecstasy, remains. 'Something' subsists, even when there is no revelation, no truth, nothing to be found.

Je ne vois rien: *cela* n'est ni visible ni sensible de quelque façon qu'on l'imagine, ni intelligible. *Cela* rend douleureux et lourd de ne pas mourir. . . . Les images de ravissement trahissent. *Ce qui est là* est à la mesure de l'effroi, l'effroi le fait venir. Il fallut un aussi violent fracas pour que *celà soit là*. (*OC*, 5:142)

I see nothing: *that* is neither visible nor sensible in any way one can imagine, nor intelligible. *That* makes it painful and heavy not to be able to die. . . . Images of ecstasy betray. *What is there* has the dimensions of terror, terror makes it come. Such a violent clash was necessary for *that to be there*. (*IE*, 122)

Pain and dread—or ecstasy and laughter—even in the absence of anyone who could experience that pain or that ecstasy, give it words and make it his or her own. All the images and ideas are repellent idealizations, impositions of meaning, when in fact there is nothing I can see or understand, and no "I" to register such seeing and understanding. Language presupposes intentions, and therefore at least a virtual (grammatical) subject; but the feeling of *what is there* has no such specificity. Language also posits a degree of universality and interchangeability, since no signification is entirely singular; but the feeling of *what is there* has no such generality. Affect precedes language, just as it precedes the constitution of a subject. It is the unbearable extremity of passion, and not the alienating intervention of language, which is asubjective and nonintentional. The "interior experience" radically disrupts self-presence. The subject seeks ecstasy, seeks to pass out of itself. Yet its existence as a subject can be defined only as its continuing endeavor to preserve itself. And so "il existe un irréductible désaccord du sujet cherchant l'extase et de l'extase elle-même [there exists an irreducible discord between the subject seeking ecstasy and the ecstasy itself]" (*OC*, 5:75; *IE*, 60).

Désaccord (discord), *déchirure* (laceration), *un violent fracas* (a violent clash). . . . Not the *cogito*, but communication. Not self-identity and self-recognition, but contingency and "improbabilité infinie [infinite improbability]" (*OC*, 1:89, *OC*, 5:84; *VE*, 130, *IE*, 69) define me. "Car si la plus infime différence était survenue au cours des événements successifs dont je suis un terme, à la place de ce *moi* intégralement avide d'être *moi*, il y aurait eu 'un *autre*' [For if the tiniest difference had occurred in the course of the successive events of which I am the result, in the place of this *me*, integrally avid to be *me*, there would have been 'an *other*']" (*OC*, 1:89; *VE*, 130). Nothing is more random, more fragile, more inessential than my "identity." I am "irreplaceable" precisely because any experience of change is an experience which no longer happens to "me," in which I am no longer "myself." Hence the primacy of affect—of a raw, asubjective experiencing of change— over consciousness *or* language. How reductive of psychoanalysis to reject the notion of unconscious affect, on the grounds that "it is hard to see how the term affect could remain intelligible without some reference to self-consciousness" and the ego (Laplanche and Pontalis, *The Language of Psycho-Analysis*, 14). For if the history of past affects is what makes the singularity of the "me" possible, it is equally apparent that—as long as this history continues—affect cannot coincide with that "me," or be present to it beyond a certain threshold. Language is a tool of social order, assigning a circumscribed "position" to the self-conscious subject, whereas the violence of affective experience de-positions the subject, exceeding its awareness, continually making it *other*. I become aware of my ecstasy only in retrospect, and even then only "comme la sensation d'un effet venant de dehors. . . . En vérité je suis *agi* [like the sensation of an effect coming from the outside. . . . In reality, I am *acted upon*]" (*OC*, 5:75; *IE*, 60).

The violent shocks of alteration are not present to me, do not appear to me. I lack the distance which would allow me to regard and evaluate them. But it is for this reason—since they have already changed me— that they are immediately *felt*; and that they can only be felt as pure "interiority." Even though this interiority is not that of "myself," and even though the shocks do not derive from within, but always supervene from outside. And this is why, in order to *affirm* exteriority, contingency, chance, and change, paradoxically "il est nécessaire de dénuder ce qui est là de toutes ses représentations extérieures, jusqu'à ce que ce ne soit plus qu'une pure violence, une intériorité, une pure chute intérieure dans un abîme illimité [it is necessary to strip away all the external representations from what is there, until it is nothing but a pure violence, an interiority, a pure inner fall into a limitless abyss]" (*OC*, 1:556; *VE*, 238; repeated with slight modifications in *OC*, 5:142; *IE*, 121–22).

I cannot apprehend the passion which fixes and moves me, makes and unmakes me, just as I cannot possess, or project myself into, the moment of my own death. Indeed, all we can say of death is that it is the extreme form, the ultimate limit, of perpetual change. Death, like all change, is necessary to, and yet infinitely alien to, the "improbability" which I now am. "La mort est en un sens vulgaire inévitable, mais en un sens profond, inaccessible [Death is in one sense the common inevitable, but in another sense, profound, inaccessible]" (*OC*, 5:86; *IE*, 71). My participation in death is incompatible with my knowledge of it. I can approach that limit, that extreme impossibility, that moment of intensest affect which is change or death, only by continually "stripping away" (*dénuder*) whatever has presence, whatever has permanence, whatever seems to constitute the essence of the world or of myself. But this process will have to continue forever; there is no moment of final nudity, no substance beneath all the layers that are stripped away.

What can it mean to *affirm* such a process, given that it is an involuntary and ungraspable one? Isn't the difference between "experience" and metaphysics precisely that between the blind immediacy of the event and the laborious process of its discursive presentation? If language is always reductive, and no transcendence of singular viewpoints is possible, then what is the perspective from which Bataille's own discourse speaks? It is not in terms of knowledge—of epistemological definition—that these questions can be answered, since the possibility of knowing, or the alternative between knowledge and skepticism, is precisely the configuration which Bataille struggles to displace. Affirmation is not simple assertion, just as contestation is not simple denial. "La 'contestation' est encore mouvement essentiel à l'amour—que rien ne peut assouvir ['Contestation' is still a movement essential to love— that nothing can satisfy]" (*OC*, 5:143; *IE*, 123). Affirmation and contestation are themselves affections, and not intellectual exercises. Bataille seems at times to be enunciating a metaphysical vision of the grounds of existence. But something else, something not definable, is always at stake: "cette fois, tout à coup, me rappellant *ce qui est là*, j'ai dá sangloter. Je me relève la tête vidée—à force d'aimer, d'être *ravi* . . . [this time, all of a sudden, remembering *what is there*, I had to weep. I get up, my head emptied—from loving, from being *ravished* . . .]" (*OC*, 5:142; *IE*, 122).

Angoisse (anguish) and *extase* (ecstasy), *douleur* (pain) and *ravissement* (rapture). Throughout Bataille's writing, there is an interminable play, an irregular oscillation, of these affects. "L'existence est tumulte qui se chante, où fièvre et déchirures se lient à l'ivresse [Existence is a tumult singing itself, where fever and lacerations are bound to drunkenness]" (*OC*, 5:96; *IE*, 81). And the subject is only a point at which these tumultuous movements are interrupted, reflected, intensified: "je ne suis et tu n'es, dans les vastes flux des choses, qu'un point d'arrêt favorable au rejaillissement [I am only and you are only, in the vast flow of things, a stopping point favoring a resurgence]" (*OC*, 5:112; *IE*, 95). Affirmation is the inscription—in the body as much as in language—of the simultaneous splendor and horror of this movement. For the passion of expenditure is irretrievably entwined with the contrary needs of self-preservation: there is no resolution to "le débat que mènent en s'opposant la volonté de prendre et celle de perdre—le désir de s'approprier et celui contraire de communiquer [the debate between opposing wills—the will to take and the will to lose—the desire to appropriate unto oneself and the opposite desire to communicate]" (*OC*, 5:165; *IE*, 142). I rapturously seek to become other than my limited self, but this becoming remains painful for the "me" which I currently am. I can neither hold on to myself, nor possess my non-self; the other which I continually become remains perpetually beyond my grasp. And this other is itself an "improbable" singularity, as limited and as contingent as I am; so that there is no conclusion, but the process of metamorphosis must start all over again. "Le sujet—lassitude de soi-même, nécessité d'aller à l'extrême—cherche l'extase, il est vrai; jamais il n'a *la volonté* de son extase [The subject—weariness of itself, necessity of proceeding to the extreme limit—seeks ecstasy, it is true; never does it have *the will* for its ecstasy]" (*OC*, 5:75; *IE*, 60).

The same violent alteration, the same affection of the body, will be pain or fear at one moment, drunken exaltation or sexual rapture at another. As perspectives shift, as experiences intensify, anguish and ecstasy play off against, and feed into, one another.

> Le non-savoir est tout d'abord ANGOISSE. Dans l'angoisse apparaît la nudité, qui extasie. Mais l'extase elle-même (la nudité, la communication) se dérobe si l'angoisse se dérobe. Ainsi l'extase ne demeure possible que dans l'angoisse de l'extase, dans ce fait qu'elle ne peut être satisfaction, *savoir saisi.* . . . Mais l'angoisse est l'horreur du dénuement et l'instant vient où, dans l'audace, le dénuement est aimé, où je me donne au dénuement: il est alors la nudité qui extasie. (*OC*, 5:66)

> Non-knowledge is first of all ANGUISH. In anguish nudity appears, which causes ecstasy. But ecstasy itself (nudity, communication) slips away if anguish slips away. Thus ecstasy only remains possible in the anguish of ecstasy, in the fact that it cannot be satisfac-

tion, *grasped knowledge*. . . . But anguish is the horror of destitution, and the moment comes when, in audacity, destitution is loved, when I give myself over to destitution: nudity then causes ecstasy. (*IE*, 52)

This interminable oscillation is the very movement of nonsubjective affect. "Le non-savoir communique l'extase [Non-knowledge communicates ecstasy]" (*OC*, 5:66; *IE*, 52), but not necessarily to me (which is why Bataille later says that such an assertion is "gratuite et décevante [gratuitous and deceptive]," *OC*, 5:143; *IE*, 123). Affects are transitions of energy, moving in any direction; they are singular rather than universal, but they do not necessarily have a privileged relation to "me." What is important is that they are movements, metamorphoses, rather than fixed states. The only conditions Bataille excludes are the teleologically defined conditions of "action" and mastery on the one hand, and the apparent stases of satisfaction, appeasement, and postcoital repose on the other. For no expenditure is great enough to put an end to itself once and for all, to obviate the necessity of eternal repetition. "Je persévère en désordre, fidèle à des passions que vraiment j'ignore, qui me dérèglent dans tous les sens [I persevere in disorder, faithful to passions which I do not really know, and which unsettle me in all directions]" (*OC*, 5:136; *IE*, 117).

The exigency that impels the "interior experience" cannot be construed as something private, personal, or subjective. For even as it denies me any repose, any fixity, any possibility of self-reflexive identification, so also it pushes me toward a community of others, in a movement of *communication*. "Chaque être est, je crois, incapable à lui seul, d'aller au bout de l'être. . . . je n'atteins pas l'extrême à moi seul et réellement je ne puis croire l'extrême atteint, car jamais je n'y demeure" [Each being is, I believe, incapable on his/her own of going to the end of being. . . . I don't attain the extreme limit on my own, and, in actual fact, I can't believe the extreme limit attained, for I never remain there]" (*OC*, 5:55; *IE*, 42). My becoming other than myself is also my giving myself, without reserve, to others; Bataille always equates communication with "perte de soi [loss of self]" (e.g., *OC*, 5:162; *IE*, 140), and insists that it can occur only when, "dans l'excès du désir nous nous donnons [in the excess of desire we give ourselves]" (*OC*, 5:160; *IE*, 139). Or as Blanchot defines the notion of sacrifice in Acéphale: "s'abandonner et se donner: *se donner sans retour à l'abandon sans limite* [to abandon oneself and to give oneself: *to give oneself without return to limitless abandonment*]" (*CI*, 30; *UC*, 15).

Communication, for Bataille, is therefore not the passing of a neutral message between the poles of sender and receiver. In the movement of communication, none of these three terms remains intact. We must think rather of an interchange between lovers, in which "ce qui communique (est pénétré en chacun d'eux par l'autre) est la part aveugle qui ne se connaît ni ne connaît [that which communicates (which is penetrated in each of them by the other) is the blind part which neither knows itself nor knows anything]" (*OC*, 5:161; *IE*, 139). What I communicate to the other is not an intention of my subjectivity. It is a literal (physical or psychological) portion of myself, but a portion which, precisely by virtue of having been communicated, is no longer myself. I do not extend myself to include or to understand the other, because this would still mean possessing the other, reducing the other to a dimension of myself. Rather, I give myself over to the other, give him/her a gift which cannot be reciprocated because the "me" who would receive in return is no longer the one who initially gave. Indeed, such a gift cannot even obligate the recipient, since he/she cannot hold onto it as property but is instead radically changed by receiving it, therefore unable to inscribe it in an economic register of debts and assets, profit and loss. Radical impropriety on the parts alike of the sender, the message, and the recipient. Communication is disequilibrating and irreversible, hence irreducible to Lévi-Strauss's, Lacan's, and Baudrillard's notions of "symbolic exchange."

A better analogy is between Bataille's writing and the feminist writing of Hélène Cixous, particularly her article "*Le sexe ou la tête?* [Castration or Decapitation?]." Cixous figures the unlimited giving of women's writing and women's sexuality in terms of vomiting and menstruation: "l'épanchement . . . qui peut apparaître dans des textes primitifs ou primaires comme une fantasmique sur le sang, sur les règles, etc., mais que je verrais plutôt comme 'rendre gorge', comme 'dégurgiter' [an outpouring . . . which can appear in primitive or elementary texts as a fantasy of blood, of menstrual flow, etc., but which I prefer to see as vomiting, as 'throwing up,' 'disgorging']" (14/54). Bataille figures a similar process in terms of shitting and ejaculation in "*L'anus solaire* [The Solar Anus]" (*OC*, 1:79–86; *VE*, 5–9): "Le globe terrestre est couvert de volcans qui lui servent d'anus. Bien que ce globe ne mange rien, il rejette parfois au-dehors le contenu de ses entrailles. . . . La terre se branle parfois avec frénésie et tout s'écroule à sa surface [The terrestrial globe is covered with volcanoes, which serve as its anus. Although this globe eats nothing, it often violently ejects the contents of its entrails. . . . The earth sometimes jerks off in a frenzy, and everything collapses on its surface]" (*OC*, 1:85; *VE*, 8).

The difference here between male and female images of bodily activity is too obvious to need extended comment. More important is the way in which Bataille disrupts the usual assumptions of phallocentric order, despite his obviously masculine and heterosexual frame of reference. For "l'amour terrestre sans condition, érection sans issue et sans règle [terrestrial love without condition, erection without escape and without rule]" (*OC*, 1:86; *VE*, 9) is posed in opposition to, and continually frustrates, the elevation and patriarchal dominance symbolized by the sun: "Le Soleil aime exclusivement la Nuit et dirige vers la terre sa violence lumineuse, verge ignoble, mais il se trouve dans l'incapacité d'atteindre le regard ou la nuit . . . [The Sun exclusively loves the Night and directs its luminous violence, its ignoble shaft, towards the earth, but it finds itself incapable of reaching the gaze or the night . . .]" (*OC*, 1:86; *VE*, 9). The sun's inability to penetrate the night, its failure to consummate its fertilizing rape, marks the limit of the traditional prerogatives of male sexuality. But this "incapacity" is precisely the condition of a new articulation of male sexuality in a different, nonhegemonic (and ultimately homoerotic) economy of desire. For what seems a "castration" from the point of view of the father/sun (whose highest value is "fecundation" or capitalist productivity) is really a multiplication of the "excessive possibilities" of free *dépense*, of nonproductive and unregulated erections, of transformations and openings. Bataille affirms the movement of "déflagrations érotiques révolutionnaires et volcaniques [erotic revolutionary and volcanic deflagrations]" which "se produisent en rupture de ban avec la fécondité [take place beyond the constraints of fecundity]" (*OC*, 1:86; *VE*, 8).

Cixous contrasts female and male economies of "loss" or mourning. For men, "'faire son deuil', ça veut dire ne pas perdre. Quand on a perdu quelque chose et que c'est une perte dangereuse, on refuse que quelque chose de soi soit perdue dans la chose perdue. Donc on 'fait son deuil', on se dépêche de réincorporer l'investissement qui avait été distribué dans l'objet perdu ['mourning' means not losing. When you've lost something and the loss is a dangerous one, you refuse to admit that something of your self might be lost in the lost object. So you 'mourn,' you make haste to recover the investment in the lost object]" (15/54). In contrast, woman "ne fait pas son deuil. Au fond, elle *relève le défi de la perte* qu'elle continue à vivre: elle la vit, elle lui donne vie, elle est capable d'une perte qui ne s'économise pas. Elle ne fait pas l'économie de la perte: elle perd sans faire l'économie de la perte. Ça donne dans l'écriture un corps qui est dans l'épanchement, le dégorgement, le vomissement au contraire de l'engloutissement masculin [does not mourn. She basically *takes up the challenge of loss* that she continues to live: she lives it, gives it life, is capable of unsparing (uneconomized) loss. She does not economize loss, she loses without holding onto (making an economy of) loss. This makes her writing a body that overflows, disgorges, vomiting as opposed to masculine incorporation]" (15/54).

I am suggesting that Bataille proposes a vision of male sexuality which breaks with the traditional masculine economy of incorporation and possession, of investment for the sake of expanded reproduction, in order to enact a process of overflow, of "non-retenue [notwitholding]" (Cixous, 15/54), of non-negative loss. This new logic of masculine desire, however unconscious and incomplete its development, may be one reason for the recent interest in Bataille in the gay male community (see, for example, the discussions by Bruce Boone). Bataille affirms an open, nonpatriarchal, "general economy" of male sexuality not by miming or appropriating any image of female sexuality—which would only continue the tradition of male domination and possession—but by affirming a rupture, a nonclosure, within male sexuality itself. His erotic writing may provide the beginnings of an alternative—for male writers and readers—both to traditional male heterosexual pornography, in which male domination and self-possession are recuperated even (or especially) in scenarios of excess, and to what Alice Jardine has called "gynesis," or the projection (in recent male avant-garde texts) of Woman as the privileged figure of a longed-for alterity, excess, and non-identity. In any case, Bataille's theory and experience of sexuality still need to be explored, in a way not regulated by psychoanalytic presuppositions, and not limited to the (undeniably present) moments in which he falls back upon the most conventional (hetero)sexual stereotyping. (In particular, one might reconsider Bataille's masochism in its *radical difference* from the economy of possession that characterizes sadism: a difference which is affirmed even in Bataille's readings of Sade, in contrast to the more familiar Surrealist readings by Breton and his circle.)

Male sexuality, for Bataille, becomes an "erection" which does not dominate from a height, but loses its "verge ignoble [ignoble shaft/

prick]" in the night which it cannot illuminate, or even encounter face to face. Ejaculation is no longer a sign of potency, but a "purement parodique [purely parodic]" (*OC*, 1:81; *VE*, 5) and unproductive movement, the living-through of a loss without recompense.

> Je suis *ouvert*, brèche béante, à l'inintelligible ciel et tout en moi se précipite, s'accorde dans un désaccord dernier, rupture de tout possible, baiser violent, rapt, perte dans l'entière absence du possible, dans la nuit opaque et morte, toutefois lumière, non moins inconnaissable, aveuglante, que le fond du coeur. (*OC*, 5:74)

> I am *open*, gaping breach, to the unintelligible sky, and everything in me rushes headlong, is accorded in a final discord, rupture of all possibility, violent kiss, abduction, loss in the entire absence of possibility, in opaque and dead night which is nevertheless light—no less unknowable, no less blinding than the depth of the heart. (*IE*, 59)

In this delirious rush of giving and self-abandonment, of refusal to economize or reinvest loss, there can be neither hierarchy (inequality) nor reciprocity (equality). For both of these imply a stability of positions, and a common unit of equivalence, which would allow me to measure myself against, or in comparison to, the other. Just as I fail to realize the "radical alteration" demanded by sacrifice when I substitute an external victim for myself, so I fail to encounter the other in the act of love when I try to *hold on to* his/her otherness, when I try to place him/her above, below, or on an equal level with, but in any case in the same homogeneous space with, myself. Whereas I encounter somebody else only when I cannot possess that other person, when I am able to lose, not only myself, but him/her as well. "C'est *prendre la perte*, la prendre, la vivre. Sauter. Ça va avec une non-retenue: elle ne retient pas [This is taking loss, seizing it, living it. Leaping. This goes with not withholding: she does not withhold]" (Cixous, 15/54). When I do not withhold, the opacity of the night is also the blinding light of communication. I communicate that which I do not myself possess or know.

The "interior experience" is an irrecuperable movement in which I give myself over to the outside and to others, and hence finally to a *community*. Bataille's notion of community has been discussed in detail by Blanchot (*La communauté inavouable*) and by Jean-Luc Nancy

(*La communauté désoeuvrée*), and I will not go over the same ground here. Suffice it to say that such a community, produced through loss, giving, and sacrifice, can never be a final, fully realized state. I communicate with and to others not when I sacrifice myself for the sake of a preexisting group or nation (which is the fascist and patriotic ideal), but when I rupture, along with myself, the limiting possibility of such a closed, stable state. "C'est le don aggressif et gratuit de soi à l'avenir, en opposition à l'avarice chauvine, enchaînée au passé [It is the aggressive and gratuitous gift of oneself to the future—in opposition to chauvinistic avarice, bound to the past]" (*OC*, 1:463; *VE*, 193). The communal moment, for Bataille, is not one of fusion, when a new and unified group is formed, but one of explosion, when the boundaries of exclusion (and also, therefore, the constraints of self-definition) are swept away.

The openness and dissymmetry of communication are equally incompatible with bourgeois individualism (self-preservation) and with the totalitarian subordination of individuals to a common (higher) unity. There can be no question of an opposition (such as Fredric Jameson proposes) between the individual and the collective. For as Blanchot notes, these two seemingly opposed principles unite in a fatal reciprocity that excludes the ruptures of radical communication (*CI*, 12; *UC*, 3). The self-enclosed individuality of the bourgeois economic subject guarantees its fixed identity, and hence ironically its interchangeability with others. We are all alike precisely to the extent that we are all individuals, all unique and internally different, and hence each possessed of the same "value." Such is the logic of the commodity. But this articulation of difference within unity applies as much to any conception of the social totality as it does to isolated individuals. The cohesion of the private self in its "alienation" has the same structure as does society idealized as an organic, unalienated whole. "Utopian" collectivity is only the image, writ large, of the very "reification" it claims to overcome. Bourgeois privacy is all too easily conciliable with, even as it is compensated by, the communal fusion of the fascist rally, the nostalgic yearning for "la communauté sanguine et l'enchaînement au passé [the blood-community and enslavement to the past]" (*OC*, 1:462; *VE*, 192).

As Bataille sarcastically comments, the romantic dream of "une existence unanime retrouvée [a unanimous existence recovered]" finds its apotheosis, not in any poetic image of perfection (the utopian hope of theorists such as Marcuse), but rather—in proper Hegelian fashion—in the imposition of obligatory military service (*OC*, 5:173; *IE*, 150). For the fascist glorification of war is the ultimate form the utopian dream of disalienation and collective identity takes.

> La guerre, dans la mesure où elle est volonté d'assurer la pérennité d'une nation, la nation qui est souveraineté et exigence d'inaltérabilité, l'autorité de droit divin et Dieu lui-même représentent l'obstination désespérée de l'homme à s'opposer à la puissance exubérante du temps et à trouver la sécurité dans une érection immobile et proche du sommeil. L'existence nationale et militaire sont présentes au monde pour tenter de nier la mort en la réduisant à une composante d'une gloire sans angoisse. (*OC*, 1:471)

> War, to the extent that it is the desire to insure the permanence of a nation, the nation that is sovereignty and the demand for inalterability, the authority of divine right and of God himself, represents the desperate obstinacy of man opposing the exuberant power of time and finding security in an immobile and almost somnolent erection. National and military life are present in the world to try to deny death by reducing it to a component of a glory without dread. (*VE*, 200)

Bataille thus proposes a more radical version of Benjamin's almost contemporaneous observations on fascism as spectacle, in which humankind "can experience its own destruction as an aesthetic pleasure of the first order" (*Illuminations*, 242). Aesthetics, like religion, derives a surplus of gratification from processes of self-destruction. And fascism, denying time and change by installing an order in which isolation and insecurity are overcome, is quite logically the heir of both. Fascism perpetrates acts of death and destruction on a massive, unprecedented scale, precisely to the extent that it is so extreme a *denial* of change and death. In the first place, fascism aesthetically distances the processes of destruction, ossifying them as objects of contemplation. Second, it posits a utopia of higher values as the justification and hidden meaning of these processes. Third, it decrees the eternity of this higher order, assured by the glorious negations of the present. We should not say, therefore, that fascism appealed to large numbers of people because it embodied, in however grotesquely distorted form, a genuine utopian impulse. We should rather note that the utopian, aesthetico-religious impulse itself, the reduction of community to unity and totality, already contains the roots of fascism.

Communal fusion and individual isolation alike negate the radical, extreme possibilities of communication. They both refuse, in terror, a Nietzschean affirmation of the ungraspable, uncontrollable future. Bataille proposes, instead, a community at the limits of human possibility, rupturing at once the closure and unity of the three Kantian Ideas of Reason: the self, the world (the social totality), and God. Bataille's community will involve a relation not of unity, but of mutual implication and contamination, of *complicity*: "sentiment de complicité dans: le désespoir, la folie, l'amour, la supplication. Joie inhumaine, échevelée, de la *communication* . . . rire, vertige, nausée, perte de soi jusqu'à la mort [sentiment of complicity in despair, madness, love, supplication. Inhuman, disheveled joy of *communication* . . . laughter, vertigo, nausea, loss of self to the point of death]" (*OC*, 5:49; *IE*, 37). Sacrifice has "la puissance de libérer des éléments hétérogènes et de rompre l'homogénéité habituelle de la personne: elle s'opposerait à son contraire, à l'ingestion commune des aliments de la même façon qu'un vomissement [the power to liberate heterogeneous elements and to break the habitual homogeneity of the individual, in the same way that vomiting would be opposed to its opposite, the communal eating of food]" (*OC*, 1:269; *VE*, 70). The communal feast, like the fascist rally, unites separate individuals into one essence. But sacrifice, or collective vomiting, creates a complicitous communal relation in which the integrity of separate individuals is lost, and yet difference as such is maintained. Community does not abolish, but is affirmed on the basis of—and in the midst of—distance and separation.

The "interior experience" of the extreme limit is that of community in this complicitous, nonrestricted sense. "Sans doute, à l'extrême, il suffit qu'arrive un seul: encore faut-il qu'entre lui et les autres—qui l'évitent—il garde un lien [No doubt, it suffices that a single individual reach the extreme limit; it is still necessary that he retain some link between himself and the others who avoid him]" (*OC*, 5:51; *IE*, 38). My isolation from others—as from myself—is the positive condition of my relationship, my communication, with them. And conversely, community itself is swept into the violence of experience at its most extreme. Not an everlasting social order, but the indefinable turbulence of the moment: "L'existence n'est pas seulement un vide agité, elle est une danse qui force à danser avec fanatisme. . . . Il faut devenir assez ferme et inébranlé pour que l'existence du monde de la civilisation apparaisse enfin incertaine. . . . Il faut refuser l'ennui et vivre seulement de ce qui fascine [Existence is not only an agitated void, it is a dance that forces one to dance with fanaticism. . . . It is necessary to become sufficiently firm and unshaken so that the existence of the world of civilization finally appears uncertain. . . . It is necessary to refuse boredom and live only for fascination]" (*OC*, 1:443–45; *VE*, 179).

What gesture is being performed here? Bataille's rhetoric has the form of an ethical imperative, but its content is a demand to dissolve all grounds and all imperative necessities, including its own. He proposes an existence of firmness, fascination and fanaticism, but only in order to turn such postures against the servilities which they usually imply. For "il est nécessaire de devenir tout autres ou de cesser d'être [it is necessary to become completely other, or to cease being]" (*OC*, 1:443; *VE*, 179). If Bataille is fascinated with the infinite movement of dying, if he sees it as the extreme form of becoming-other or communication, this is out of his concern to reject bourgeois society's murderous logic of appropriation, fixation, and static determination. Modern Western culture, culminating in fascism, is a culture of negativity and the death instinct. We both employ and limit violence in the interest of social order. We reproduce our own comforts (if we belong to the more privileged strata of society), but only on condition of reproducing the regimes of exploitation and domination that guarantee them. We worship self-destruction precisely to the extent that we believe in eternal life: such eternity is the final form which things attain in their death. It is in opposition to this fatal logic that Bataille seeks to destroy culture, to turn violence against the cult of domination and preservation, to affirm change—even to the point of dying—against the propriety and finality of a perfected death. One cannot oppose fascism by reasserting the civilized values of which fascism is only the final and most massive growth; but only by reaffirming the gratuitousness of catastrophe which the fascist rage for order strives to repress.

Bataille's strategic, theatrical use of metaphysical speculation allows him to affirm a nonconceptualizable experience of catastrophe. Far from reacting defensively to a purported situation of existential finitude or metaphysical uncertainty, he actively seeks to provoke conditions of violence, anxiety, and chaos. This self-dissolving project is what sets him apart, on the one hand from the existentialists and deconstructors who are paralyzed by what Nietzsche's Zarathustra calls the "*abgründliche Gedanke* [abysmal thought]" (*Thus Spoke Zarathustra*, 178) of the indeterminacy of value and meaning, and on the other hand from the pragmatists who smugly deny that such a thought is of any importance. For Bataille does not posit that we are suffering from a crisis of rationality; he tries insidiously to create one. His complains not that values have collapsed, but that they retain their efficacy and authority. He aims to disrupt every equilibrium, to deny us our peace of mind, to infect society or exacerbate its disease, to make impossible any cure. "La recherche de Dieu, de l'absence de mouvement, de la *tranquillité*, est la peur qui a fait sombrer toute tentative de communauté universelle [The search for God, for the absence of movement, for *tranquillity*, is the fear that has scuttled all attempts at a universal community]" (*OC*, 1:473, *VE*, 201). The perpetual motion of Bataille's discourse continually resists and upsets such tranquillity.

This is not to deny that the fearful search for peace and stability is in some sense unavoidable, and is at the heart, not only of much philosophy and theology, but above all of bourgeois "common sense." Nothing is more difficult than projecting the absence of any project, recording in discourse the disappearance of discourse. Language is inadequate to communication: it is the pacifying recuperation of communication. But neither can communication take place without language, or outside of it. How do I speak, when I no longer have the security of being myself? It is like being alive and dead at the same time. "A l'extrémité fuyante de moi-même, déjà je suis mort, et *je* dans cet état naissant de mort parle aux vivants: de la mort, de l'extrême [At the fleeting extreme limit of myself, I am already dead, and in the coming-to-birth of this state of death, *I* speak to the living: about death, about the extreme limit]" (*OC*, 5:58; *IE*, 44). The lure of tranquillity and stability, of the finality of death, arises out of the very movement which denies it.

"Etre dans la nuit, sombrer dans la nuit, sans même avoir assez de force pour *le voir*, se savoir dans cette obscurité fermée, et malgré elle *voir clair* . . . [To be in the night, to founder in the night, without even having enough strength to *see it*, to know oneself to be in this closed obscurity, and despite it to *see clearly* . . .]" (*OC*, 5:59; *IE*, 45–46). But once I can see clearly that I cannot see, the game is lost (or won), the abolished "me" has been restored, the discredited *cogito* returns. "Le sujet dans l'expérience en dépit de tout demeure [The subject in the experience in spite of everything remains]" (*OC*, 5:76; *IE*, 61). If death is the most extreme form of sacrifice, communication, and change, it is also the illusory terminus that can never be actually reached. I cannot escape from my compromised identity, any more than I can retain it and assert it. Such is the haunting experience of the Eternal Return: "mais en moi tout recommence, jamais rien n'est joué. Je me détruis dans l'infinie possibilité de mes semblables: elle anéantit le sens de ce moi. Si j'atteins, un instant, l'extrême du possible, peu après, j'aurai fui, je serai *ailleurs* [But in me everything begins again, nothing is ever played out. I destroy myself in the infinite possibility of my fellow beings; this possibility annihilates the sense of this *me*. If I attain, for an instant, the extreme limit of the possible, soon after, I will have fled, I will be *elsewhere*]" (*OC*, 5:48; *IE*, 36).

What returns, however, what always comes back because it is always elsewhere, is not just me. But "un moment de *rage* [a moment of *rage*]" (*OC*, 3:381), a violence, a "will" which is not my will. A refusal of the servitude alike of being "myself" and of subordinating myself to something allegedly greater than myself. There is no way of exorcising these confusions, these incoherencies, these ambiguities. What we should beware of is the attempt to cover them over, to *harmonize* them. "Le souci d'harmonie est une grande servitude. . . . L'harmonie, comme le projet, rejette le temps au dehors; son principe est la répétition par laquelle tout possible s'éternise [The concern for harmony is a great servitude. . . . Harmony, like the project, throws time back into the outside; its principle is the repetition by which every possibility is made eternal]" (*OC*, 5:70; *IE*, 56). An unforeseen repetition disrupts our expectations of finality, of clarity, of order. But repetition itself becomes a principle of identity, of boredom, of eternity, of order. "Le désir revient, mais, tout d'abord, c'est le désir d'annuler le temps (d'annuler le désir). . . . [Mais] s'il est d'abord désir d'annuler le désir, à peine est-il parvenu à ses fins qu'il est désir de rallumer le désir [Desire returns, but first of all it is the desire to annul time (to annul desire). . . . But if it is at first the desire to annul desire, scarcely has it arrived at its goals, than it is the desire to rekindle desire]" (*OC*, 5:71; *IE*, 56). The ignoble search for tranquillity cannot be excluded from desire, but only because to exclude it would be to accomplish its goal of harmonizing or tranquilizing desire.

Which is why there is no reconciliation or conclusion, why the "vertiginous fall," the act of murdering God or cutting off the king's head, is alone important. For it is the sole point at which communication, radical *heterogeneity*, is able to erupt: "C'est le TEMPS qui se déchaîne dans la 'mort' de Celui dont l'éternité donnait à l'Etre une assise immuable [TIME is unleashed in the 'death' of the One whose eternity gave Being an immutable foundation]" (*OC*, 1:510; *VE*, 220). The glorious, revolutionary moment of decapitation is a singular event not yet harmonized and recuperated, not yet assimilated into the "durée indifférente [indifferent duration]" of homogeneity and habit. "L'expérience intérieure est la dénonciation de la trêve, c'est l'être sans délai [inner experience is the revocation of a truce; it is being without respite]" (*OC*, 5:60). Only this violent rupture, this immediacy of "la joie devant la mort [joy before death]" successfully "prive de sens tout ce qui est *au-delà* intellectuel or moral, substance, Dieu, ordre immuable ou salut. Elle est une apothéose de ce qui est périssable, apothéose de la chair et de l'alcool aussi bien que des transes du mysticisme [robs of meaning everything that is an intellectual or moral *beyond*, substance, God, immutable order, or salvation. It is an apotheosis of that which is perishable, apotheosis of flesh and alcohol as well as of the trances of mysticism]" (*OC*, 1:554; *VE*, 237).

The problem still remains how such an acephalic existence—whether on a social or an individual level—is to be attained. But the question, in this form, is poorly posed. A purely acephalic existence (one of unlimited expenditure) cannot be *achieved* or *sustained*, "la destruction révolutionnaire étant régulièrement suivie de la reconstitution de la structure sociale et de sa tête [since revolutionary destruction is regularly followed by the reconstitution of the social structure and its head]" (*OC*, 1:469; *VE*, 199). "L'existence se situe constamment à l'opposé de deux possibilités également illusoires [Existence is constantly situated in opposition to two equally illusory possibilities]," those of pure fascist organization and pure revolutionary disorganization (*OC*, 1:468; *VE*, 198). The former, despite all its efforts, cannot entirely suppress resistance; it is never firmly in place once and for all. But the latter is radically *impure*; it denies the power that would allow it to purify and perpetuate itself. The creative ferment of "decomposition" lasts only for an instant—or not even for an instant. To institute a regime of disorderly, nonproductive expenditure, to insert it within linear temporality, is again to reduce it, hence to fail to confront it. The *event* of decapitation cannot be an efficacious action. It leads to nothing, or what it leads to is a new order in which it has no place. Headless existence is "rien qui constitue une *substance* à l'épreuve du temps, tout au contraire, ce qui fuit aussitôt apparu et ne se laisse pas saisir. . . . rien n'apparaît plus misérable et plus mort que la chose fixe, rien n'est plus désirable que ce qui va aussitôt disparaître [the opposite of a *substance* that withstands the test of time, it is something that flees as soon as it is seen and cannot be grasped. . . . nothing seems more miserable and more dead than the stabilized thing, nothing is more desirable than what will soon disappear]" (*OC*, 1:560; *VE*, 241).

The death of God, the cutting off of the head, is an action which is not an action, an action without a determinate object. "J'en arrive à cette position: l'expérience intérieure est le contraire de l'action. Rien de plus [I come to this position: inner experience is the opposite of action. Nothing more]" (*OC*, 5:59; *IE*, 46). It is an act, then, which cannot ever be accomplished, but only endlessly repeated. This frenzied repetition of a movement without conclusion and without duration is a radical experience of TIME. Pure intensive time, a time of incessant metamorphosis, freed from stasis as from progression: the time of "tout ce qui existe se détruisant, se consumant et mourant, chaque instant ne se produisant que dans l'anéantissement de celui qui précède et n'existant lui-même que blessé à mort [everything that exists destroying itself, consuming itself and dying, each instant producing itself only in the annihilation of the preceding one, and itself existing only as mortally wounded]" (*OC*, 1:556; *VE*, 238). TIME as a movement of disaggregation, in which the objects which we think we recognize "sont rendues à l'obscurité de l'inconnu. Non seulement le temps les altère, les anéantit . . . mais le mal qu'est en elles le temps, qui les domine de haut, les brise, les nie, est l'inconnaissable même, qui, à chaque succession d'instant, s'ouvre en elles, comme il s'ouvre en nous qui le vivrions si nous ne nous efforcions de le fuir en de faux-semblants de connaissance [are returned to the obscurity of the unknown. Not only does time alter them, annihilate them . . . but the evil which is time within them, which dominates them from above, breaks them, negates them, is the unknowable itself, which at the succession of each instant, opens itself within them, as it opens itself within us who would experience it if we didn't force ourselves to flee it in false pretenses of knowledge]" (*OC*, 5:158–59; *IE*, 137).

Time as ordinarily conceived—whether linear and progressive, or closed, cyclical, and mythic—is a reactive assertion of permanence, a denial of radical temporality. "Dans les conditions communes, le temps est annulé, enfermé dans la permanence des formes ou les changements prévus. Des mouvements inscrits à l'intérieur d'un ordre *arrêtent* le temps, qu'ils figent dans un système de mesures et d'équivalences [In common conditions, time is annulled, enclosed within the permanence of forms or of changes which are foreseen. Movements inscribed within an order *stop* time, which they freeze in a system of measures and equivalences]" (*OC*, 5:89; *IE*, 74). Such is the denial of change in favor of being and essence, the philosophers' "lack of historical sense, their hatred of even the idea of becoming" castigated by Nietzsche (*Twilight of the Idols*, 35). But such is also the more subtle rationalization of change, the identification of becoming with being in dialectical thought. And perhaps the most insidious of these denials of TIME is that of Heidegger, who links the very openness of the future to the recuperative project of comprehension (which is the source of Bataille's profound revulsion for Heidegger—cf. *OC*, 5:19; *IE*, 7).

Against all such representations, the radical experience of TIME is that of an immediacy so intense that it cannot be captured by any presence, and all the less by any projection. The past has already vanished, the future is radically other and unknowable. Bataille likes to quote Nietzsche's formula: "Ich liebe die Unwissenheit um de Zukunft [I love the ignorance of the future]" (*Gay Science*, 231, #287; cf. *OC*, 1:463; *VE*, 196). And the 'present' is less a bridge linking past and future than it is an abyss in whose convulsive depths the knowledge— the presence—both of past and of future are lost: "cette venue impérative, toute-puissante et déjà anéantie [this imperative, all-powerful and already annihilated arrival]" (*OC*, 5:89; *IE*, 74). Everything is transformed, to the point where we cannot point to any subsisting thing and say that it is *that which* has been transformed. TIME opens itself within me, external to me and yet constituting me: I am born and I die in *catastrophe*.

> Quelque chose d'immense, d'exorbitant, se libère en tous sens avec un bruit de catastrophe; cela surgit d'un vide irréel, infini, en même temps se perd, dans un choc d'un éclat aveuglant. . . . La 'catastrophe' est la révolution la plus profonde—elle est le temps 'sorti des gonds': le squelette en est le signe, à l'issue de la pourriture, d'où se dégage son existence illusoire. (*OC*, 5:88–89)

> Something immense, exorbitant is liberated in all directions with a noise of catastrophe; it surges from an unreal, infinite void, and at the same time loses itself in it, with a blindingly brilliant

shock. . . . 'Catastrophe' is the most profound revolution, 'time out of joint'; the skeleton is its sign, the outcome of decay, from which its illusory existence emerges. (*IE*, 73–74)

To love change and uncertainty, to embrace catastrophe, to affirm metamorphosis and TIME. Nietzsche's *amor fati*, love of fate. "Ne pas vouloir [être le tout], c'est vouloir le temps, vouloir la chance. Vouloir la chance est l'*amor fati*. *Amor fati* signifie vouloir la chance, différer de ce qui était. Gagner l'inconnu et jouer [Not to want to be everything is to want time, to want chance. To want chance is *amor fati*. *Amor fati* means wanting chance, differing from what has been. Winning the unknown, playing it]" (*OC*, 6:140). In order to affirm a rich and heterogeneous existence, it is necessary, again and again, to "se précipiter vivant dans ce qui n'a plus d'assise ni de tête [throw oneself headlong into that which has no foundation and no head]" (*OC*, 1:513; *VE*, 222). Bataille, like the madman who announces the death of God in Nietzsche's parable, *plays, performs* this unending fall into an unattainable void. A paradoxical intervention within a context (that of language, or that of a stabilized, hierarchical society) from which it is quite rigorously excluded, Bataille's discourse is a performative utterance of a particularly radical sort: the simulation of an action which is consumed by its enactment.

A simulated action, a happening without an object, the "chute vertigineuse [vertiginous fall]" (*OC*, 1:513; *VE*, 222) into TIME also necessarily abolishes the subject. "Je me représente couvert de sang, mais transfiguré et d'accord avec le monde, à la fois comme une proie et comme une mâchoire du TEMPS qui tue sans cesse et qui est sans cesse tué [I imagine myself covered with blood, broken but transfigured and in agreement with the world, both as prey and as a jaw of TIME, which ceaselessly kills and is ceaselessly killed]" (*OC*, 1:557–58; *VE*, 239). If it is the head which initiates action, then the cutting off of the head, as Blanchot notes, also implies the impossibility of willed action, the abandonment even of the calculated decision to remove the head (*CI*, 31–32; *UC*, 15–16). This is why inner experience is not action. Or better, action can only take place in the loss or abolition of the agent. It is radically contingent, absolutely singular, without a model. It can never be referred back to itself. "Car l'existence universelle est illimitée et par là sans repos: elle ne referme pas la vie sur elle-même mais l'ouvre et la rejette dans l'inquiétude de l'infini [For universal existence is unlimited and thus restless: it does not close life in on itself, but instead opens it and throws it back into the uneasiness of the infinite]" (*OC*, 1:473; *VE*, 201). In this opening, and this disquietude, there is no place for agency or initiative. Action, at its most alive, its most intensely "active," can only be an uncontrollable *passion*.

We must say, then, of Bataille what Pierre Klossowski says of Nietzsche: passion is "la force impulsionnelle qui, précisément, excède le 'vouloir' du suppôt et *déjà le modifie*, donc *menace son identité stable* [the driving force which, precisely, exceeds the agent's 'will' and *already modifies* it, thus *threatens its stable identity*]" (*Nietzsche et le cercle vicieux*, 112). The agent who performs a glorious action is always *already* other than itself. Theseus can no longer thread the labyrinth in order to confront the monster. For the confrontation has already taken place as soon as Theseus is lost in the labyrinth; and he is already lost in the labyrinth even before he makes the decision to enter. The acephalic man "n'est pas moi mais il est plus moi que moi: son ventre est le dédale dans lequel il s'est égaré lui-même, m'égare avec lui et dans lequel je me retrouve étant lui, c'est-à-dire monstre [is not me but he is more me than me: his stomach is the labyrinth in which he has lost himself, loses me with him, and in which I discover myself as him, in other words as a monster]" (*OC*, 1:445; *VE*, 181). Philosophy and criticism can seek, as always, to normalize this monstrosity. They can stand around the bier and argue over the remains. But they will never be able to abolish—or, on the other hand, to conceptualize or formalize—the "vertiginous fall" in which the violent heterogeneity of existence is ecstatically affirmed at the very point of its annihilation. The "*excessive* possibilities" of life are celebrated and consumed in such a catastrophe; "le reste est ironie, longue attente de la mort . . . [the rest is irony, a long wait for death . . .]" (*OC*, 3:31).

Le mystique athée, conscient de soi, conscient de devoir
mourir et de disparaître, vivrait, comme Hegel le dit
évidemment de lui-même, "dans le déchirement absolu"; mais, pour lui, il ne s'agit que d'une période:
à l'encontre de Hegel, il n'en sortirait pas, "contem-
plant le Négatif bien en face," mais ne pouvant jamais le transposer en Etre, refusant de le faire et se
maintenant dans l'ambiguïté.
—Georges Bataille

CHAPTER 5

Impersonal Obsessions

L'arrêt de mort *and the Passion of Thought*

I

"Je ne puis dire quel malheur envahit l'homme qui une fois a pris la parole. Malheur immobile, lui-même voué au mutisme; par lui, l'irrespirable est l'élément que je respire [I cannot say what pain invades a man once he has begun to speak. It is a motionless pain, that is itself pledged to muteness; because of it, the unbreathable is the element I breathe]" (*AM*, 57; *DS*, 33). The urgency and intensity of Blanchot's fiction, the difficulty of its speech, comes from its obsessive exploration of those events that transpire in silence, in isolation, in the darkness of the night. His *récits* enter the abysses of death, of pain and suffering, of privacy, vulnerability, and loss. And they do not emerge victorious from those abysses but remain forever lost within them. Hence the difficulty of reading Blanchot. It is almost unbearable to be brought face-to-face with the ambiguity and the blindness of our own passions, to confront the darkness of affective experience on so naked and so unmediated a level. "Il est effrayant parce qu'il y a en lui quelque chose qui méprise l'homme et que l'homme ne peut pas supporter sans se perdre. Mais se perdre, il le faut [It is terrifying because there is something in it which scorns man and which man cannot endure without losing himself. But he must lose himself]" (*AM*, 108; *DS*, 67). Blanchot's *récits* do not endeavor to palliate or recompense this impossible sacrifice, this *losing of oneself* in the labyrinths of passion. They offer no false comforts, no humanistic consolations, no spiritual conquests. Their force, their affirmation, is entirely *other*.

L'arrêt de mort [*Death Sentence*], in particular, is the narration of a nameless and motionless *malheur* (misfortune, pain, unhappiness); the forced recollection of something that cannot be remembered, the recounting of what cannot ever be said. The narrator is transformed by an overwhelming encounter (or series of encounters) from which he cannot free himself, but which he is unable to come to terms with, or even adequately to describe. He is continually tormented by an obsession he can neither satisfy nor evade. His life and death are consumed by a *thought*, "une pensée superbe que j'essaie en vain de mettre à genoux [a splendid thought, which I am trying in vain to bring to its knees]" (*AM*, 55; *DS*, 31). Retreat or disengagement is impossible: "Mais la règle le veut et l'on ne saurait s'en affranchir: dès que la pensée s'est levée, il faut la suivre jusqu'au bout [But this is the rule, and there is no way to free oneself of it: as soon as the thought has arisen, it must be followed to the very end]" (*AM*, 67; *DS*, 39). In thrall to this thought, the book circles around a deep and intimate pain, or rather one which exceeds all measures of depth and intimacy. For the more the narrator descends into his own psychological recesses, the more he is exiled from the complacencies and certitudes of the "self." This is his unhappiness, and also his greatest affirmation. He discovers an exteriority at the heart of all self-communion, a distance at the heart of all intimacy, an irreparability at the heart of all willed action.

Such *malheur*, such impossibility, is the element in which Blanchot's fiction moves. The great illusion of Western culture is that somehow, through art, experience can be purified, sanctified, and redeemed. Blanchot's writing, to the contrary, affirms "lived experience" in all its density and materiality: experience insofar as it is not subject to idealization, and cannot be illuminated by the penetration and insight of the intelligence. His narration does not provide catharsis or compensate for loss; its only effect is to precipitate and intensify the recognition of irreversibility, of the moment when "l'irrémédiable était arrivé [the irremediable had happened]" (*AM*, 65; *DS*, 38). Nothing could be further from the aestheticism which sees liberation in the act of objectification, which praises the artist for giving outward form to an inner torment. Writing, for Blanchot, is passion itself, and not action, expression, or representation. The importance, the obsessive concentration, and the greatest merit of writing lie precisely in this, that it is not an exercise in mastery, and that it does not admit of resolution, formalization, or articulation.

The indeterminacy, and interminability, of writing is what denies the aesthetic realm any form of spiritual authority, higher truth, or special privilege, and instead identifies it with the indescribable affective intensities of ordinary life. Blanchot is obsessed with the inaccessibility of the quotidian, of precisely that which is most familiar and most immediate. "Le quotidien: ce qu'il y a de plus difficile à découvrir. . . . Il ne se laisse pas saisir. Il échappe. Il appartient à l'insignifiance, et l'insignifiant est sans vérité, sans réalité, sans secret [The quotidian: that which is most difficult to uncover. . . . It does not let itself be grasped. It escapes. It belongs to insignificance, and the insignificant is without truth, without reality, without secrets]" (*EI*, 355–57). The quotidian has no center, no inner meanings, no deep structure. It is not apparent only because it is not even hidden. And this is what makes it so difficult for interpretation to define it, or authority to control it. "Insignificance" links the most extraordinary passions and the most banal incidents of daily life. When all our rationalizations are stripped away, the mute and inert insistence of the quotidian is what remains. The narrator describes this residual existence, at one point, as "une sorte de relent étrange . . . une odeur froide de terre et de pierre que je connaissais à merveille parce que dans la chambre elle était ma vie même [a sort of strange musty smell . . . a cold smell of earth and stone which I was perfectly familiar with because in the room it was my very life]" (*AM*, 106; *DS*, 66). It is the aroma of minor habits I no longer even notice, but also of major events (like the approach of my own death) that remain unimaginable at the same time they are excessively familiar. This is the fatality of a never extinguished subsistence, and of a never fulfilled imminence. There are experiences which will not go away, which are not healed by time. They are overly insistent, it is impossible not to recognize them, and yet they cannot ever be articulated in the clarity of a supposed presence.

I know that it is not customary to read Blanchot in this way, to focus so insistently on the affective and experiential dimensions of his texts. And yet nothing could be more important. It will not do to set up oppositions between experience and textuality, between life and death on one hand and language on the other. The subject is subverted, but not to the benefit of any free play of the signifier or any order of representations. As Foucault puts it, Blanchot's texts do not participate in a supposed modernist project of "auto-reference" and linguistic internalization. The experience of language for Blanchot is that of a radical *dispersion*, an exteriority into which the order of significations disappears together with the subject that speaks (*The Thought from Outside*, 11–13). Blanchot's writing is abstract, impersonal, and radically "intransitive" because it is a writing of what he calls *l'expérience-limite*, engaged with those experiences that lie at the limits of human possibility, at the limits of language, thought, and consciousness. Death and intimacy (like the quotidian) are movements that cannot directly be written *about*. In a very real sense, they are inexpressible; they occur at the point at which language has been exhausted, and at which our ability to contain and appropriate experience, our power of comprehension and expression, has broken down. Such experiences are irreducible to the cultural norms of narration and conceptualization: incompatible with the social or Symbolic realm of representation no less than with that fictional (grammatical) center, or semblance of identity, which is the self or ego. They strike only when I am not yet ready to receive them, or when "je ne suis plus maître d'en parler [I am no longer able to speak of them]" (*AM*, 53; *DS*, 30).

Limit-experiences alter everything; hence they leave no survivors. In the throes of passion no less than in those of dying (and dying, too, is a passion), I am not the same person I was. Indeed, I am not quite a "person," an individual or a subject, at all. "Mais, sachez-le, là où je vais, il n'y a ni oeuvre, ni sagesse, ni désir, ni lutte; là où j'entre, personne n'entre [But know this, that where I am going there is neither work, nor wisdom, nor desire, nor struggle; there where I enter, no one enters]" (*AM*, 86; *DS*, 53). None of my most intimate possessions and attributes can be sustained in the face of this ultimate intimacy, this *malheur* which suffuses and transforms my being. I must lose myself, but I cannot expect to find myself again at the end, let alone to be enriched or fortified by the experience. Such is the radical intransitivity of the event: it approaches me, it happens *to* me, but it can never *belong* to me. I am thrust to one side; its hyperbolic presence exceeds and excludes my own. And so the most intensely personal experiences are also the most inaccessible, the most rigorously impersonal. I am truly marked by an experience only when I no longer have the solidity, the self-presence, that would allow me to refer it back to myself. In the movement of passion, at the approach of death, in the proximity of an Other, the "I" is no longer there. Surely, someone is there, but this Someone is not myself, is not anybody in particular. "Quelqu'un est ce qui est encore présent, quand il n'y a personne. . . . Je ne suis pas là, il n'y a personne, mais l'impersonnel est là [Someone is what is still present when no one is there. . . . I am not there, there is no one there, but the impersonal is there]" (*EL*, 24; *GO*, 74, *SL*, 31). Impersonality is not the general or the universal: it is what is most singular and irreplaceable, what remains when every possibility is exhausted, at the limit of my capacity to experience and to imagine.

L'arrêt de mort does not—could not—*represent* such limit-experiences; but it *communicates* them and communicates with them, in a vertiginous and incessantly repeated contact. It recounts a series of overwhelming yet almost impalpable events, of violent, impersonal passions; and the process of writing is itself one of these events, one of these passions. The narrator suffers the double burden of being compelled to speak and of not being able to speak. He writes his account, tears it up, writes it again. He is literally suffocated by the story he tells, by his complicity with it and his distance from it, by the "loyalty" which, without reciprocity, it demands from him: "une pensée exige une loyauté qui rend difficile toute ruse. Elle-même est parfois fausse, mais derrière ce mensonge je reconnais encore quelque chose de vrai que, moi, je ne puis pas tromper [a thought demands a loyalty which makes any ruse difficult. Sometimes it is itself false, but behind this lie I still recognize something true which I cannot betray]" (*AM*, 55; *DS*, 32).

In response to this "truth," the narrator wants nothing more than to get the story told, to say everything that has to be said. He wants to "mettre fin à tout cela [put an end to it all]," to "en finir bientôt [be done with it soon]"; nothing is more "noble et important" (*AM*, 7; *DS*, 1). But nothing is less possible. He cannot come to the end, because no matter what has happened, and no matter what story he tells, "tout ne s'est pas encore passé [not everything has yet happened]" (*AM*, 54; *DS*, 31). What has not yet happened is, if nothing else, the recounting of what has happened. The narrator has "perdu la silence [lost silence]" (*AM*, 57; *DS*, 33); he has been seized by a compulsion to speak, a restless agitation which can never again be quelled. The time of the story is prolonged in the time of telling the story, and his inability to come to the end of the one echoes his inability to come to the end of the other. "Après ces événements, dont j'ai raconté quelques-uns—mais maintenant encore, je les raconte . . . [After these events, several of which I have recounted—but I am still recounting them now . . .]" (*AM*, 56; *DS*, 32). It is a self-defeating situation: every effort he makes to reach the end only estranges him further from it. For action cannot extinguish action, and silence cannot be recovered by piling on more and more words. The narrator is trapped in a vicious circle: because he speaks, he cannot regain silence, but because he has lost his silence, he cannot avoid speaking. He cannot stop speaking until he reaches the end; but he will not reach the end, as long as he continues speaking. The moment of ultimate silence is continually being projected, but for that very reason it is the one moment that never arrives.

This vicious circle or double bind is the key to Blanchot's radically de-idealized and non-voluntaristic view of writing. The narrator's dilemma in *L'arrêt de mort* is one instance of the situation of the writer which Blanchot describes in more general terms in "La solitude essentielle [The Essential Solitude]," the first chapter of *L'espace littéraire* (*EL*, 9–28; *GO*, 63–77, *SL*, 19–34). In the state of radical passivity, of beautiful and appalled fascination, to which the writer is reduced, "écrire, c'est se livrer à l'interminable. . . . Ecrire, c'est se faire l'écho de ce qui ne peut cesser de parler [to write is to surrender to the interminable. . . . To write is to make oneself the echo of what cannot stop talking]" (*EL*, 17–18; *GO*, 69, *SL*, 27). Writing is at once highly charged and impalpable, all-encompassing and indecisive. It testifies not to a glorious strength, a positive power of creation, but to a weakness and a fatality, an inability to keep silent. I do not give myself over to the interminable by virtue of a heroic, resolute decision. I write only out of the impotence of my wish to say nothing, or the failure of my efforts to say something. I write because I cannot extinguish the echoes propagated even by my attempts to impose silence. The solitude into which the writer retreats is populated with strange simulacra, inconclusive phantoms of discourse.

> Cette solitude elle-même s'est mise à parler . . . au-dessus d'elle veille une plus grande qu'elle et au-dessus de celle-ci une plus grande encore, et chacune, recevant la parole afin de l'étouffer et de la taire, au lieu de cela la répercute à l'infini, et l'infini devient son écho. (*AM*, 57)

> This solitude has itself begun to speak . . . a greater solitude hovers above it, and above that solitude, another still greater, and each,

taking the spoken word in order to smother it and silence it, instead echoes it to infinity, and infinity becomes its echo. (*DS*, 33)

Writing, then, is a kind of echolalia, in which I lose my own voice as I am seized by the impersonal. This phenomenon of echoing is not an action, a new initiative, but only an *effect*; the effect of an absent or infinitely distant cause. The uncanniness of an echo is that it does nothing but literally reproduce a prior impression; and yet its multiplication of that impression blurs and effaces it. Radical repetition, echoing to infinity, makes representation impossible. An echo does not say anything new, and yet its very persistence produces an alteration. The phenomenon of the echo cannot be adequately described, then, in the usual terms of correspondence, *or* the lack of it, to a prior model. Experience is not an origin or model for what would then be recounted in language; but the interminability which already infects what we call experience finds a continuing derisive echo, an equivalent or relay, in the infinite distance between the event and the narration of the event. "Il se peut que tous ces mots soient un rideau derrière lequel ce qui s'est joué ne cessera plus de se jouer [It may be that all these words are a curtain behind which what happened will never stop happening]" (*AM*, 54; *DS*, 31). The echoing can never come to an end, because it has never had a beginning. The experience the narrator tries to recount, the shock of the events from which he cannot free himself, is already an infinite series of echoes and repetitions.

Echoing, or repetition, supervenes whether one wants it to or not. But this repetition is a compulsion and a temptation, a *malheur* and an affirmation, far exceeding the parameters of language and interpretation. Echoing endlessly, repeating itself without saying anything, the movement of writing is *impossible* and *interminable*. It is not unfinished, so much as it renders vain and irrelevant the very notion of accomplishment. The radical impossibility of not speaking does not turn speech itself into a productive or existentially possible act. The double negative does not become a positive; it marks rather the "faiblesse de négatif [weakness of the negative]" (*EI*, 225), the failure even to attain a true negation. This is why Blanchot describes writing as a movement in the *neuter* (in a voice which neither posits nor denies), which can only be approached by means of oxymorons. For writing is not a real action, but only its compulsive echo. When I write, my language becomes the infinite reverberation of a murmur without an origin, an alien discourse, one which is not originally mine, nor anybody else's. Whatever form the writer seeks to impose upon the work, "l'oeuvre, à la fin, l'ignore, se referme sur son absence, dans l'affirmation impersonnelle, anonyme, qu'elle est—et rien de plus [in the end, the work ignores him, it closes on his absence, in the impersonal, anonymous affirmation that it is—and nothing more]" (*EL*, 12; *GO*, 65, *SL*, 23). Such an "affirmation" cannot be characterized or qualified, which means also that it cannot be appropriated or possessed. The work is not concerned with or for the writer, even though the writer is necessarily concerned (occupied, obsessed) with it. Writing, as a limit-experience, is a movement without an object, and without reciprocity or transitivity.

All this should help to clarify the links between writing, impersonality, and passion. Writing is passive or involuntary, but this of course does not mean it is the necessary consequence of determinate causes. It is compulsive rather than compulsory. Without being what can properly be called an action, writing is yet a condition of ceaseless agitation. The writer is Echo in the absence of Narcissus: never present in the writing, but never able to gain any respite from the writing. To write is not to record or represent a given action, but to lose one's capacity to be the subject or initiator of that action. "L'écrivain . . . perd le pouvoir de dire 'Je' [The writer . . . loses the power to say 'I']" (*EL*, 17; *GO*, 69, *SL*, 27). Or again, "l'un des traits caractéristiques de cette expérience est de ne pouvoir être assumé, comme sujet à la première personne, par celui à qui elle arrive [One of the characteristic traits of this experience is that the one to whom it happens cannot take it up as a first person subject]" (*EI*, 32). I cannot express or articulate *my own* desires in this writing; what is strange about this experience is precisely that nothing of it is my own. When I enter the space of writing, I cannot speak for myself any longer; I cannot recollect or reconstitute myself.

This is not to say, however, that when I write I simply vanish into the story I am telling. The impersonality of writing is not an Eliotic escape from personality. The writer does not transcend individuality in the direction of the universal, the objective, the dispassionate, the beautiful, and the true (*EL*, 19–20; *GO*, 70–71, *SL*, 28). I must lose myself, but losing myself is not as easy as all that. I do not escape the fatality of the event, its weight and its irreversibility, merely because I cannot claim it for myself. What is alien to me, what deprives me of myself, by that very fact continues to haunt me. When I write, "ce qui m'arrive n'arrive à personne, est anonyme *par le fait* que cela me concerne [what happens to me happens to no one, is anonymous *insofar as* it concerns (affects) me]" (*EL*, 27; *GO*, 76, *SL*, 33; emphasis mine). What happens to me happens to no one, because what happens is my exclusion from what is happening. The approach of the impersonal, the loss of myself, is also the loss of my ability to change, the loss of my power to transcend or to project myself. I am no longer able to participate in this transformation; it leaves me behind. I cannot escape from myself, in the sense that I cannot escape from—I am not released or liberated by—the loss of myself. I am bound irrevocably to the loss of myself, by my very inability to take part in it. Even as it excludes me and ignores me, the movement of writing marks me, fatally alters me, seizes me and does not let me go. I must continually discover myself *becoming* an infinite echo; I must repeatedly suffer my own radical inability to achieve an identity or to initiate an action.

Impersonality is not a goal to be projected and attained, but the passion of an unending metamorphosis. Its pain is that of a double incapacity, a double exclusion. In the passivity of writing, I lose myself so radically and so utterly that I am deprived of the power to abolish myself, no less than of the power to preserve myself. I am able neither to be nor not to be, neither to speak nor to remain silent. I am no longer myself, but I subsist as an anonymous "someone" consumed by passion. I am condemned to the indefinite continuation of an existence that is no longer my own. I remain suspended in a strange sort of half-life, like a zombie: "Qui fait que maintenant, chaque fois que ma tombe s'ouvre, j'y réveille une pensée assez forte pour me faire revivre? Le propre ricanement de ma mort [What makes it happen that every time my grave opens, now, I rouse a thought there that is strong enough to bring me back to life? The very derisive laughter of my death]" (*AM*, 86; *DS*, 52). I no longer have the power to say "I," but the "I" continues to resound obsessively, a derisive echo, an obscure fatality. I am never present to the world or to myself, but I am perpetually brought back from the brink of effacement by a strange and menacing force that I can neither recognize nor claim.

The distance could not be greater between this bizarre mode of subsistence and the notion of identity that underlies phenomenological and dialectical models of self-reflection. In the experience of the limit, it cannot be said that I am alienated from myself and from my possessions. The concept of alienation still implies a norm of self-presence and self-possession, even if this norm is unattainable in practice. But in writing or any other movement at the limit, it is precisely the possibility of reference to such a norm which has been irretrievably lost. My rupture with immediacy is itself radically immediate, that is, not susceptible of being bridged or covered over by a series of mediations. Nor can I recuperate my empirical experience of loss by positing (as Descartes, Kant, and Husserl do in varying ways) a transcendental subjectivity as the foundation, or condition of possibility, for these disruptions, incapacities, and doubts. For again, it is such self-reflexive structures first of all that are contested and broken at the limit, in the movement of a thought that remains stubbornly exterior to itself. The experience that affects me most profoundly cannot be adequated to any of my schemas of experience. This is why I am shaken so powerfully by such an experience, but also why I am unable properly to receive it, and why in happening to me it happens to no one.

In the experience of the limit, accomplishment and dialectical progression are impossible because time itself no longer has a linear and cumulative structure. The time of writing, or of passion, is "le temps de l'absence de temps . . . sans présent, sans présence [the time of the absence of time . . . without a present, without presence]" (*EL*, 22; *GO*, 73, *SL*, 30). But this strange mode of temporality is itself a kind of positive subsistence (and not merely the negation of presence). Rather than being alienated from my passions, it is as if I were waiting perpetually for them to arrive, or forever recollecting their departure, without ever being in place at the moment of their occurrence. The narrator speaks, therefore, not of estrangement, but of a more radical and more original "étrangeté [strangeness]" (*AM*, 66, 79, 112; *DS*, 39, 48, 70), the pathos of a distance which is not opposed to, or removed from, intimacy, but which inhabits it, and hollows it out from within. This strangeness is associated with "le phénomène de la vitre [the phenomenon of the shop window]" (*AM*, 79; *DS*, 48), the "immense plaisir [immense pleasure]" of experiencing the world at a distance, as if through a plate of glass, as when the narrator sees Simone D. for the first time in many years (*AM*, 72; *DS*, 43). This distance invests people and objects with a peculiar fascination.

> Par exemple, si je lisais un livre qui m'intéressait, je le lisais avec un vif plaisir, mais mon plaisir lui-même était sous une vitre, je pouvais le voir, l'apprécier, mais non l'user. De même, si je rencontrais une personne qui me plaisait, tout ce qui m'arrivait avec elle d'agréable était sous verre et, à cause de cela, inusable, mais, aussi, lointain et dans un éternel passé. (*AM*, 79–80)

For instance, if I read a book that interested me, I read it with vivid pleasure, but my very pleasure was behind a pane of glass, I could see it, appreciate it, but not make use of it (not use it up). Similarly, if I met a person who pleased me, everything pleasant which happened to me with that person was behind glass, and as a result, inexhaustible (not able to be worn out), but also distant and in an eternal past. (*DS*, 48)

The phenomenon of the plate of glass indicates a strange doubling, a radical ambiguity and duplicity at the base of all experience. A doubling which, in time without a present, forever precedes any unity or any movement of identification. The "I" is not lost to itself (which would imply that it could be found again) so much as it is always already dis-placed: "abréviation canonique, représentant la loi du même, par avance fracturé [canonical abbreviation, representing the law of the same, fractured in advance]" (*Le pas au-delà*, 15). The narrator continues to say "I," but he speaks out of the fundamental incompossibility of this "I" and the movements that affect it. The plate of glass at once heightens experience for the narrator, and removes him from that experience. On one side of the glass, experience is impersonal and unforeseeable. It never corresponds to my anticipation, never measures up to my powers of apprehension, passes me by, is over before it has even properly begun. I am changed without knowing that I have changed, and without being able to remember who I was before being changed. On the other side, "I" am able to appreciate the experience only because of my strange separation from it. This is what both permits me to savor it aesthetically, and tempts me to become tied to it in a compulsive movement that transgresses the limits of aesthetic detachment. Behind the plate of glass, the event that I am unable to experience becomes an object of contemplation, "devient une figure souveraine [becomes a sovereign figure]" (*AM*, 72; *DS*, 43), becomes the obsessive focus of my thought even as it is endowed with a disturbing sterility. The pleasure I take in such an image is as vain as it is flawless: a pleasure which cannot be worn down or used up, because it cannot be used or experienced directly, in the present, at all. It is preserved forever in a funereal perfection which testifies to its original "strangeness," but which is also the source of every idealization. Such is the seduction, the fascination of the image. It beckons from the distance of an "eternal past" which echoes endlessly, but which is not for all that ever brought into the moment when the "I" would be able to encounter it.

The time proper to experience is thus radically split: between an impersonal event which cannot even be constituted as "present" because it is too immediate to be anticipated or recalled, and the *désoeuvrement* ("worklessness") of an "I" that has always already lost the present, since it can do nothing but anticipate or recall an instant that never arrives. And in the separation and distance imposed by the pane of glass, passion is similarly divided. The narrator is drawn in two directions at once, losing himself in the distance at the same time that he tries to possess or master that distance. This irreducible ambiguity is manifested in a small way as the narrator recalls Simone: "ayant eu cette chance de la voir à travers une vitre, je n'ai jamais, pendant le temps que je l'ai rencontrée, cherché plus qu'à ressaisir sur elle 'l'immense plaisir' et aussi à briser la vitre [having had the luck to see her through a pane of glass, the only thing I wanted, during the whole time I knew her, was to feel that 'immense pleasure' again through her, and also to break the glass]" (*AM*, 73; *DS*, 44).

The "immense pleasure" of distance, the pleasure of viewing Simone through a pane of glass, is inflated to a degree all the more "excessif, déraisonnable [immoderate, absurd]" (*AM*, 73; *DS*, 43) in that it is so inconsequential in itself. The narrator hardly knows Simone; it is not herself, but only her return, that moves him. She appears after he has forgotten her, as if she had been preserved eternally behind that plate of glass. The shock of her "return" at a distance creates a false semblance of identity. Everything has changed for her (her husband has died; she is about to get married again), and yet the narrator regards her as if she were the same person she was before. And there is more: even the "chance" of having seen her again is not enough for him. He wants to regularize what is the result of a random encounter, "ressaisir [recapture]" and repeat an emotion that can only arise out of sheer fortuitousness. His desire is the echo of an echo, the citation (hence the quotation marks around "immense pleasure") and attempted re-evocation of an already missed encounter. Her falsely idealized image is initially an aestheticization, projected out of the surprise of her reappearance. But this image quickly becomes something much more intense, a signpost for the narrator's descent into an abyss of obsessive repetition. He seeks to recover what he never possessed in the first place, and which allures him only by virtue of its insurpassable distance.

This desire will eventually drive the narrator to enter Simone's room, unbidden, in the middle of the night. But the need to impose mastery, to "ressaisir" a lost object, is not the full measure of his passion. He also wants to "briser la vitre [break the glass]," to abolish the distance, to reach through and establish immediate contact. Such a movement, however, can take place only at the price of extinguishing the narrator's own subjectivity. The space he wants to traverse and destroy is the space of contemplation, the interval in which the "I" recollects and establishes itself. The paradox of impersonality, of the distance between the "I" and its passions, can also be stated this way: that the "I" never participates, but is essentially "aesthetic" and contemplative. It embodies the *notion* of willed action, of initiative; but this notion is only produced after the fact, from a position of disengaged observation and reflection. My misfortune is that I only see things at a distance, through a pane of glass; but this pane of glass is what permits me to see in the first place. If I break the glass, what is left? Not even my own action as one who breaks the glass. "Les murailles sont tombées, celles qui nous séparent, celles aussi qui nous permettent de communiquer, celles enfin qui nous protègent en nous tenant à distance [The walls have fallen, those which separate us, those also which permit us to communicate, those finally which protect us by keeping us at a distance]" (*EI*, 86; cf. also *EI*, 256, and *Le dernier homme*, 28). When the walls have fallen, when the glass is broken, I finally make contact; but the "I" is no longer present to experience the "immense pleasure" of such a contact.

This configuration recalls the culminating nonrevelation of one of Blanchot's earlier works of fiction, the novel *Aminadab* (1942):

Mais tout à l'heure nous serons définitivement unis. Je m'étendrai les bras ouverts, je t'enlacerai, je roulerai avec toi au milieu des grand secrets. Nous nous perdrons et nous nous retrouverons. Il n'y aura plus rien pour nous séparer. Quel dommage que tu ne puisses assister à ce bonheur!

But in a moment we will finally be united. I will stretch out with open arms, I will embrace you, I will roll with you in the midst of great secrets. We will lose ourselves and find ourselves again. Nothing more will separate us. What a pity that you cannot be present at this happiness! (225; this passage is also quoted by Georges Bataille at a crucial point in *Le coupable*: *OC*, 5: 323–25; *Guilty*, 81–82)

In this movement beyond the capabilities of the "I," passion itself is utterly transformed, since it no longer corresponds to a need for finding what has been eternally lost. It can no longer be measured by the standards of recapture and possession. It no longer chases the lure of an idealized image, since that image vanishes along with the subject that apprehended it. This is the abyss, not of fixation, but of metamorphosis. I no longer seek to impose repetition; instead I am shaken and altered by a repetition which carries me along, of which I am the effect and not the subject. Passion is no longer my own desire, but "la passion du dehors [the passion of the Outside]" (*EI*, 64ff.), the impersonal movement through which I become Someone or no one.

II

There is no way of resolving this ambiguity, this duplicity (in both the etymological and the derived sense of the word) of the movement of passion. It is an impulsion both of possession and of dispossession. Who can say what motivates, what impels or causes, the intrusions, the transgressions, the repeated entries of one person into another person's chamber, which echo throughout *L'arrêt de mort*? When the narrator visits Simone, in her room, after having himself received an unexpected and unwanted visit from Nathalie, he can only say that "cette pièce sombre et inconnue maintenant me fascinait; le but était bien là, dans ce noir [that gloomy and unfamiliar room now fascinated me; my goal was certainly there, in that dark]" (*AM*, 74; *DS*, 44). But this recognition can only be stated after the fact; and it is futile to try to determine to what extent his goal is some particular thing that could be found in and retrieved from the dark, and to what extent this goal is nothing but the impenetrability of the dark itself. The narrator's "fascination" takes the place of any prior motivation, and marks the obsessive point at which each of these alternatives is transformed into the other.

The encounter with Simone is only a small incident in the book, but its duplicitous pattern is characteristic of all of the narrator's experiences. The supposed subject of passion is lost in its perpetual fluctuations, or in what one of Blanchot's later works of fiction describes as "ce mouvement absolument lent, oscillation immobile, que je devancerais en vain [this absolutely slow movement, immobile oscillation, which it would be futile for me to anticipate]" (*Celui qui ne m'accompagnait pas*, 171). When the darkness approaches me, I am swallowed up by its depths; when it recedes, everything fades into the triviality of distance. In the latter case, I retain my mastery, my sense of myself, but at the price of losing all contact, being deprived of all opportunity to exercise that mastery. It is in its indecisive "oscillation" between these positions that passion might be said to be (as currently fashionable literary theory would have it) "undecidable." But there is really no question of even trying to make a decision. The "I," the power of initiative and decision, is itself only one of the terms of the alternative. I am not yet, or no longer, present, when the alternative as such is posed. Passion offers no possibility of choice. In its absolute ambiguity, the incompatible terms of its movement are affirmed simultaneously. What is undecidable from the point of view of logic, is approached in impersonal experience as the intolerable pressure of metamorphosis. "Mais se perdre, il le faut; et celui qui résiste sombre, et celui qui va de l'avant, devient ce noir même, cette chose froide et morte et méprisante au sein de laquelle l'infini demeure [But one must lose oneself; and whoever resists will founder, and whoever goes forward will become this very blackness, this cold and dead and scornful thing in the very heart of which lives the infinite]" (*AM*, 108; *DS*, 67–68). I may think to respond either by rejecting the darkness or by going forward into it. But my options are not open; no matter what I do, I cannot escape the terror of this call. The darkness envelops me in any case, and as I lose myself within it, I am no longer the one who might have chosen either to deny or to accept it.

It is not that my decision is irrelevant, in the face of an overriding fate; but rather that the darkness, the force of what I am not, *at once* impels my decision and excludes me from participating in it. Nothing in fact could be more decisive than the steps the narrator takes: the calling of J.'s name in the first part (*AM*, 36; *DS*, 20), and the "Viens [Come]" (*AM*, 111; *DS*, 69) which he addresses to Nathalie in the second. Yet in both cases, the decision is a repetition and a response, and not a free initiative. The narrator is *compelled* to decide, to respond, by the disturbing immobility of J.'s corpse, as by the violent "certitude" (*AM*, 109; *DS*, 68) of Nathalie's presence in the room. He is *summoned* by J. out of the infinite distance of her death, and by Nathalie out of the infinite distance of the darkness. And even then his "decision" consists only in a kind of patience tinged with fear, his willingness to *become* the darkness that will swallow him in any case, or the fortitude with which he affirms, after it has already engaged him, "ce mouvement infini qui me portait à sa rencontre [that infinite movement which drew me towards her]" (*AM*, 36; *DS*, 20). The decision is generated, not by the subject, but from within the darkness which attracts the subject. A strange reversal of normal narrative causality seems to be at work: the decision has already been effected, prior to my making the decision or becoming cognizant of it.

Ce qui arriva était arrivé depuis longtemps déjà ou depuis longtemps était si imminent que de ne l'avoir pas amené en plein jour, alors que dans mon existence de chaque nuit je l'éprouvais, c'est là le signe de mon accord secret avec ce pressentiment. (*AM*, 107)

What happened had already happened long ago, or for a long time had been so imminent that not to have revealed it, when I felt it every night of my life, is a sign of my secret agreement with this premonition. (*DS*, 66–67)

This "secret agreement" impels or attracts me even as it precedes my own willed action, and escapes my conscious, daytime awareness. Its perpetual imminence is that of a thought at the very threshold of consciousness, a pre-sentiment rather than a sentiment. A thought too close to become an object of thought, which I can only *éprouver* (sustain, suffer) and not possess or enjoy. For thought itself is a passion, and not the expression of some supposed spontaneity or reflective power of consciousness. It finds its origin and its conclusion outside of itself, at a point which it cannot grasp, and with which it is never able to coincide. I do not think, I do not come to a decision, except by approaching "cette *impossibilité* de penser qu'est, en cette réserve, la pensée pour elle-même [this *impossibility* of thinking which, in this reserve, thought for itself is]" (*EI*, 173). Thought is not self-sufficient; it involves an indecisive encounter with "ce que *je ne puis pas* penser [what *I cannot* think]" (*EI*, 75). And this encounter can never be brought to a conclusion, since it is "non pas l'événement de la rencontre devenue présente, mais l'ouverture de ce mouvement infini qu'est la rencontre elle-même [not the event of an encounter which has become present, but the opening of the infinite movement which is the encounter itself]" (*Le livre à venir*, 18; *GO*, 112). To think or to write, to retreat into myself, or on the contrary to emerge out of myself, to be intimate with another person's life or to witness another person's death—all this is possible only by virtue of a prior and greater impossibility. Thought arises only at the limit of thought, in the restless agitation of contact with a "présence-absence dont la pensée se tourmente, sur laquelle elle veille douloureusement, avec soupçon, avec négligence, ne pouvant que s'en détourner, si tout ce qui l'en approche l'en écarte [presence-absence which thought frets over, watches over painfully, suspiciously, carelessly, able only to turn away, since anything which brings thought near to it also pushes thought away from it]" (*EI*, 173). Thought arises as it watches over its limit, its *other*, circling a point it is never able to attain, but which occupies it and fascinates it for that very reason.

What are the implications of describing thought in this way? Blanchot agrees with the dialectical and phenomenological traditions that thought is not an objective content, but an event, an encounter, the passion of the experience of thinking. Yet this encounter is an infinite movement into an irreal or neutral space, not something that can ever take place or be accomplished in the present. And the *passion* of thought, correspondingly, is too passive to be called subjective either in a psychological or a phenomenological sense. Thought is impersonal, meaning that it is radically separate from—and incompatible with—the "I" which it stimulates but which cannot claim to inaugurate or intend it. It occurs at the limit, meaning that it is not the expression of a potentiality (neither mine nor the world's), but the exhaustion of all possibility. It is entirely contingent and unforeseeable, since I cannot master it in any way, predict it, or control it. It is singular, which is to say that it is never equal to itself, corresponds to no model, and cannot be subsumed under any generalities or categories. And yet it is not in any sense original, for its form is that of an echo or interminable repetition, so that no matter how far we trace it back, we never come upon an initial impulsion, but always something which is in its turn only a relay or repetition. And finally, thought is not spontaneity or reflection, but compulsion, because I think only insofar as I unwillingly take on the burden of this interminable repetition, and insofar as, far from making it my own, I am altered and irrevocably marked by its violently monotonous insistence.

And so, in Blanchot's perverse reinscription of the *cogito*, subjectivity is infinitely and irreparably dependent upon the otherness of a thought that for its part is never subjective, never to the subject's own measure. I am unable to think the thought that is yet never absent from my thoughts, and that makes me what I am. There is a word for such a condition, and that word is: obsession. When I am in the grips of an obsession, I am unable to take any positive action, but I am also unable to desist from an irrational, repetitive movement which convulses me at every moment. Blanchot calls this phenomenon "préhension persécutrice [persecutive prehension]," as in the case of the hand which cannot write, which has nothing to write, but which nonetheless continually writes, grasps the pencil and will not let it go: "cette main éprouve, à certains moments, un besoin très grand de saisir: elle doit prendre le crayon, il le faut, c'est un ordre, une exigence impérieuse [at certain moments, this hand feels a very great need to grasp: it must take the pencil, this is necessary, this is an order, an imperious exigency]" (*EL*, 15; *GO*, 67, *SL*, 25).

I do not have the power to *decide* to obey (or disobey) such an order; and I do not accomplish anything by obeying it. I find myself already obeying it, prior to all reflection. Compulsion anticipates all other aspects of experience; it is included in advance in everything I think, say, or do. The "sick" hand seems to have a life of its own, or rather a life which, terrifyingly, is not its own. What I think of as willed action takes place only in the shadow of this obsession, this alien life, when my second or "healthy" hand seizes the first one, in order to stop it from repetitively grasping and writing, or in order to control its motions and thereby transform its futile scribblings into intelligible symbols. I seek to change compulsion into freedom, to turn a futile, illusory gesture into a real and efficacious action. But my exercise of mastery is secretly conditioned, and therefore strangely compromised, by the very force it seeks to subdue. The imposition of order is itself the most compulsive, the most unfree and inauthentic, of actions. When the "great" writer imposes his will on the text, "cette maîtrise réussit seulement à le mettre, à le maintenir en contact avec la passivité foncière [this mastery only manages to put the writer in contact, keep him in contact, with a fundamental passivity]" (*EL*, 15; *GO*, 67, *SL*, 25). In seeking to establish order, I bind myself to a movement whose senselessness and lack of direction undermines all notions of order. The first hand's grasping movement is a simulacrum of action, a mocking, ruinous parody of the second hand's act of mastery. But this is a case where the "parody" precedes the "original." When the "healthy" hand seizes the "sick" one, by that very movement it mimics and perpetuates the latter's passive agitation. Voluntary action ironically echoes the involuntary. I conquer repetition only by giving way to it, again and again. My will is subject to a fatality of which it can know nothing. And not only writing, but everything we accomplish, everything we regard as possible, natural, or normal, is secretly marked by "le caractère anormale et le terrible origine [the abnormal nature and the terrible source]" (*AM*, 103; *DS*, 64) of such irrational compulsion.

We would like to separate consciousness, as a force which expresses mastery, which imposes order, which founds possibility—we would very much like to dissociate consciousness from all this morbidity. We would like to deny the materiality and contingency of thought. We would like to believe that our thought is spontaneous, or that its conditions are themselves produced by our own legislation and reflection, or at the very least that its extrinsic determinants can be comprehended and seized, thematized or theorized, by rational reflection and inquiry. But we discover, again and again, that it is only in indescribable movements of passion, only in the obscurity of impersonal compulsion, that our fantasies of mastery, our highest ideals and our notions of freedom, are born. We find that our achievements, our moments of satisfaction, only lead us into a more profound and intimate contact with the nocturnal world of passivity and obsession. My very lucidity becomes compulsive, and leads me astray: "Qui m'a donc aveuglé? Ma clairvoyance. Qui m'a égaré? Mon esprit droit [What then blinded me? My clear-sightedness. What misled me? My straightforward spirit]" (*AM*, 86; *DS*, 52). Behind every action, beneath every initiative, lurks the *pressentiment* that "une trahison invisible allait s'accomplir, un de ces actes déchirants dont personne ne sait rien, qui commencent dans l'obscurité et finissent dans le silence, et contre lesquels le malheur ignoré n'a pas d'arme [some secret treason was going to take place, one of those harrowing acts which no one knows anything about, which begin in darkness and end in silence, and against which an unknown misery has no weapon]" (*AM*, 76; *DS*, 46).

"Treason," in its fatality and anonymity, is the consequence and the fatal echo of the fiercely personal "loyalty" which every true thought demands. Both loyalty and betrayal are dimensions of, or responses to, the impersonal fascination which alone initiates thinking. To think is not to be the master of a form or a technique but to fall prey to an obsession, to live intimately with an ever-present, yet strangely inaccessible, *pensée*. The narrator's life is consumed by a thought that tempts him, seduces him, cajoles him, torments him, misleads him, but never abandons him. It is an experience of radical passivity, but one which for this very reason involves jealousy and rage, impatience and struggle and fatigue. There is no time, and no breathing room, for that patient hearkening to the mystery of Being that Heidegger so magisterially recommends. When I encounter so *"superbe* [splendid]" a thought, it makes an absolute demand for my loyalty, a demand expressed sometimes as a harsh exigency, and sometimes as a (dangerous or seductive) temptation. And indeed I respond to this demand; it is something to which I cannot fail to respond. But at the same time, my loyalty is insufficient; I do not respond rightly. To live intimately with such a *pensée* "exigerait de moi ce qu'un homme ne peut pas conceder [would demand something of me that a man cannot give]" (*AM*, 56; *DS*, 32). What is demanded is absolutely beyond my powers as a subject, something to which nothing in the first person, nothing I say or do, could ever adequately correspond. And this is why every thought, every experience of passion, in a sense ends in betrayal or failure. "Il eût fallu que je sorte vraiment de ma personne et, par ma vie, que je donne vie à ces mots. Mais j'étais faible, quelle faiblesse, quelle misérable impuissance [What I had to do was to emerge truly out of myself, and with my life give life to these words. But I was weak, what weakness, what miserable impotence]" (*AM*, 120; *DS*, 75).

But although the narrator berates himself for his incapacity (and it would be impossible for him not to do so), weakness, impotence, and treason are not merely negative terms. They must be affirmed, just as loyalty is affirmed, as irreducible aspects of the very experience of passion. There is no telos of passion, no repose or fulfillment, in comparison to which my "failure" could be regarded as an instance of giving up, turning away, or falling short. Betrayal is itself a response, and a particularly intense one, to the inordinate demand for loyalty.

> L'infidélité est bien, est mal, je n'en juge pas: mais son mérite—du point de vue de la terre—est de réserver l'histoire, en préparant un sentiment qui éclate au jour quand il a perdu tous ses droits. (*AM*, 91)

> Infidelity may be good, may be bad; I am not passing judgement on it: but its merit—as far as earthly things are concerned—is to keep the story in reserve, as it prepares a feeling that will burst into view when it has lost all its rights. (*DS*, 56)

Faithlessness or failure illuminates, and makes possible, the very exorbitance of passion's demand. The life of the passion that animates me is not quite my own, and this makes it all the more difficult for me to give my own life over to it. My attachment to myself, to what seems to be my own life, to what I cannot realize is already not my own—all this is an inevitable error. My cowardly or dishonorable weakness is a function of the subsistence of the "I," not of its disappearance. I am too weak, not by lack of strength, but by excess of strength and by the continuation of selfhood. It is not that I am too weak to act, but rather that I am forever too weak to give up my claim to action, my vain pretension to sufficiency and mastery. Passion demands infinite self-abandonment, and I loyally abandon everything that is mine to it; but as long as I am strong enough to abandon everything to it, as long as "I" remain the one who does the abandoning, I remain too weak to abandon myself.

It is important to insist, over and over again, that this is not a matter of moral weakness or failure. Moral judgment is a language-game that we apply to a specific realm, that of the actions (and sometimes the wishes) of the "I"—but it is the limits of this realm that are in question here. There is a situatedness, and hence a political specificity, to everything that happens; but we should beware of too facilely translating the political into the moral, or of using either of these as an alibi. The narrator suggests precisely that, in the pressure of the great events (the beginning of the War) which coincide with his narrative, "je cherchais dans la folie du sang et des armes l'espoir d'échapper à l'inévitable [I sought in the madness of blood and arms hope of escaping the inevitable]" (*AM*, 99; *DS*, 61). When the *récit* obstinately refuses to be subsumed in the course of public events—even as it deliberately calls attention to such events—this is not out of any attempt to separate the so-called private realm from what is social, political, and historical. The boundary line it draws is quite different. Private and personal life, the petty concerns of the bourgeois subject no less than the aesthetic and moral sublimities by virtue of which it justifies itself to itself—all of these are on the same side as the social, the realm of public affairs. The narrator's activity as a political journalist is continuous with his rather ludicrous concern with such things as his friend's duel, with "l'honneur selon le monde [the 'worldly' conception of honor]" (*AM*, 118; *DS*, 74). The point is that such activities, which are necessary and inescapable, and in relation to which moral judgments can and should be made, are themselves always betrayals from the point of view of passion. Which is to say, yet again, that passion is only realized in the world, as it must be realized, by virtue of such betrayals.

The limit-experience of passion separates the integrity of the self and the totality of the world, not from one another, but from what is inaccessible and irreducible to either. What is beyond the limit (but "beyond" is no longer an acceptable term here) is only "un sentiment qui . . . a perdu tous ses droits [a feeling which . . . has lost all its rights]." And such a "sentiment" cannot arise out of myself (whether I act in the loneliness of my supposed selfhood or in communion and solidarity with others), but only out of the radical unfamiliarity of others, in a summoning, an interpellation that exceeds my capacity to respond. It is necessary for Nathalie to compel the narrator to leave behind the security of the self (even at its most miserable) and the world (even at its most horrifying and deadly): "Il se peut que, lassée de me voir persévérer avec une sorte de foi dans mon rôle d'homme du 'monde', elle m'ait brusquement, par cette histoire, rappelé la vérité de ma condition et montré du doigt où était ma place [It may be that she was tired of seeing me persevere with a kind of faith in my role as man of the 'world,' and that she used this story to recall me abruptly to my true condition and point out to me where my place was]" (*AM*, 126; *DS*, 79). And this place can only be the darkness; or better, it is nowhere, the "lieu sans lieu [place-less place]" (*EI*, 565; *GO*, 141) of the *neuter*, which the narrator, to the extent that he continues to say "I," to insist on himself, cannot occupy.

Whatever the events of the story—and the narrator notes on several occasions that even if the facts are changed, "ils prennent le même sens et l'histoire est la même [they take on the same meaning and the story is the same]" (*AM*, 126; *DS*, 79)—what counts is only the passion which draws the narrator to the limit-point where his ability to initiate action ceases. At the limit, "une pensée persévérante est tout à fait à l'abri de ses conditions [a persistent thought is completely beyond the reach of its conditions]" (*AM*, 87; *DS*, 53). This thought possesses me prior to my own will, rather than with or against my will. Such is the purity of its infinite demand. Every step I take is conditioned by an insistence which, for its part, is unconditional (admitting of no exceptions) and unconditioned (not affected or determined by any prior or external circumstances). I must refer everything I do to an ultimate point that escapes all reference. I am totally occupied, reduced to a state of passive absorption that leaves no room for anything else: "Quand elle se lève, cette pensée, il n'y a plus ni souvenir ni crainte, ni lassitude ni pressentiment, ni rappel d'hier ni projet pour demain [When this thought arises, memory is no longer present, nor fear, nor weariness, nor foreboding, nor any recalling of yesterday, nor any plan for tomorrow]" (*AM*, 55; *DS*, 32).

Such is the overwhelming, obsessional encounter in which all thought, all experience, and all subjectivity are born. When the *pensée* arises, I live entirely in the moment, and entirely in the presence of the most profound and most singular emotion; and yet nothing could be more removed from what we conventionally regard as "identity" or "presence." For I live with this thought, which utterly consumes me, in a curious sort of intimacy without intimacy, a contact which at once exceeds and precludes any degree of closeness. "Je la regarde. Elle vit avec moi. Elle est dans ma maison. Parfois, elle se met à manger; parfois, quoique rarement, elle dort près de moi [I look at it. It lives with me. It is in my house. Sometimes it begins to eat; sometimes, though rarely, it sleeps next to me]" (*AM*, 55–56; *DS*, 32). Nothing could be more immediate; nothing could penetrate more profoundly the very details of my quotidian experience. When the thought sleeps next to me, or hovers over my chair as I sit and write—and this physical proximity is not merely a metaphor—then my own proper gestures, the rhythms of my own body and mind, are agitated and disturbed. The *pensée* is not just a representation or an *idée fixe*, but "quelque chose dont tout ma personne était physiquement occupée [something which my entire person was physically engrossed in]" at every moment (*AM*, 56–57; *DS*, 33).

And yet this extreme closeness also involves a constraint of formality and distance. Even in the midst of daily contact, "la familiarité, voilà ce qui entre nous s'est à jamais perdu [familiarity is just what has disappeared forever between us]" (*AM*, 55; *DS*, 32). Intimacy, like silence, is lost as soon as it has been found. I cannot become "familiar" with the *pensée*, I cannot reduce it to my own measure, even though (or because) it accompanies me everywhere, forever guides me and torments me. It asks everything of me, but has no regard for me. It moves me, but whatever I do leaves it unmoved. I cannot appease it, or inflect it, or affect it in any way. I *respect* the *pensée* too much, I cannot help putting it at a distance by the very strength of my obedience and the promptness of my response. And this is why it is characterized by "une sorte de dureté, la distance infinie entre son respect pour moi et mon respect pour elle [a sort of hardness, the infinite distance between its respect for me and my respect for it]" (*AM*, 87; *DS*, 53).

The most intense proximity is marked by a fundamental dissymmetry, an "infinite distance" that effectively prohibits communion or identification. When I come close to this thought, what I come close to is "une *interruption d'être* . . . l'inconnu dans son infinie distance [an *interruption of being* . . . the unknown in its infinite distance]" (*EI*, 109). Its immediacy serves only to accentuate its irreducible strangeness: "Et moi, insensé, je me croise les mains et je la laisse manger sa propre chair [And I, a madman, fold my hands and let it eat its own flesh]" (*AM*, 56; *DS*, 32).

The narrator's drive toward idealization is met only by action this incongruous, this bizarre. He wants to be *impressed* by the *pensée*'s distance, by its inflexibility: "A la vérité, c'est sa droiture qui me fascine [Its uprightness is what actually fascinates me]" (*AM*, 55; *DS*, 32). Such is the hardness and permanence with which we always invest the ideal. But the narrator is compelled to recognize that such rigor is in fact only a function of his own "weakness" or subsistence: "Dureté n'est pas un mot juste: la dureté venait de moi, de ma personne [hardness is not the right word; the hardness arose from me, from my own person]" (*AM*, 87; *DS*, 53). He blames himself for elevating the thought, for making it into something extraordinary, for trying to live with it in "l'intimité orgueilleuse de la terreur [the proud intimacy of terror]," and failing to realize "la misère et le peu de prix de cette intimité [the misery and worthessness of this intimacy]" (*AM*, 56; *DS*, 32). He is able to understand now, after the fact, that he over-valued the terror of the thought's advent in order to retain for himself the pride of having been the one who faced that terror. If only he could have maintained a sense of the *pensée*'s quotidian reality, of its presence in the most modest as well as the most extravagant circumstances, "ni la familiarité ne nous aurait manqué, ni l'égalité dans la tristesse, ni l'absolue franchise [we would not have lacked familiarity, nor equality in sadness, nor absolute frankness]" (*AM*, 88; *DS*, 54).

But of course understanding is always after the fact, and the narrator's "mistake" is involuntary and unavoidable. It is the error, or the imposition, at the root of all aestheticization and idealization. An obsession is too pressing, too overwhelming an experience for me to accept its presence in the very fabric of the quotidian. Its urgency leads me to regard it as something grander and more special. I translate this particular image, or this particular thought, into a realm of hardness and distance, of ideality and glory, because when I do so my disquieting sense of being so utterly dependent on it, and so exclusively occupied with it, becomes easier to bear. The insistent pressure of a compulsion impels me to magnify the object of that compulsion, to transform my daily encounter with it into "une intimité de quelques instants où tous ses pouvoirs orgueilleux se montraient et où les miens la saisissaient avec un orgueil encore plus grand [an intimacy of several seconds during which all its proud powers were revealed, and during which my own powers seized it with an even greater pride]" (*AM*, 87–88; *DS*, 53–54). This is an attempt to maintain myself in the face of dissolution: my own powers are recuperated, at whatever cost, in the heart of the movement which limits or denies them.

Such is the odd duplicity of obsession. Obsession marks an absolute limit to freedom, initiative, and mastery; but it is out of obsession that I desire to dominate, to impose my mastery. I am compulsively driven to idealize; and this is why idealization systematically denies its roots in compulsion. To idealize is to present the radical contingency of obsession, the randomness and irrelevance of its object, as something eternally necessary; and at the same time to present the involuntariness of compulsion as something freely chosen. And yet it is only the uncontrolled violence of irrational compulsion that impels me to distort and deny it in this way. It is in impersonal movements of passion, themselves beyond the reach of any mastery, that the forces of power and domination are born. The imposition of order, the generation of form, is not an escape from the constriction and darkness of obsession, but its most total and horrifying expression. Only in this sense is thought an ordering of reality.

My proud self-aggrandizement in the face of disaster is the inevitable "treason" with which I respond to every true thought. The *pensée* makes an infinite demand for my loyalty, but the zeal of my obedience ironically marks my failure to meet this demand. For my treason is not the abandonment of the thought (an abandonment which the thought itself invites me to) so much as it is my attempt to realize it. To sublimate the thought, to impose moral necessity or aesthetic form and measure upon it, to transform it into a higher actuality—all this is the symptom of a continuing desire to assert and maintain the power of the "I," and beyond it the larger structures of power and domination that define the "world." In his account of the myth of Orpheus, Blanchot insists on the sovereign lightness and *insouciance* (unconcern, carelessness) of the descent into darkness—the moment when Orpheus ruins his labors by looking back at Eurydice—in deliberate opposition to the existentialist high seriousness of dread and *souci* (care, concern, Heideggerian *Sorge*), by which Orpheus struggles to master the darkness and repossess Eurydice (*EL*, 233; *GO*, 103, *SL*, 175). Giving way to passion, Orpheus loses the possibility of possession (as defined by the dominant, masculine economy) and instead insures his ultimate dismemberment. But the opposite dimension of this experience is equally unavoidable: I betray passion to the extent that I transform it into a project capable of fulfillment. In my desire to accomplish what the thought demands, I impose an economy of possession there where there can be no possession. My very concern for the *pensée* betrays it. And this concern marks the complacency and vanity, or the unhappy persistence, of the "I."

Le Dehors (the Outside), the place-less place from which the *pensée* arises, is the ground on which every relation of power and domination is inscribed, but only because it is first of all the groundlessness through which all such relations can be subverted. In this sense, Blanchot's delineation of the economy of passion in relation to the subject is no different from the social economy of power and resistance as analyzed by Foucault. (To my knowledge, the only study of Foucault which has done justice to his closeness to Blanchot in this respect is that of Gilles Deleuze; see his *Foucault*, 88–99 and passim.) Institutionalized technologies of power, as Foucault has shown, are generated from the interplay of multiple relations of forces that run everywhere and threaten to exceed, undermine, or pervert the dominant order in all directions. That is to say, domination presupposes, and nourishes in spite of itself, the anarchic proliferation of forces that oppose domination. And this is why resistance is always possible, why power can always be undone. When Foucault says that power is everywhere, he is not saying that we are condemned to the ubiquity of totalitarian surveillance, but rather that every place is a site of struggle, that everything can be contested, that the disruptive passion of the Outside can irrupt anytime and anywhere. And when Foucault refuses a rationalist politics (such as that of Habermas), which would impose the norms and goals of an idealized social communication, this does not mean that he fails to offer us grounds for social change, but rather that he is rightly suspicious of the way in which all such "grounds" themselves serve as structures of domination, with the pragmatic function of managing and reducing revolutionary energies. Foucault is not denying the possibility and the imperative of political struggle; but he *is* locating the rationalism that posits utopian ideals, as well as the voluntarism that sees power as something to be acquired and possessed, as alibis for domination and impediments to radical social change.

Blanchot's concerns in *L'arrêt de mort* may seem radically different from Foucault's in *The History of Sexuality*, but the two writers share a focus on the double movement of *la passion du dehors* as that which at once generates and limits power and possession. Power arises out of resistance, and not the reverse; just as the demand for possession arises out of passion, and not the reverse. Power and possession, whether embodied in larger social structures and technologies or simply in the "I," seek to regulate and control the very forces and movements which have invested them, but which remain for all that irreducibly exterior to them. And this is why, if passion alone makes domination and possession possible, it is also passion that limits and reverses every form of domination and possession. The confining structures of power and subjectivity never altogether disappear, but the *chance* of contestation can forever alter and displace them. In radically interrogating the limit-experience, Foucault and Blanchot seek to undo the maneuver by which Kant transformed compulsion into a specious and self-enslaving appearance of freedom, and the limits of reason into its regulative ideas. The directly political dimensions of this interrogation, which are Foucault's main interest, are for the most part merely implicit in (although by no means absent from) Blanchot's writing. He is occupied instead with tracing the strangely impersonal affectivity, the pain and joy, of these movements, as they traverse different levels of violence and intensity.

All this only returns us with greater urgency to the question of the subsistence of the "I" in face of the impersonality of passion. The difficulty is that passion arouses a demand for possession, and yet is incompatible with possession. I desire mastery, which is to say that I want to impose and accomplish the aim of my passion. But passion is precisely a movement without an aim. In its grasp, I am carried away from myself, carried away from the state in which mastery and possession are possible. It is not that my desire is frustrated by a cruelly indifferent fate: that, in itself, would be easy enough to bear. But much harder to endure is the discovery that the force which defeats me is the very one which sustains me. Only the movement that impels me, that inhabits the deepest recesses of my body and mind, has the ability to anticipate and circumvent my own powers of initiative and action. The misery of subjectivity is that it remains so intolerably, suffocatingly close to the *dehors*, to an irreducible exteriority, an infinitude which "scorns" it, which continually forestalls it and exceeds its grasp, but which it cannot do without. My deepest experience, my most intimate passion, the most authentic, the most crucial, the one which makes me what I am—it is precisely this which I am unable to desire, and into which I am unable to enter. I *must* lose myself in the darkness— and this "must" has the force both of a command and of a necessity— but this is the one thing that the "I" can never do. I try to lose myself, and by dint of my effort to do so I find myself preserved; but when I try to preserve myself, I am swept away by the movement in which I lose myself.

Such a double impossibility, the weakness and passivity in which I can neither assert nor evade my own subsistence, defines the irreducible *malheur* of my thought. In this sense, *malheur* is Blanchot's equivalent for what Nietzsche calls nihilism, *ressentiment*, or the becoming-reactive of forces. *Malheur* lies, not in any personal loss I suffer, but in the loss of the personal itself: "un malheur important, aussi silencieux qu'un vrai malheur peut l'être, étranger à tout secours, inconnu, qui rien ne pouvait faire apparaître [a great unhappiness, as silent as a real unhappiness can be, beyond all help, unknown, and which nothing could cause to appear]" (*AM*, 63; *DS*, 37). The impersonality of passion is a *malheur* for the one who bears witness to that passion, who is excluded from it at the very point of suffering it. And if my *malheur* lies in this exclusion, then that *malheur* is a passion in its own right, from which I am yet again excluded. The subject mourns, less its own deprivation, than its absence even from the scene of deprivation. The "I" suffers impersonality, a passion which is always the passion of others, not by virtue of sympathetic identification, but in the very radicality of its separation. My subsistence as a voice which says "I" is all the more desolate in that I am even deprived of the residual gratification of weeping over myself, of saying that the loss, the *malheur*, is mine.

This means that *malheur* cannot be defined in terms of lack or negativity. My narcissism is wounded and offended, not by the failure of my desires to be satisfied, but by the very fact that I am agitated by passion at all. For to be moved by passion is to be shaken by forces which cannot be confined to my own—or anyone else's—personality. The "I," in its unhappiness, its lingering subsistence, is (in Nietzschean terminology) not the locus of a force, but a marker of the belatedness and reactivity which is the counterpart of all force. When force, or metamorphosis, abolishes all presence, the "I" is what is left behind to testify to the impossibility of presence. The *malheur* of being a subject, and *therefore* of not possessing the powers which subjectivity would like to arrogate to itself, is a *physical* sensation more than it is a metaphysical anguish. It is an uncloseable wound, like the bizarre "cicatrice [scar]" or "boursouflure transversale [diagonal swelling]" which covers the hand of the narrator's neighbor Colette (*AM*, 60; *DS*, 35); or better, like the "ligne de chance [line of fate]," "le profond coup de hache [the deep hatchet stroke]" which mysteriously marks J.'s palm (*AM*, 21; *DS*, 10). Or it is the "altération de sang [change in the blood]" (*AM*, 78; *DS*, 47), which the narrator experiences as a result of the doctor's experiments, and which leaves him overly sensitive to his outside environment, and subject to "brèves nausées au cours desquelles se produisaient des espèces de froides avalanches, un écroulement écoeurant d'images vides [brief bouts of nausea during which there were a sort of cold avalanches, a sickening collapse of empty images]" (*AM*, 88; *DS*, 54). And again, it is the "impression de froid absolu [impression of absolute cold]" which the narrator feels in his absurdly overheated room (*AM*, 77; *DS*, 47), and which is akin to the strange coldness of bodies at the moment of the most intimate contact (*AM*, 112; *DS*, 70).

The most overwhelming, and irreversible, impressions or affections are also the most impervious to any form of comprehension. The narrator's blood becomes entirely "énigmatique, d'une instabilité qui étonne l'analyse [mysterious, and so unstable that it was astonishing to analyze]" (*AM*, 79; *DS*, 48). Its radioactive "fluctuations" (*AM*, 78; *DS*, 47) seem to remove it from any usual connections of cause and effect. (The doctor's motivations in injecting him are equally unclear.) As for the marks on J.'s and Colette's hands, they are similarly indeterminate: wounds which have never been inflicted, which have always been there, which have never been preceded by the integrality of an unmarked body. The deep line in J.'s palm "ne se montrait bien qu'au moment de l'éclipse de toutes les autres [did not become distinct except at the moment when all the others were eclipsed]" (*AM*, 21; *DS*, 10), that is to say when she regains that astonishing youthfulness in which she seems exempt from the ordinary course of events, but only because it marks the imminence of her death. It is a line of "chance," of an outcome which the narrator regards as preordained and tragic (*AM*, 22; *DS*, 11), but which remains arbitrary and unpredictable. The imprint which marks me most deeply, the force which overwhelms me and determines my fate, is not an expression of my character, but a pure, external contingency.

All these marks are imprinted physically on the flesh. They are there, with a silent, enigmatic insistence, like the *pensée* which absorbs the narrator. His relation to the world becomes entirely physical, a contact no longer mediated by mental or symbolic representations, as at the moments of his bouts of nausea, and of his sensations of extreme cold. The "écroulement [collapse]" of all his images leaves him defenseless, in the grips of the most intense materiality. All fixity of forms is abolished, and he is unable to resist the flux of external forces—the physical more-than-presences—which enter the space of his privacy without his being able to recuperate them in any way. *Le dehors* (the Outside) has moved inside, and made my own interiority into a realm more distant and alien than the external world could ever be:

> Le froid de ces corps est une chose très étrange. . . . ce peu de froid est profond, non pas le léger rayonnement d'une surface, mais pénétrant, enveloppant, il faut le suivre et, avec lui, entrer dans une épaisseur sans limite, dans une profondeur vide et irréelle où il n'y a pas de retour possible à un contact extérieur. (*AM*, 112)

> The coldness of these bodies is something very strange. . . . this little bit of cold is profound; it is not a slight radiation from the surface, but penetrates, envelopes, one must follow it and with it enter an unlimited thickness, an empty and unreal depth where there is no possible return to external contact. (*DS*, 70)

All of these physical intrusions—wounds, spasms, cataleptic seizures—are *traces* in the sense made familiar by Levinas and Derrida. They are gaps, discontinuities, heterogeneous marks, interrupting the self-sufficiency and internal coherence of my thought. They are residues that mark the intrusion within me of an inaccessible and unthinkable exteriority. They are non-absences which 'present' the radical impossibility of presence. They fail to function as indices in the semiological sense. They cannot be accounted for in and of themselves, in their own proper terms; therefore they must refer to forces that exceed or precede their own existence. But however insistently they refer beyond themselves, the referential movement they initiate can never be completed. They stubbornly refuse to disappear into their references. And so their otherness, their disruption of closure, does not lead back to some absent origin or cause.

These traces are points of physical contact, not in the usual empirical sense, but in that they manifest a life not subordinated to thought, a materiality that—by virtue of this very insubordination—incessantly provokes thought. Such is the life of the body, apart from all our images and representations of the body: "une vie qui n'est pas la vie, mais qui est plus forte qu'elle et que nulle force au monde ne pourrait vaincre [a life which is not life, but which is stronger than life and which no force in the world could ever overcome]" (*AM*, 107–8; *DS*, 67). The marks or traces of this life are themselves its only life. They have no proper presence, and no signification, but only the strange coldness of "l'existence sans l'être [existence without being]" (*La part du feu*, 317; *GO*, 47), the disturbing and alien insistence of things that are not subordinated to our use, and whose life is not our own. The life which agitates me remains neutral, impersonal and distant. It cannot be reduced to an attribute or potentiality of anything that would still be "myself." And yet it is this life which upholds and transforms my own; this life, this passion, is the only one I have. Its distance is that of something which is "absolument proche, d'une proximité que les êtres ignorent [absolutely near, of a proximity that people are not aware of]" (*AM*, 107; *DS*, 67). This life is inscribed in my very flesh, nearer to me than I myself am. Passion "happens" in the vertiginous closeness of the death that I cannot assume, or the other person whom I can never become.

Souvent l'inconnu nous donne de l'angoisse, mais il est la condition de l'extase. L'angoisse est peur de perdre, expression du désir de posséder. C'est un arrêt devant la communication qui excite le désir mais qui fait peur. Donnons le change au besoin de posséder, l'angoisse, tout aussitôt, tourne à l'extase.
—Georges Bataille, *L'expérience intérieure*

CHAPTER 6

Impossible Encounters

Passion, Intimacy, and Affirmation in Blanchot

Blanchot subversively suggests, in *L'espace littéraire*, that reading is in fact the lightest and most irresponsible of tasks. For reading is not directed to discovering the form or meaning of the book being read, nor even the absence or indeterminability of form or meaning. It is not a process of interpretation at all: "lire se situe au-delà ou en-deça de la comprehension [reading is situated beyond or before comprehension]" (*EL*, 261; *GO*, 96, *SL*, 196). The two *récits* that I will be discussing in this chapter—*L'arrêt de mort* and *Au moment voulu*—do not seem to be appropriate subjects for interpretation. Not because they are "undecidable," so that interpreting them would be an endless process, but because the seriousness of the labor of interpretation seems oddly beside the point. In "l'affirmation violente, impersonnelle [the violent, impersonal affirmation]" (*EL*, 256; *GO*, 93, *SL*, 193) of the *œuvre*, there is simply no place for hermeneutical or rhetorical considerations. On one side, there is the torment, the obsession, the passion, the fascination, in short the "essential solitude" of one who is no longer the author. On the other side, there is the spontaneous, uncritical "Yes" of an anonymous and unconcerned reader. On neither side is there room for the spirals of linguistic or phenomenological self-reflexivity.

Of course, it is not really a question of opposed sides. The same "innocence of becoming," the same *insouciance* and *désœuvrement* (worklessness), characterize the torment of the writer and the liberty and *légèreté* (lightness) of the reader. There are no fixed positions in the text, no opposed poles of subjectivity. There is only a violent, catastrophic moment of *contact*, the vanishing point of a perpetual and always reversible metamorphosis. Reader and writer do not exist outside of the movement which deprives them of being and identity, transforming them into one another. In the instant of reading, "ne se laisse admettre dans la légèreté d'un Oui libre et heureux que ce qu'on a supporté comme l'écrasement d'un néant sans consistance [only what has been borne as an oppressive nothingness without consistency can be admitted into the lightness of a free and happy Yes]" (*EL*, 260; *GO*, 96, *SL*, 195). A strange and terrible affirmation, this "Yes," which affirms only what is impossible and unsupportable, and yet which never ceases—lightly and carelessly, but also violently and passionately—to affirm. Every event in Blanchot's *récits* partakes of this doubleness of affirmation, "exaltation sans mesure, profondeur d'amertume et de cruauté, et pourtant qu'était-ce? la frivolité de l'image la plus gaie [boundless exaltation, depth of bitterness and cruelty, and yet what was it? The frivolity of the most cheerful image]" (*MV*, 125; *WT*, 55). The narratives continually approach "cette rapide condensation de la clarté en feu, du feu en un Oui, Oui, Oui brûlant autour d'un noyau froid ["his quick condensation of the brightness into fire, and of the fire into a Yes, Yes, Yes burning around a cold core]" (*MV*, 126; *WT*, 55). What weight can be given to this "Yes"? The oxymoronic intensity of a language that erases its own postulates, problematizes its own conclusions, and thereby asserts nothing and denies nothing— this is not the undecidable suspension of affirmation but its positive and necessary condition.

In exploring and repeating this affirmation, Blanchot is concerned less with language and signification than with joy and pain, affect and passion. The pathos of Blanchot's texts is a pathos of intimacy and excess, and not an anxiety of ignorance or interpretation. Nearly everything is obscure and uncertain in a *récit* such as *Au moment voulu*; but even uncertainty is violently consumed and transformed by passion, in the supreme moment of Judith's "*Nescio vos*." Such words are indeed a text, repeated from a distant past, "un écho d'autrefois [an echo of another time]." But what is important is neither the provenance nor the "vérité de grammaire [grammatical fact]" of these words; it is the immense "travail des ténèbres [labor on the part of the shadows]" which throws them back at the narrator "comme la bénédiction et la malédiction de la nuit [as the benediction and malediction of the night]" (*MV*, 137; *WT*, 60). He is affected by these words that reject him, that thrust him aside and push him infinitely far away, just as he is affected by looks and touches and other forms of sensible or physical contact. What counts in speaking and writing, as in touching and looking, is the impossible and unsituable movement of *being-affected*, and not any subsequent possibilities of reinterpretation. I am trying to suggest that the "lutte profonde [profound struggle]" (*EL*, 256; *GO*, 93, *SL*, 193) between writer and reader has no privileged or paradigmatic status. In its more-than-ambivalence, it is not all that different from other kinds of quotidian *rencontres* (encounters), such as Nathalie's visits to the narrator's hotel room in *L'arrêt de mort*, or the narrator's stay with Judith and Claudia in *Au moment voulu*. It is in the gaiety and triviality of everyday life and in the most simple relationships with others that one encounters "ce terrifiant contact, cette catastrophe démentielle [this terrifying contact, this mad catastrophe]" (*MV*, 135; *WT*, 58) which is the source and subject of Blanchot's obsessive, impassioned meditations.

These intense encounters, at once quotidian and extraordinary, are affirmed in the *neuter*, in a *voix narrative* (narrative voice) that is neither the author's nor the narrator's. As Blanchot comments with regard to some of his earliest fictional works,

> Avant toute distinction d'une forme et d'un contenu, d'un signi-fiant et d'un signifié, avant même le partage entre énonciation et énoncé, il y a le Dire inqualifiable, la gloire d'une 'voix narra-tive' qui donne à entendre clairement, sans jamais pouvoir être obscurci par l'opacité ou l'énigme ou l'horreur terrible de ce qui se communique. (*Après Coup*, 97–98)

> Before all distinctions between form and content, between signi-fier and signified, even before the division between enunciation and statement, there is the unqualifiable Saying, the glory of a 'narrative voice' that speaks clearly, without ever being obscured by the opacity or the enigma or the terrible horror of what it communicates. (*Vicious Circles*, 68)

Blanchot's narratives get their startling force from the splendor of this Saying, this affirmation which has no positive content of its own but which also cannot be reduced to an interpretation of whatever may or may not have been said. Such a Saying exceeds all categories of expression or signification; it is entirely singular, and may not be allegorized, figured, or personified in any way. It neither transcends nor unifies the text, but is "plutôt comme un vide dans l'œuvre [rather a kind of void in the work]" (*EI*, 565; *GO*, 141): a rupture of plenitude, a point of forgetfulness, a moment when the dialectic of decision and comprehension comes to a halt.

The singularity of this point of rupture cannot be contained by any play of rhetorical substitution. The "détournement perpétuel [perpetual turning-away]" (*EI*, 564; *GO*, 141) of a language in the *neuter*, which neither asserts nor negates, and the radical exteriority of thought to itself, make it impossible to approach language and thought merely in terms of figuration. The *neuter* is "cela qui porte la différence jusque dans l'indifférence, plus justement, qui ne laisse pas l'indifférence à son égalité définitive [that which carries difference right into indifference, more precisely, which does not leave indifference in its definitive evenness]" (*EI*, 450). It is always excessive, always *de trop* (*EI*, 458); it marks an irreducible dissymmetry, an *interruption*, an irrecuperable break in continuity. It is the point of an "expérience de ce qui n'obéit pas à l'ordre régnant de l'expérience [experience of that which does not obey the ruling order of experience]" (*EI*, 613), and whose only "law" is that of "cet oubli premier qui précède, fonde et ruine toute mémoire [this first forgetfulness that precedes, initiates, and destroys all memory]" (*EI*, 564; *GO*, 140). Beyond any movement of substitution, thought is impelled by a sovereign instance—the *pensée*—which cannot itself be thought, which cannot be anticipated or remembered, which cannot be made the object of a figure any more than of a reference, and which cannot be reciprocated or reflected in thought. Blanchot cites the emptily resonating "mot-trou [hole-word]" which absorbs all subjectivity and all discourse in Duras's *Le ravissement de Lol V. Stein* (*EI*, 565; *GO*, 141): a point of rupture that can never be attained once and for all, in the fullness of any presence.

This sovereign instance is "expressed" by an interminable repetition, less because it is caught in a web of endless textual exchange, than because it is, as Klossowski says of Nietzsche's thought of the Eternal Return, always already subtracted from such exchange. (Klossowski's astonishing reinvention of Nietzsche, in *Un si funeste désir* and *Nietzsche et le cercle vicieux*, is frequently cited by Blanchot: most notably in "Sur un changement d'époque: l'exigence du retour," *EI*, 405–18; in "Le rire des dieux," *L'amitié*, 192–207; and in *Le pas au-delà*, passim). Never identical to itself, the unthinkable thought of the Return is unique and inexpressible—and hence inexchangeable. It is an "absolue ambiguïté [absolute ambiguity]" (*L'amitié*, 206) which is yet not ambivalence or undecidability. For the very intensity of this thought—an intensity that precedes and exceeds its content—renders it incompatible with the unity and stability of the self which would (ambivalently) receive it, or of the world in which it would be (undecidably) communicated and interpreted. I cannot realize this thought, or exhaust it, but only reiterate the movement by which I approach it. It is a point of absolute surprise, a point that cannot be intended or thematized by thought, that cannot be figured or personified in any way.

Recent criticism has emphasized that identity cannot be thought without difference, just as the literal cannot be thought without the figurative. The former term necessarily presupposes, even as it disavows, the latter. Identity is an effect of difference, and the illusion of the literal is a product of figuration. But the thought of the Eternal Return marks the extreme point, and therefore also the limit or breaking point, of the very movement of figuration. In the uncanny *singularity* of the "highest thought," of the dizzying moment when Nietzsche discovers the Eternal Return, it is the *failure* of figurative substitution, rather than its ubiquity, that disqualifies the claims of identity and presence. The Eternal Return ruptures immediacy in the very movement by which it refuses the continuing play of figures and mediations. No substitution, no figuration, can be adequate to express the "revelation" that overwhelms Nietzsche at this moment—and that is why the Return ruptures every possibility of presence, to the point that it cannot itself be actualized, cannot be rendered present. The affirmation of the Return is "toujours hors de la pensée qu'elle affirme et où elle s'affirme, expérience de la pensée comme du Dehors et, par là, indiquant le point de disjonction—de non-coherence—où son affirmation, toujours l'affirmant, déjà la destitue [always outside of the thought which it affirms and where it is affirmed, experience of thought as of the Outside, and thereby indicating the point of disjunction—of non-coherence—where its affirmation, always affirming it, already dismisses it]" (*EI*, 408).

The Eternal Return, then, supervenes only as a trace, only by "disjunction." It cannot be *figured*. It has no corresponding signs with which to manifest itself; it leaves no space for its own assertion. It affirms everything, without exception, but so exorbitantly that it undermines the authority of this affirmation. "Qu'est-ce qui reviendra? Tout, *sauf* le présent, la possibilité d'une présence [What will return? Everything, *except* the present, the possibility of a presence]" (*Le pas au-delà*, 27). Everything returns, but not in the mode of identification and possession. And so repetition produces difference, rather than confirming the identity of something that would return. The *retour* can be accomplished only as a *détour*, "tournant qui se répète, répétition qui se produit par son propre détour [turning which repeats itself, repetition which produces itself by its own detour (turning-away)]" (*EI*, 410). This *détour* is a movement of alteration, rather than one of figuration. As Klossowski says, it is impossible for an identical self to affirm the Eternal Return: "à revouloir, le moi *change*, devient *autre* [in re-willing, the self *changes*, becomes *other*]" (*Nietzsche et le cercle vicieux*, 106). The idea of the Return is not merely a content of my thought, but an impulsion from the Outside, a "will" invading and affecting my own will, so that I become different from what I was by the very fact that I think it. The subject becomes other than itself, but without ever transcending the singularity of particular perspectives. The identity and self-enclosure of any given individual perspective is ruined, but not to the benefit of some universalizing or mediating movement. The Return is a perpetual becoming-other and not merely a rhetorical referring-elsewhere, "une éternelle scintillation où se disperse, dans l'éclat du détour et du retour, l'absence d'origine [an eternal scintillation where, in the brilliance of detour and return, the absence of the origin is scattered]." The subject which thinks the Return is uprooted, swept away in a restless agitation "nous invitant à en appeler à l'inépuisable capacité de metamorphoses [inviting us to appeal to the inexhaustible capacity of metamorphoses]" (*L'amitié*, 205).

The "lesson" of the Eternal Return is that no postulation of identity is stable or sufficient unto itself. Time is radical alteration: no moment is able to perpetuate itself, or project itself beyond itself. The continuities of past and future, of memory and anticipation, are subverted, and together with them the construction of a living "present." The undoing of origin and identity forever precedes any movement in which origin and identity might be constituted. The Eternal Return initiates a theater of simulations, an "eternal scintillation" in which the play of figuration first becomes thinkable. But the Return, in itself, is not so thinkable. It belongs to a future I will never be able to realize, and to "un passé effroyablement ancien [a frightfully ancient past]"

(*Le pas au-delà*, 33): to a time which can never become mine. The *moment* when Nietzsche apprehends and "re-wills" the Return is of supreme importance precisely because it is nonpresent and insituable: it marks the absolute rupture of the present, the subject's *contact* with a time that is incompatible with, and not contemporary with, its own. Pure alteration, without presence or identity, the thought of the Return is therefore *singular* and *irreversible*.

The Eternal Return disrupts, even as it parodically asserts, the economy of the Same. Similarly, the Saying of language in the *neuter* subverts, even as it generates, the possibilities of narrative closure. In both of these instances, the shock of rupture and the compulsion to repeat testify to an *encounter* that provokes thought, but continually escapes it. The intrusion of the Outside is less the insistence of a language which I do not own, of an alien thought within my thought, than it is—yet more radically—an encounter with something altogether irreducible to language and thought, which I can never conceive, which I cannot interpellate even as a *pensée*. It is not that Language or Being "speaks" me or speaks through me, but that an instant of intense contact, a limit-experience, marks the catastrophic failure of these possibilities. The most profound moment of Orpheus's inspiration comes, not when the forces of night and death are modulated through his lyre, but when, by giving way to those forces and looking back, he ruins in one moment the majesty of the underworld, the power and coherence of his song, and the personal hopes of Eurydice and of himself (*EL*, 230ff.; *GO*, 101ff., *SL*, 173ff.) Orpheus's sacrifice, like Nietzsche's exaltation in Sils Maria—or his collapse in Turin—affirms the extravagance of a passion that can neither be satiated by presence nor adequately sustained by infinite substitution.

II

Blanchot's fiction is written in the trace of such inordinate desires, such overwhelming encounters. It affirms the singularity of extreme passion, the uniqueness not of personal identity, but of impersonality and the rupturing of identity. His *récits* are focused on moments of excessive and unbearable *contact*, moments that exceed representation and therefore literally defy description. Such is the instant in which the narrator of *L'arrêt de mort* receives the gaze of a woman who is already dead: "quelque chose de terrible dont je ne parlerai pas . . . le regard le plus terrible qu'un être vivant puisse recevoir [something terrible which I will not talk about, the most terrible look which a living being can receive]" (*AM*, 36; *DS*, 20). This gaze is terrible because it is unreturnable and even, strictly speaking, unreceivable. The look of the Other's death is that of a distance so great as to preclude all hopes of reciprocity, let alone any pretensions to mastery.

> Qu'est-ce donc qui me met le plus radicalement en cause? Non pas mon rapport à moi-même comme fini ou comme conscience d'être à la mort ou pour la mort, mais ma présence à autrui en tant que celui-ci s'absente en mourant. (*CI*, 21)

> What then calls me into question most radically? Not my relation to myself as finite or as the consciousness of being before death or of being for death; but my presence for an Other who absents him/herself by dying. (*UC*, 9)

But what does it mean to be present to another's dying, to witness the death—or even simply the absence—of someone I love? The narrator regrets not having been present at the instant of J.'s death. He arrives, as always, too late. Yet this belatedness is not merely accidental. The instant of transition which is death is quicker than any apprehension of it could ever be; so fleeting and impalpable as to evade any possibility of presence. J.'s dying scarcely lasts as long as the time necessary to communicate its occurrence to the narrator: "elle se mourait, elle était presque morte, l'attente n'avait pas commencé à ce moment-là; à ce moment-là elle avait pris fin [she would die, she was almost dead, the wait had not begun at that moment; at that moment it had come to an end]" (*AM*, 34; *DS*, 19). I anticipate and wait for the other person's death; but his/her actual dying never corresponds to the time of my waiting. The strange temporality of dying can no longer be represented by internal time-consciousness. It is not only J.'s pulse, but also the onlookers' apprehension of it, which—twice—"s'éparpilla comme du sable [scattered like sand]" (*AM*, 34, 52; *DS*, 19, 30). The narrator is not able to observe J.'s spring into death, but only the trace of that movement, which is to say her remains: "Elle n'était déjà plus qu'une statue, elle absolument vivante [She was already no more than a statue, she (who had been) absolutely alive]" (*AM*, 35; *DS*, 20).

What is uncanny about a cadaver is its appearance of being alive and dead at once. "Le cadavre a beau être étendu tranquillement sur son lit de parade, il est aussi partout dans la chambre, dans la maison.

A tout instant, il peut être ailleurs qu'où il est, là où nous sommes sans lui, là où il n'y a rien, présence envahissante, obscure et vaine plénitude [It is in vain that the cadaver lies tranquilly in state on its bier, it is also everywhere in the room, in the house. At any moment, it can be elsewhere than where it is, where we are without it, where there is nothing, an invading presence, an obscure and vain fullness]" (*EL*, 353; *GO*, 84, *SL*, 259). The corpse is no longer the person whose mute resemblance it bears; but *as* a resemblance, it cannot be reduced to the status of an object, of inert matter. It is the *trace* of a vitality that can no longer be rendered present. And so the narrator is troubled by the strange contrast of liveliness and immobility in J.'s corpse, by the signs of a desperate struggle for life in which he was unable to assist her. He has been excluded from her dying, but he is all the more sensitive to being present at the scene of this exclusion. Feeling the weight of this ambiguity, he calls out her name; and receives, in response, an intolerable look which reinforces the disjunction of life and death (far from abolishing it).

The death of the Other is an "error," a *hantise* (haunting, obsession), a bizarre fascination from which I cannot free myself. The clichés of existentialism tell us that each of us is absolutely alone at the moment of death. Blanchot reminds us, rather, that I "share" in the other person's death precisely by not being able to share it. The trauma of my separation from somebody else is, paradoxically, what prevents me from ever being altogether alone. The Other's definitive estrangement ties me to him/her, creates a silent complicity between us. I cannot accompany, much less console, this Other, I cannot relieve his/her suffering, I cannot exempt him/her from the necessity of dying—and this impotence binds my consciousness to him/her irrevocably.

The look that J. accords the narrator—like so many other gazes throughout the *récit*—arises out of this impossibility, this infinite distance in which there is no communion. Elsewhere in the book, the narrator evokes "un sentiment absolument douleureux, dépossédé et comme privé de lui-même; son souvenir devenait le désespoir sans expression, qui se cache sous les larmes mais ne pleure pas, qui n'a pas de visage et transforme en masque celui qu'il emprunte [an absolutely distressing feeling, dispossessed and as if bereft of itself; the memory of it became inexpressible despair, despair which hides in tears but does not cry, which has no face and changes the face it borrows into a mask]" (*AM*, 81; *DS*, 49). J.'s look is similarly impersonal: abstracted from or deprived of itself. It is blank and expressionless, without any of the signs that would indicate sympathy or human warmth. It does not restore J. to the world of the living, so much as it upsets the narrator's own sense of belonging comfortably to this world. He is brought into contact with an experience which he cannot himself imagine, much less assume. He is forever affected by this unwilling transgression, by the "fait que j'avais vu et surpris ce que je n'aurais pas dû voir [fact that I had seen and taken by surprise something I shouldn't have seen]" (*AM*, 37; *DS*, 21).

This glance, this transgression, implicates the narrator in a relation and an economy that the individual consciousness is unable to intuit, construct, or intend. J.'s look overwhelms him because he is unable to assimilate or appropriate it in any way. And indeed, although the entire narrative of the first part of *L'arrêt de mort* is centered upon that look, the look itself is absent. It has no *place* in the story which recounts it. It is not, it cannot be, described or talked about. Instead, it is abolished by being reabsorbed into the usual order of things. Once J. has been restored to life, any reference to her return, or to her having been dead, is put under erasure: "À partir de ce moment, elle fut non seulement tout à fait vivante, mais parfaitement naturelle, gaie et presque guerie. . . . Elle se détendit aussitôt et redevint absoluement humaine et vraie [From that moment on, not only was she completely alive, but perfectly natural, gay, and almost completely recovered. . . . Right away she relaxed and became absolutely real and human again]" (*AM*, 36–37; *DS*, 20–21). She is not someone who has come back, a *revenant*, but someone still alive, who has to approach the impossible limit of dying, yet again—as if for the first time. The *contact* opened by J.'s gaze is effaced by the very fact of its having been accomplished. Everything returns to its place, as if that unreceivable glance had, in fact, never been received.

And so, it may be said that in bringing J. back to life the narrator accomplishes nothing at all. Of course, this "nothing" is not without importance: it affirms the obscurity and banality of the quotidian against all attempts to endow death with some sort of metaphysical or supernatural prestige. But the narrator gives J. a day of surplus existence only at the price of compelling her to pass through the torment of dying for a second time. His living relation to her culminates in his helping her die, shortening her agony by means of an injection. In recalling her to life, he does not exercise a power he possesses, but experiences all the more poignantly the pain of her loss. This is why he does not see anything extraordinary in his having revived J., but admires only the violence and the valor of her own struggle to hold death at bay (*AM*, 52–53; *DS*, 30).

The strangeness of J.'s glance is immediately lost, because it does not indicate a superior power, the sublimity or authority of another order of being. There is no other order, nothing on the other side of the limit. The "crossing" into death is not a passage to another realm, nor even to another order of significations. "Ici, le *sens* ne s'échappe pas dans un autre sens, mais dans l'*autre* de tout sens [Here, *meaning* does not escape into another meaning, but into the *other* of all meaning]" (*EL*, 359; *GO*, 89, *SL*, 263). The limit-experience that we call death is a vain and inauthentic movement, which ratifies nothing and leads nowhere. It throws thought back on itself, since it cannot be *aufgehoben* (sublated) or surpassed in any way. The only accomplishment of J.'s overwhelming look is therefore—to be forgotten. The economy of dying, like that of the Eternal Return, or of the writing of the *neuter*, is necessarily one of *oubli* (forgetfulness). But this *oubli* is precisely the way in which it affects me. In the uncanny presence of death, I myself am drawn away from presence. J.'s look cannot be preserved or recollected, for it alters too profoundly and too irrevocably the one who would remember. "Oublier la mort n'est pas se rapporter d'une manière inconsidérée, inauthentique et fuyante à cette possibilité que serait la mort; c'est au contraire entrer dans la considération de l'événement nécessairement inauthentique, présence sans présence, épreuve sans possibilité [To forget death is not to relate to the possibility which is death in a thoughtless, inauthentic, and fleeting manner; on the contrary, it is to take into consideration the necessarily inauthentic event, presence without presence, trial (ordeal) without possibility]" (*EI*, 291). (Blanchot's rejection of Heidegger's idealization of death should especially be noted here.)

All this helps to explain why I am implicated, or put into question, much more fundamentally by the death of the Other than by my own death. "On ne *veut* pas mourir, on ne peut pas faire de la mort un objet pour la volonté, on ne peut pas vouloir mourir [One does not *want* to die, one cannot make of death an object of the will, one cannot want to die]" (*EL*, 128; *SL*, 105). To will death is to will the absence of the very situation in which one would be able so to will. Such is the insurpassable contradiction which Blanchot describes in the case of suicide. (Suicide could therefore be called the nightmare inversion, or *mise en abîme*, of Kant's categorical imperative.) Suicide is an *épreuve* of impossibility, all the more so because it does in fact empirically occur. For even if I will my own death, I am still demanding it from the point of view of continuing life. Thus it is J.'s living force and energy—the power which enables her to hold off the moment of death—which is also behind her demand for a quick death, for the avoidance of needless suffering. Dying is always involuntary, even when I am able to choose the manner and the moment of my own death. Dying can never be an intentional object of consciousness. Which is also to say (in opposition not only to religious thought but also to any philosophy of human finitude) that I am unable to project an authentic relation to myself in death.

This incapacity testifies to the shocking, radical *otherness* of dying: of a death which is never "my own." Death is inaccessible to the subject: "car en elle *je* ne meurs pas, je suis déchu du pouvoir de mourir, en elle *on* meurt, on ne cesse pas et on n'en finit pas de mourir [for in it *I* do not die, I have fallen from the power to die, in it *one* dies, one does not stop and does not finish dying]" (*EL*, 204; *SL*, 155). The "on [one]" who dies is not anyone in particular, since the person who dies is precisely stripped of his/her living particularity; but it is always *someone else*, someone other than myself. Blanchot suggests that I suffer the death of the Other but not my own death, very much as Wittgenstein says that "Ich kann wissen, was der Andere denkt, nicht was ich denke [I can know what someone else is thinking, not what I am thinking]" (*Philosophical Investigations*, IIxi, 222). This is not to say that the other person's thought, or the other person's death, becomes immediately and transparently "my own." But rather: when I witness the death of the Other, I suffer a pain that can never be my own. I am "present" at an event which is the ruin of all presence. I am *implicated* by the irreducible otherness of the other person, precisely because that person is no longer there. In loss, in separation from the one I most love, I am touched by that infinite *difference* that alone makes love possible.

III

The death of the Other is one of those overwhelming *events* which reverberate throughout *L'arrêt de mort*, and indeed all of Blanchot's fiction. In such events, the Other affects me, or concerns me, and at the same time escapes my scrutiny. The traditional directionality of Western thought is inverted. I am no longer able to refer the advent of the other person to my thought of that person, or to a space of figural substitution in which my fantasy is able to play freely. Instead, my thought is taken away from me, estranged, singularized, and necessitated, by the Other's attraction. Metaphor gives way to metamorphosis. I am altered, and drawn outside of myself, in an *encounter* that does not even occur in the time of my own interiority but precedes the constitution of myself as someone capable of having such an encounter. Just as my thinking is sustained by a *pensée* that exceeds my capacity to think it, so in its turn that *pensée* is generated in the violence and surprise of a happening that it is unable adequately to formulate. Just as writing is not a self-sufficient action, but is drawn into and impelled by a broader movement of compulsion, so the obsessive repetition that initiates thought is itself exceeded in a moment of *contact*. The impersonality and nonintentionality of passion implies, not isolation, but engagement with an Other. Before the unhappy subsistence of the "I," there is the shock of the Other's touch. Prior to the very constitution of my subjectivity in obsession, there is the singularity of a glance or a voice that summons me.

The events that concern Blanchot's narrator in *L'arrêt de mort* are unwelcome and unanticipated, but unavoidable: strange nocturnal intrusions that shatter his illusions of privacy, independence, and self-containment. In the proximity of others, he lives a life, dies a death, and is consumed by a passion, which are not his own. The Outside invests his privacy not in the form of a revelation of Being, but as an experience of *intimacy*. For again and again, and in spite of his craving for solitude, he is drawn into the space of "une intimité qui fait voler en éclats la présence, l'abolissant en quelque sorte ou l'exaltant jusqu'à sa destruction [an intimacy which makes presence explode into pieces, abolishing it in some manner or exalting it to the point of its destruction]" (*Le pas au-delà*, 101). Intimacy is the hyperbole of presence, which by its very intensity ruptures the possibility of presence. I cannot maintain my selfhood in the face of someone who is simply *too close*. The other's intrusion interrupts the movement by which I establish a relation to myself. I no longer have the freedom that comes from reflection and distance. The disturbing singularity of the Other's approach, the insistence of his/her ambiguous and unintended gestures, is a shock yet more radical than that of the Eternal Return. Excess is the effect of the Other's provocation and seduction— or merely of the Other's appearance—and not of a private vision. Intimacy overwhelms presence, for the more-than-presence of the Other is a *surplus* which I am absolutely unable to absorb or reduce. The

Other resists my impulse to translate everything into exchangeable figurations, into metaphysical or ontological generalities.

Intimacy is a relation that cannot be contained by presence, but that also does not afford the one affected by it the luxuries of distance and doubt. Just as it is not entered into voluntarily, so it cannot be suspended by the vagaries of interpretation. When the narrator returns to his room, at the most intense moment of *L'arrêt de mort*, he already knows the fatality that weighs over him. He does not first have to discover Nathalie sitting in the darkness; there is no perceptual process by which he becomes aware of her presence. "Qu'il y eût quelqu'un dans cette chambre, je n'avais pas besoin de faire encore un pas pour le savoir. . . . Tout à coup, la certitude que quelqu'un était là qui me cherchait fut si forte que je reculai devant elle . . . [I did not have to take another step to know that there was someone in that room. . . . All of a sudden the certainty that someone was there who had come to find me became so intense that I drew back from her . . .]" (*AM*, 107–9; *DS*, 67–68). He does not have to apprehend her, because he cannot possibly avoid or ignore her. Whatever he does, she is already *there*; she has always preceded him, she is waiting for him in the very place he thinks is most authentically and inalienably his own. He has made it clear that he does not like other people violating his privacy by coming into his room (*AM*, 64–65; *DS*, 38); and the room he now enters is precisely the one which he had sealed off because he was tormented by the scent of Nathalie's perfume, and by other lingering traces of her previous visit: "Je me dis que je ne sortirais plus de cette chambre, mais que personne non plus n'y entrerait [I told myself that I would not leave that room any more, but also that nobody any more would enter it]" (*AM*, 88; *DS*, 54). He wants to maintain his privacy by establishing absolute closure, by making change impossible. But he cannot close himself off, without also including Nathalie. As is the case with the animal protagonist of Kafka's story "Der Bau [The Burrow]," the narrator's dwelling is the locus of his most intense privacy and self-communion; and, as in Kafka's story, it is just here that the Other's proximity becomes inescapable (see Blanchot's discussion of "Der Bau," *EL*, 223–26, *SL*, 168–70; and Joseph Libertson's commentary, *Proximity*, 96–105).

The Other appears in the vacant space of my own privacy and selfhood. His/her intrusion takes the form, first of all, of a *look*. Someone is already looking at me, before I have had a chance to look back.

I am seen, I am pierced by a glance, even in darkness and absence, even when I cannot myself respond. This look summons me, even as it rejects me or fails to recognize me. Eyes emerge out of the darkness: "Les yeux s'ouvrent, les yeux les plus vivants, les plus profonds du monde, et qui me voient [The eyes open, the most alive, the most profound eyes in the world, and they see me]" (*AM*, 108; *DS*, 67). But this living gaze, so close to me, and which interpellates me so urgently, is also oddly absent, withheld and subdued, "cette flamme morte et vide de ses yeux [that dead and empty flame in her eyes]" (*AM*, 109, 111; *DS*, 68, 69). Nathalie's eyes are "tantôt passifs et vides, tantôt enflammés par une brûlure dont on ne voyait que l'inquiétant reflet [sometimes passive and empty, and sometimes inflamed by a burning of which only the disquieting reflection was visible]" (*AM*, 122; *DS*, 76–77). Insistent and reserved at once, her gaze is altogether ordinary, entrenched firmly in the quotidian, and yet even more unsettling than J.'s look from the space of death. "Un regard est très différent de ce que l'on croit, il n'a ni lumière ni expression ni force ni mouvement, il est silencieux, mais, du sein de l'étrangeté, son silence traverse les mondes, et celui qui l'entend devient autre [A look is very different from what one might think, it has neither light nor expression nor force nor movement, it is silent, but from the heart of strangeness its silence crosses worlds and the person who hears that silence is changed (becomes other)]" (*AM*, 109; *DS*, 68). This look is singular not in spite of, but by virtue of, its impersonality. It affects me not by its expression, but in its mere, mute insistence: what counts is not *what* it says, but simply *that* it says.

If I could attribute an intention or an expression to this look, if I could consider it to be open to the possibilities and uncertainties of interpretation, then I would not so be affected by it. It would have a force commensurate with my own, against which I could struggle, or with which I could collaborate. But the unsignifying blankness of the look marks the limit of these ruses of consciousness. When all the maneuvers of projection and identification, of interpretation and conflict, are exhausted, the gaze subsists in its passivity and neutrality. It is not that it cannot be interpreted, but that it exceeds, it abstracts itself from, all the potentialities to which it gives rise. It can be opposed but not abolished, explained but not explained away. However I respond to it, however I interpret it, it simply continues to regard me; it is *there*, apart from any demands it might make or any thoughts it might express. In tracing the disturbances provoked by such an unaccountable and unsituable "presence," Blanchot is necessarily closer to Levinas than he is to Nietzsche:

> Levinas donne précisément le nom de *visage* à cette 'epiphanie' d'autrui. Lorsque autrui se révèle à moi comme ce qui est absolument en dehors et au-dessus de moi, non parce qu'il serait le plus puissant, mais parce que, là, cesse mon pouvoir, c'est le visage.

> Levinas precisely gives the name of the *Face* to this 'epiphany' of the Other. When the Other is revealed to me as the one who is absolutely outside and above me, not because he would be the more powerful, but because, there, my power ceases—this is the Face. (*EI*, 77)

Blanchot is rightly suspicious of Levinas's ethical and theological vocabularies, his hasty rendering of the experience of impossibility into the derivative form of a prohibition (*EI*, 78–80, 89–93). But Blanchot is close to Levinas in discovering intimacy at its highest pitch in the passive and neutral contact of the Face. The greatest feeling is also the most distant, since it is the one in which I am most removed from my own stable presence or being-in-the world. There is a strange blankness and tonelessness at the heart of passion, an "absence" corresponding to what Levinas calls the "nudity" of the Face. The Other intrudes upon my privacy, but with a featurelessness that always eludes my grasp. The powerlessness and impassivity of this Face, this look, abstracts me from my own powers. It is on account of this blankness, nourished and sustained by it, that intimacy is an infinite relation of desire, which cannot be reduced to measures of negativity and possession. Intimacy marks the point at which my power ceases, but not because it is overpowered by another power. This experience cannot be understood simply in terms of constraint and limitation. For at the limit that is the Other's approach, the forces that constrain me are contested together with those that I claim to wield or possess. As Blanchot writes in another context (referring to the strange absence of force that characterizes the modern work of art): "Elle n'est pas forte au regard de ce qu'elle est, elle est sans pouvoir, impuissante, non pas qu'elle soit le simple revers des formes variées de la possibilité, mais parce qu'elle désigne une région où l'impossibilité n'est plus privation, mais affirmation [It is not strong with respect to what it is, it has no power, it is impotent, not because it is simply the obverse of the varied forms of possibility, but rather because it designates a region where impossibility is no longer deprivation, but affirmation]" (*EL*, 300; *SL*, 223).

Intimacy is a "weakness" that is yet an affirmation. The insistent approach of the Other is incompatible with any measures of self-definition, self-possession, or self-preservation. And yet this loss of self is neither a privation which the self might experience, nor an absolute negation of the self. It is rather an infinite movement, which can never conclude in the ecstasy (or the horror) of total identification. Closure is as radically unattainable in the forms of communion or effacement as in that of solipsism. Intimacy is not an achieved state, but an *event* exceeding presence, the shock of an *encounter*, forever unexpected, forever unconsummated, and forever to be renewed.

> La rencontre: ce qui vient sans venue, ce qui aborde de face, mais toujours par surprise, ce qui exige l'attente et que l'attente attend, mais n'atteint pas. Toujours, fût-ce au coeur le plus intime de l'intériorité, c'est irruption du dehors, l'extériorité ébranlant tout. La rencontre perce le monde, perce le moi.

> The encounter: that which comes without advent, which approaches head on, but always by surprise, which demands waiting and for which waiting (expectation) waits, but which it never attains. Always, even in the most intimate heart of interiority, it is an irruption of the Outside, exteriority shaking up everything. The encounter pierces the world, pierces the self. (*EI*, 608)

The encounter is Blanchot's radicalization of the surrealist notion of *chance*. It is the throw of the dice, the disposition of randomness that determines everything (or more precisely, as Blanchot puts it, "in-determines" everything—*EI*, 610), because in itself it is unique and indeterminable. Its shock is that of the unexpected, of something that cannot be anticipated or prepared for in any way. This is why it "pierces" not only the self, but the very world in which that self is accustomed to move. Everything in my life is altered, when a particular person enters my room at a particular moment, for reasons that remain obscure, and are in any case irrelevant. Even if I can explain it after the fact (as when the narrator proposes several explanations for Nathalie's first visit to his room), the *surprise* of the encounter remains unaccountable, and ruptures the linearity and homogeneity of cause and effect. What is affirmed in the encounter is the "hétérogenéité des phénomènes, leur radicale *distance* au lieu même de leur croisement [heterogeneity of phenomena, their radical *distance* at the very place of their crossing]" (*EI*, 609). The encounter is singular and irreversible, an irreducible irruption of exteriority, because the terms it brings into relation cannot be adequated to one another. My own life is determined by this other life, because everything I say or do is affected by its imprint; but the trace that penetrates my very being nonetheless remains outside my grasp. This determination is also an "indetermination," since what it determines is a future as inevitable, yet as open and unpredictable, as the advent of death itself.

The encounter bespeaks a moment of intimacy, my contact with an Other who remains apart from me at the very point of his/her approach. Without this separation, there would be no intimacy; I do not encounter the more-than-presence of the other person if I remain capable of containing that person within the homogeneous space of my own perceptions. In intimacy, the *distance* of the Other, his/her irreducibility to myself, itself becomes suffocatingly close. The nearness of the Other exceeds all measure, denying me the leisure of a space for self-reflection. But the distance of the Other is also beyond all measure, as I am confronted with the alien insistence of somebody who is assuredly not myself, and whose will and desire do not coincide with my own. If the Other's intrusion upon my privacy is intimated in a look, then his/her continuing alterity at the point of greatest contact is manifested in a touch.

> Elle était debout, presque contre moi, je voulais lui prendre le bras, mais elle ne faisait aucunement attention à ma personne tout à coup rejetée extrêmement loin. . . . Lentement je posai ma main sur la sienne, ce contact était comme un souvenir amer, une idée, une vérité froide, implacable, contre laquelle la lutte n'avait qu'un sens mesquin. (*AM*, 122)

> She was standing, almost against me, I wanted to take her arm, but she was not paying any attention to my person, which had suddenly been flung extremely far away. . . . Slowly I put my hand on hers; this contact was like a bitter memory, an idea, a cold, implacable truth, and to fight against it could only be a shabby thing. (*DS*, 77)

Intimacy at its highest pitch can be conveyed in the lightness of a touch, and yet this touch is enough to alter my world irrevocably. For I am put in immediate contact with a person, a body and a thought, with whom I have nothing whatsoever in common. When the narrator grazes Nathalie's flesh, he feels how far that flesh is from anything of his own. I make contact, but this contact does not seem directed toward me: "Tout cela se passait infiniment loin, ma propre main sur ce corps froid me paraissait si éloignée de moi . . . [All this was taking place at an infinite distance, my own hand on this cold body seemed so far away from me . . .]" (*AM*, 111; *DS*, 69). There is no meeting ground, no general category that subsumes both of us, no common terrain. I am together with the Other only to the extent that I am separated from myself. Contact occurs in the coldness, and not the warmth, of a hand that lies on another hand; or in the sadness of an exchange of glances that do not cross. To touch another person is also, immediately, to be pushed away (this is a recurring pattern in *L'arrêt de mort*). In intimacy, I discover the distance and the strangeness—the radical otherness—of the other person: as I never could have done, had he/she remained a stranger.

It is all too easy to mistake the forces at work here, to translate Blanchot's affirmations into the clichés of alienation and the unhappy consciousness, or to assimilate his descriptions of the gaze and the encounter to existentialist formulations such as Sartre's. But the movement that intrudes upon the integrity of the subject also paralyzes the ruses of the dialectic. In the encounter, "L'autre, surgissant par surprise, oblige la pensée à sortir d'elle-même, comme il oblige le Moi à se heurter à la défaillance qui le constitue et dont il se protège [The Other, looming up by surprise, obliges thought to come out of itself, as it obliges the ego to run up against the weakening which constitutes it and against which it guards itself]" (*EI*, 450). Distance and *défaillance* do not mark the limits of intimacy; they are its positive and necessary conditions. The touch or the gaze arises out of an immense distance, because its contact occurs entirely without mediation. Nothing in the approach of this body lessens its radical strangeness, its incompatibility with the sphere of things that I can claim or recognize as my own. Intimacy therefore precludes reciprocity: I cannot respond adequately, or in kind, to the exorbitant movement by which the Other approaches me. Contact is a relation which preserves the dissymmetry and the "non-contemporanéité [non-contemporaneousness]" (*EI*, 609) of the terms put into relation. Intimacy abolishes the homogeneous space in which the dialectical struggles of master and slave, subject and object, self and other, could take place.

This movement that exceeds possession cannot itself be made into an occasion for possession. It draws me "hors de l'ordre des choses [outside the normal order of things]" (*AM*, 67; *DS*, 40), and into the space of "quelque chose qui n'avait rien à voir avec la vie et le cours du monde [something which had nothing to do with life and the course of the world]" (*AM*, 83; *DS*, 50). It deprives me of my "world" and strands me in a place apart from any place, apart from any possibility of expression, apart from any *order*. And there is indeed beauty, as well as terror, in this movement. I am released, freed from the nostalgic regrets of the past, from the responsibilities of the project, and from the anxieties of futurity, more than I am bound by any servitude. In the midst of his distress, the narrator accedes to the glory of Nathalie's triumph, and to "l'appel de l'affirmation toute-puissante qui est unie à moi [the summons of the all powerful affirmation which is united with me]" (*AM*, 126; *DS*, 79).

But this "freedom," this affirmation, this intimacy, is not a state that can be perpetuated or preserved. It is not a utopian moment, not an imaginary, transcendent, or otherworldly compensation for actual suffering. It does not restore finality in the form of communion. It has no future and no past; it is without presence, without permanence, without a fixed site, and without any guarantees. It does not repair a loss, but affirms the irreparability of loss itself. Intimacy is foredoomed to failure; and it is only *within* its failure that it is *affirmed*, that its infinite movement exceeds any measure of success. Thus Blanchot comments on the final phrase of Duras's *La maladie de la mort*: "Ainsi cependant vous avez pu vivre cet amour de la seule façon qui puisse se faire pour vous, en le perdant avant qu'il soit advenu [Thus nevertheless you were able to live this love in the only manner possible for you, by losing it before it came to pass]." For Blanchot, such a movement marks "l'accomplissement de tout amour véritable qui serait de se réaliser sur le seul mode de la perte, c'est-á-dire de se réaliser en perdant non pas ce qui vous a appartenu mais ce qu'on n'a jamais eu [the accomplishment of all veritable love, which would be to realise itself exclusively in the mode of loss, that is to say realizing itself by losing not what has belonged to you but what one has never had]" (*CI*, 71; *UC*, 42).

Every passion, every love ends badly. In his/her singularity and inaccessibility, the Other whose contact affects me is always already lost to me, lost even before having been found. But this loss is the very tie that unites us, the point at which our absolute incompatibility, our difference from one another, is brought into contact. Loss is therefore not lack or deprivation, but the "expression" of a surplus of life and being. It cannot be coded in the conventional (psychological) terms of anticipation or nostalgia (*CI*, 71–72; *UC*, 42). When the Other reaches out to me, nothing positive is gained or accomplished; and yet, in the unrealizable instant of this gesture, expended and not possessed, I am outside the relations of power (domination and exploitation) that have defined—and continue to define—my life and world. As the narrator says of Judith's gaze in *Au moment voulu*:

M'assujettir? elle ne le voulait pas; se laisser orienter? elle ne le pouvait pas; me toucher, oui; c'est ce contact qu'elle appelait le monde, monde d'un seul instant devant laquelle le temps se cabre. (*MV*, 150)

Subjugate me? She didn't want that. Let herself be guided? She couldn't. Touch me? Yes; it was this contact that she called the world, world of a single instant, an instant before which time rears up. (*WT*, 66–67)

IV

Au moment voulu repeats these affirmations and these encounters, and in so doing alters them. Again and again, this *récit* brings us to the excruciating brink of "willed moments," events which supervene "at the right time," instants of simultaneous happiness and unhappiness, overwhelming in their very poverty. These moments range from the narrator's entry into the corridor to Judith's exaltation and collapse, including along the way such scenes as Claudia's building of the fire, and the glances through the snowy window which unite and separate the three protagonists. The question is not how one interprets these moments, but how one responds to them, how one is affected by them, how one endures or repeats them. For such events are everything and nothing: overwhelming, unforgettable, and yet transparent, frivolous, irreal. They are barely noticeable, over before they have properly begun; and yet one can say of them, as the narrator says of his stay in the corridor, "j'y suis encore, j'en suis resté lá [I'm still there, I stayed there]" (*MV*, 15; *WT*, 4). One cannot get beyond them, for they rupture the continuity of linear time. They are indeed "événements humains [human events]"—nothing could be more vivid, more deeply felt, or more "real"—and yet they do not "take place," do not happen once and for all, but "construisent indéfiniment leur retour [indefinitely construct their return]" (*MV*, 165; *WT*, 73). *Au moment voulu* is the nonlinear narration of "une intrigue profonde, immobile, que je ne dois pas regarder, ni même apercevoir, dont je ne dois pas être occupé et qui cependant exige toutes mes forces et tout mon temps [a profound, static intrigue, one that I mustn't look at, or even notice, that I mustn't be occupied by and that nevertheless requires all my strength and all my time]" (*MV*, 153; *WT*, 68).

If we do need some clue for entering—although we can never leave it—the labyrinth of this "intrigue," then perhaps our best guide is the scene in which Claudia sings a *Lied* by Schumann. She sings "en blanc," in a voice deprived of the *pathétique* of theatrical artifice, as of all individuating characteristics: a voice "indifférente et neutre, repliée en une région vocale où elle se dépouillait si complètement de toutes perfections superflues qu'elle semblait privée d'elle-même [indifferent and neutral, hidden away in a vocal region where it stripped itself so completely of all superfluous perfections that it seemed deprived of itself]" (*MV*, 68–69; *WT*, 29). And yet such a voice, by virtue of its "extraordinaire retenue [extraordinary restraint]" is all the more profoundly engaged "à la recherche du seul bonheur de chanter [in search of the simple happiness of singing]" (*MV*, 71; *WT*, 30). Claudia's singing is like that of the Sirens, as Blanchot describes it in "La rencontre de l'imaginaire [Encountering the Imaginary]": "Elles chantaient, mais d'une manière qui ne satisfaisait pas, qui laissait seulement entendre dans quelle direction s'ouvraient les vrais sources et le vrai bonheur du chant [They sang, but in a way that did not satisfy, that only implied in which direction lay the true sources of the song, the true happiness of the song]" (*LV*, 9; *GO*, 105). In stripping everything away, depriving itself even of itself, this singing points toward that perpetual imminence that is the song's sole affirmation. So much passion and force, even in the infinite *usure* (wearing away) of all passion and all force. This blankness and neutrality, at once the "law" of the *récit* and that which the *récit* recounts, ruins all distinctions and all desires; but it enacts, in its very effacement, the excess and the singularity, the vanity and avidity, of pure desire. In a similar way, it is Judith's fixed and absent gaze of which the narrator says, "Je ne pense pas avoir jamais vu un regard aussi avide [I don't think I've ever seen a look as avid as that one]" (*MV*, 131; *WT*, 57–58).

The voice in which Claudia sings is not a personal, expressive voice, but a voice in the *neuter*: a speech neither of fixed distinctions nor of indifference, but of "pure extravagance" (*EI*, 567; *GO*, 143). The most intense passion is the most radically impersonal, since it is both the one which alters or annihilates the subject most completely, and the one from which the subject remains at the furthest remove, like a spectator at its own funeral. The nonidentification and forgetting that passion requires, the deprivation even of deprivation that it implies—this is what makes for its tonelessness, "une soudaine froideur, une évocation plus abstraite semblable à une imperceptible éloignement de la voix [a sudden coldness, a more abstract rendering, like an imperceptible distancing of the voice]" (*MV*, 68; *WT*, 29). An asubjective blankness is a mark, not of world-weariness or existential anomie, but of the most violent and powerful affect.

I am attempting to evoke the affective dimension of *Au moment voulu*, the passive force of its desire. For of what else does the narrator try repeatedly to speak? "Il est vrai que je parle d'anxiété, mais c'est du frémissement de la joie que je parle,—et de détresse, mais c'est de l'éclat de cette détresse [It is true that I'm talking about anxiety, but it is the shiver of joy that I'm talking about—and distress, but the luster of this distress]" (*MV*, 146; *WT*, 65). One never comes to the end of such explanations, of the joy and distress which they contain. In a sense, nothing is less mysterious than these moments of affective intensity; they happen every day. One could speak of them so easily, if only. . . . But as the narrator concedes, at such moments, "la parole ne m'appartenait pas [It wasn't up to me to speak]" (*MV*, 83; *WT*, 36). There are points beyond which it becomes impossible to speak—and it is to this "beyond," this "plus loin encore [even further]" (*MV*, 76; *WT*, 32), that passion incessantly strains. If at such moments we cannot speak, it is not on account of any personal weakness: "Je ne manquais pas de forces. . . . Je vivais à peu près normalement [I did not lack strength. . . . I was leading a more or less normal life]" (*MV*, 141; *WT*, 62). Nor is it the effect of any defect in the symbolizing power of language; if nothing can be spoken, there is nothing ineffable either. "Plus loin" does not indicate some mystical or transcendent realm. It marks a limit beyond which no "place" exists—and yet a limit which is perpetually transgressed. It is not that "self" and "language" are too weak, but that the violent, affirmative forces of passion are too strong—too strong for us, but also too strong for themselves: "Mes forces me trahissaient, mais infidèles à qui? à leurs limites: démesurées plutôt, désespérérément grandes [My strength was betraying me, but what was it being unfaithful to? To its own limits: it was excessive, hopelessly great]" (*MV*, 78; *WT*, 33). The most one can accomplish in the presence of such forces—and even this requires an amazing, superhuman strength—is to scream out two forgotten words—and then collapse.

The supposedly fixed structures of subjectivity and language are traversed and shaken by affects they are unable to limit or contain. It is simply that passion exceeds our capacity to experience it, exceeds all standards of pleasure and pain. Passion is "impossible," in the sense that it is irreducible to satisfaction or accomplishment. Its violence cannot be exhausted by any measure of expression or effectuation. There is nothing more powerful and more *alive* than the force and passion, the "vivacité prodigieuse [prodigious vivacity; amazing spirit]" of Judith's exaltation (*MV*, 132; *WT*, 58). But the vivacity of desire is also what makes it so literally *unbearable*. Such an excess of life and force cannot be sustained, even for the duration of a single instant. It is incompatible with the integrity and continuity of the subject that would encompass it, or of the language that would represent it.

The "impossibility" of passion is therefore its most striking and necessary confirmation. Judith achieves an incredible triumph, and her collapse "n'appartenait pas moins à l'exaltation, c'en était l'évidence, le moment où il ne s'agissait plus d'adorer la majesté d'un débris, mais de saisir et de déchirer [was just as much part of the exaltation, was proof of it, the moment when one no longer worshipped the majesty of a piece of debris, but seized it and tore it apart]" (*MV*, 133; *WT*, 58). There can be no question of frustration, deprivation, or lack, since this "saisir et déchirer [seizing and tearing apart]," this violent transgression of the merely possible, is precisely what passion affirms, what it most profoundly *wants*: "C'est pourquoi aimer est terrible et nous ne pouvons aimer que le plus terrible. . . . [To attain the point] où toute ressemblance succombe et se brise, c'est cela que veut la passion [That is why it is terrible to love and we can love only the most terrible. . . . (To attain the point) where all resemblance yields and is shattered—that is what passion wants]" (*MV*, 161; *WT*, 71–72). Passion leaves no space, and has no time, for recognition and reflection. It ignores possibility, ignores and destroys even its own possibility.

Judith's avid *regard*, says the narrator, "ne se souciait ni de la possibilité ni du moment [(was) unconcerned about either possibility or the moment]" (*MV*, 150; *WT*, 66). Such is the violence and impatience of desire, but such is also its *légèreté* and *insouciance*. What is most unlivable is life in its purest and highest intensity. And passion is the inconsiderate, destructive consummation, the expenditure (*dépense*) without reserve of this intensity. And it is this intensity, this expenditure, which *Au moment voulu* so powerfully affirms:

> Son exigence ne se détournait pas de la vie, mais, la consumant dès qu'elle la touchait, elle paraissait invivable, exactement comme la passion est vivre, bien que l'être touché par la passion détruise aussi la possibilité qu'est la vie. (*MV*, 144–45)

> Its exigency did not turn away from life but rather consumed it the moment it touched it and appeared unlivable, in exactly the same way that passion is living, even though the creature touched by passion also destroys the possibility that is life. (*WT*, 64)

The violence of this affirmation ruptures the presence of the living present in the very act of affirming it. The event, the moment of passion, is "absolument présent [absolutely present]" (*MV*, 155; *WT*, 69), present so absolutely that it is "trop forte pour les jours et . . . fait d'eux une pure dissipation [too strong for the days, turning them into pure dissipation]" (*MV*, 157; *WT*, 69). Dissipation, unlimited metamorphosis, becoming without being, "la pure passion du temps, la pure puissance du jour [the pure passion of time, the pure power of the day]" (*MV*, 144; *WT*, 64). This excess of presence, its instability, its irreducibility to the merely present, is what distinguishes the *now*: "'Maintenant,' étrange rayon. Maintenant, force furieuse, pure vérité privée de conseil ['Now'—strange ray. Now—furious force, pure truth deprived of counsel]" (*MV*, 149; *WT*, 66). Desire is not concerned with the long term of success or failure. For it is always *maintenant* [now]: it demands consummation in the instant, be this at the price of the loss of the instant itself. In the throes of passion, all one can do is to consume oneself in order to glorify the moment, to become "cette torche allumée en vue d'éclairer un seul instant [this torch lit in order to illuminate a single instant]" (*MV*, 143–44; *WT*, 63). And this is why it is never possible to narrate the history of passion, to trace its unfolding in linear time. And more: such a narration is as undesirable as it is impossible: "Personne ici ne désire se lier à une histoire [No one here wants to be connected to a story]" (*MV*, 108; *WT*, 47].

"Now" is the conflagration of time (which does not mean its accomplishment). It interrupts the continuity of any *histoire*, but not to the benefit of that ideal suspension of time we call "eternity." For nothing is more distasteful than the religious and aesthetic attempt to eternalize the moment, to make it last forever or bring it back to life: "Lorsque se montre la figure d'un tel moment, il ne faut pas la respecter. . . . Cet instant fût devenu l'humiliation et la honte, si j'avais essayé de le perpétuer ou essayé de le retrouver [When the face of such a moment shows itself, one mustn't respect it. . . . that instant would have been turned into humiliation and shame, if I had tried to perpetuate it or tried to find it again]" (*MV*, 139–40; *WT*, 61–62). "Now" seeks least of all to be respected. It is the moment when a passion that exceeds the will, and even the knowledge, of the subject who enacts it, nonetheless *is* acted and not just reacted: "la profondeur de maintenant, là où la passion signifie aimer et non pas être aimé. Qui aime est la magnificence de la fin; qui est aimé, avare souci, obéissance à la fin [the depth of now, where passion means loving and not being loved. One who loves is the magnificence of the end; one who is loved is miserly care, obedience to the end]" (*MV*, 149; *WT*, 66). Passion wants more than eternity; even infinite time is not enough to contain it. As the narrator says of Judith, "L'illimité ne lui suffisait pas. C'est pourquoi elle m'appelait éternellement hors de l'infini [The limitless was not enough for her. That is why she was eternally summoning me out of the infinite]" (*MV*, 148; *WT*, 66). Beyond the infinite and the eternal comes the insistent call of the *moment voulu*, "le flamboiement de cette parole: voici qu'elle arrive, quelque chose arrive, la fin commence [the conflagration (blazing) of this speech: now it is happening, something is happening, the end is beginning]" (*MV*, 146; *WT*, 64).

Passion wants the now, it flares up only for the now and for the end which is proclaimed in the now. In its excess, which is to say its affirmation, it can only announce the end. But such excess is also its insubordination, its nonreciprocity, its sovereign refusal of the constraint of any end. Desire certainly does not obey any master, just as it does not correspond to any teleology or to any symbolic structure. "Un ordre? Le désir transperce tous les ordres [An order? Desire transfixes (pierces through) all orders]" (*MV*, 148; *WT*, 65). The instant of desire is that of "la liberté du pur caprice [the freedom of a pure caprice]" (*MV*, 133; *WT*, 59). Such freedom is not in any traditionally voluntaristic sense "mine." I cannot possess or control it, even as I cannot sustain or endure it. And yet to be swept away by such "caprice" is not to be enslaved to any power, but to expend oneself in the moment, and to be able to say, as Judith is able to say, "'C'est moi seule qui l'ai fait' [It was I alone who did it]" (*MV*, 148; *WT*, 65).

To proclaim the end and yet not to serve the end. To will the moment when an excess of passion destroys any identity, any capacity to will. To enact an infinite passivity, to grasp, in the present, "un avenir qui ne serait jamais plus à nouveau, de même que le passé refusait d'avoir lieu une fois [a future that would never again be new, just as the past refused to have taken place once]" (*MV*, 135; *WT*, 60). One never comes to the end of so violent a consummation, so exalted and furious an instant. "Le flamboiement d'une signification dernière [the blaze of a final meaning]" (*MV*, 136; *WT*, 60) never burns down, but continues triumphantly to announce its own extinction. In its impatience, its more-than-presence, passion is always ahead of itself, and so it endlessly, fatally renews itself, preceding any origin, surpassing any end. Such is the strange, divided temporality of the now, of the *moment voulu*. On one hand, "personne ne pourrait jamais dire qu'elle [cette scène] avait déjà eu lieu; elle était arrivée une première et une unique fois [no one could say of such a scene that it had ever taken place before; it had occurred a first time and only once]" (*MV*, 133; *WT*, 59). On the other hand, the uniqueness of such a scene is precisely what requires its eternal repetition, "l'écho d'un événement souverain se répercutant à travers l'infinie légèreté du temps où il ne peut se fixer [the echo of a supreme event reverberating through the infinite lightness of time, where it cannot settle]" (*MV*, 163–64; *WT*, 73). The event only happens once, but how could anybody ever fix and locate this "once"? The moment can never be exhausted, because it can never be reduced to an indifferent equality with itself.

Thus the narrator is condemned to the vain and sterile repetition of moments and images which can never coincide with themselves, which can never present themselves once and for all.

Terribles sont les choses, quand elles émergent hors d'elles-mêmes, dans une ressemblance où elles n'ont ni temps pour se corrompre ni origine pour se trouver et où, éternellement leurs semblables, ce n'est pas elles qu'elles affirment, mais, par-delà le sombre flux et reflux de la répétition, la puissance absolue de cette ressemblance qui n'est celle de personne et qui n'a pas de nom et pas de figure. (*MV*, 160–61)

How terrible things are, when they come out of themselves, into a resemblance in which they have neither the time to corrupt themselves nor the origin to find themselves and where, eternally their own likenesses, they do not affirm themselves but rather, beyond the dark flux and reflux of repetition, affirm the absolute power of this resemblance, which is no one's and which has no name and no face. (*WT*, 71)

From the perspective of a society in which affect is referred back to the "self," and in which desire is measured by the standards of lack and possession, such a fate can only be a tragedy, and the *affirmation* of such a fate can only be the sheerest madness. And yet how wrong it would be to read *Au moment voulu* as a tale of misery, of alienation, of the frustration of an alleged drive to mastery: "Je dois le rappeler: de tels jours ne sont pas consacrés à un malheur inconnu, ils n'affirment pas la détresse d'une décision mourante; au contraire, ils sont traversés par l'immensité joyeuse, autorité rayonnante, lumière, pure frivolité . . . [Such days are not devoted to an unknown misfortune, they don't confirm the distress of a moribund decision; on the contrary, they are traversed by joyful immensity, a radiant authority, luminescence, pure frivolity . . .]" (*MV*, 156–57; *WT*, 69). Madness, perhaps. "Mais si c'est une folie, je le vois, j'y prends part [But if it is madness, I can see that I participate in it]" (*MV*, 153; *WT*, 68).

Au moment voulu affirms this madness, this exorbitance of passion which is irreducible precisely to the extent that it is *not* the correlate of a self-identical subject. Desire is a movement, not of self-possession, but of intimacy and contact: "l'intimité de l'ébranlement [the intimacy of the shock]" (*MV*, 147; *WT*, 65), "l'intimité d'un tutoiement mystérieux [the intimacy of a mysterious familiarity (saying *tu*)]" (*MV*, 134; *WT*, 59). Passion is a *rencontre* (encounter), albeit one whose violence and surprise exclude all recognition and all communion. "Je rencontrai cette femme que j'ai appelée Judith; elle n'était pas liée à moi par un rapport d'amie ou d'ennemie, bonheur ou détresse; elle n'était pas un instant désincarné, elle vivait [I met this woman I called Judith; she was not bound to me by a relationship of friendship or enmity, happiness or distress; she was not a disembodied instant, she was alive]"

(*MV*, 147; *WT*, 65). It is out of Judith's separation from the narrator, out of their ignorance of one another (even if they have been lovers)— out of this non-relation that her gaze confronts and summons him: "ce regard, étrangement effronté, était une constante violence pour me saisir, sommation ivre, joyeuse . . . [that look, oddly brazen, was a constant, violent attempt to seize me, a drunken, joyful challenge]" (*MV*, 150; *WT*, 66). Nothing is important except for the vivacity of this gaze, this contact, the way it alters the one who gives it and the one who receives it. The instant of the gaze is the instant of uncontainable metamorphosis, of an unlimited being-affected, and it doesn't matter if one "experiences" this contact only in the form of catastrophe, it doesn't matter if our only intimacy is that of an "ébranlement [shock]." The moment is eternally too strong for us, but this doesn't matter either. For "jamais cet instant ne fut troublé, ni prolongé, ni différé, et peut-être m'ignorait-elle, et peut-être était-elle ignorée de moi, mais il n'importait, car pour l'un et pour l'autre cet instant était bien le moment voulu [This instant was never disturbed, or prolonged, or deferred, and maybe she didn't know me, and maybe she was unknown to me, but it didn't matter, because for one and for the other this instant really was the awaited moment (the *moment voulu*), for both of us the time had come]" (*MV*, 139; *WT*, 61).

L'être, le plus souvent, semble donné à l'homme en dehors des mouvements de passion. Je dirai, au contraire, que nous ne devons jamais nous représenter l'être en dehors de ces mouvements.
—Georges Bataille, *L'érotisme*

Cette parole égale, espacée sans espace, affirmant au-dessous de toute affirmation, impossible à nier, trop faible pour être tue, trop docile pour être contenue, ne disant pas quelque chose, parlant seulement, parlant sans vie, sans voix, à voix plus basse que toute voix: vivante parmi les morts, morte parmi les vivants, appelant à mourir, à ressuciter pour mourir, appelant sans appel.
—Maurice Blanchot, *L'attente l'oubli*

CHAPTER 7

Without an End

Conclusions

—Is this, then, a work of criticism?

—In some respects yes, in others no.

—That's too easy to say. Ambiguity is a cheap art-school trick. You'll have to explain.

—To come to a conclusion? To summarize what I've already said? That seems pointless. Why make the same assertions all over again? Besides, if I *could* say everything all at once, here, now, then I might have saved myself the trouble of writing the rest of the book. But my argument—if that's what it is—is changed when it is stripped of all the repetitions, variations, and detours which constitute it, or of all the textual citations which go into it. A conclusion, an explanation, is ridiculous on two counts: it is not only superfluous, but impossible as well.

—Superfluous and impossible: that is to say, what Bataille would call a movement of pure expenditure. A gift to the reader, albeit a gift which I do not want to give. Critical writing, like fiction or poetry, involves this unwilling gift, this abandonment of logic and rigor, this pure extravagance. But it also mobilizes (as do fiction and poetry in their own ways) something which says "I," which congeals into an author, which solidifies an identity: and which thereby denies heterogeneity and difference, and blocks communication.

—Which leads us back to the same question. Is this a work of criticism? Does it conform to the laws of the genre? What have you accomplished by writing it?

—Well, I suppose this *is* a work of criticism insofar as we retain the distinction between primary text and commentary, between original and derivative discourses. (Not to mention the distinctions between literary discourses and those with pretentions to be philosophical, historical, scientific, and so forth.) My own text is dependent upon—or parasitic upon, as recent literary theory is prone to put it—previously existing texts which in their turn are classified as literature: the collected writings of Georges Bataille and Maurice Blanchot.

—Hold it right there. For one thing, the writings of Blanchot and Bataille themselves contain a high proportion of critical discourse or commentary. . . .

—Drawing us into an infinite regress in which there is no original or primary text. Ah, the complacencies of the abyss. Far be it from me to uphold the notion of an Original, a primal Word, a sacred text in relation to which everything else would be merely commentary. But it seems to me that much recent literary theory remains in complicity with this hackneyed theological construct. Contemporary theory continues to endow language with a metaphysical aura, last glimmer of the mysterious prestige of the Origin. Isn't the current obsessive focus on *reading*, on *interpretation*, on *rigor*, merely an inverted, negative form of the hermeneutical insistence on recovery of lost meanings, or of the Western religions' superstitious reverence for the Word?

—Yes, Foucault's comments on this point seem particularly apt. "In granting a primordial status to writing, do we not, in effect, simply reinscribe in transcendental terms the theological affirmation of its sacred origin or a critical belief in its creative nature? . . . Is this not to reintroduce in transcendental terms the religious principle of hidden meanings (which require interpretation) and the critical assumption of implicit significations, silent purposes, and obscure contents (which give rise to commentary)? Finally, is not the conception of writing as absence a transposition into transcendental terms of the religious belief in a fixed and continuous tradition or the aesthetic principle that proclaims the survival of the work as a kind of enigmatic supplement of the author beyond his own death?" ("What is an Author?" 120).

—Foucault criticizes the very hypostatization of language which Blanchot more summarily denounces as "un transcendentalisme vicieux que Heidegger nous rappellera en deux phrases trop simples: le langage n'a pas à être fondé, car c'est lui qui fonde [a vicious transcendentalism that Heidegger would recall for us in two excessively simple propositions: language does not need to be founded, for *it* is what founds]" (*Michel Foucault tel que je l'imagine*, 23; *Michel Foucault as I Imagine Him*, 72).

—And so the insistence on language instead of subjective expression, on an uncontrollable rhetorical drifting, or on a social and Symbolic medium with its own opacities and its own laws, simply doesn't go far enough. It doesn't really rupture the hegemonic structures of utility and interiority, it doesn't bring us far enough Outside. It merely folds back on itself. The academy is the modern successor of the Church, and the same processes of decipherment and interpretation, of unfolding multiple significations, of making visible what was hidden, continue unabated. What better alibi for scholasticism and pedantry could there be than the claim that everything is secondary, everything is commentary? At least we are no longer dragged back to the pure interiority, the fascist authority, of an absolute Origin; but we never get Outside either. In its seamless ubiquity, infinite in scope and yet self-referring and self-validating at every moment, the web of textuality resembles nothing so much as the absent face of God.

—And that defines one sense in which this book is not a work of criticism. It does not present itself as a "reading" of Blanchot and Bataille. I have tried to avoid interpretation as much as possible. I offer neither a questioning of their language, nor an exposition and critique of their ideas. I have resisted the imperialist urge to construct a meta-discourse which would take their writings as its target or object.

—But what alternative is there? How can you escape the processes which you decry? This is certainly a book *about* Blanchot and Bataille. You quote them repeatedly, explain them, expound them, weave your words around theirs. You seem to be advocating their ideas, unfolding their implicit meanings, or translating them into a more contemporary idiom. This book is criticism, or it is nothing.

—Let me try to state the point a bit differently. Of course this book is written in relation to, and is altogether dependent upon, the words and texts signed (although sometimes pseudonymously) by Bataille and Blanchot. But what sort of relation has been established? Have I paraphrased, systematized, interpreted, revealed repressed contents? Have I twisted, distorted, selectively rearranged material, quoted out of context? Rather, I have tried to write a book in which the questions of interpretive accuracy, adequacy, and faithfulness to the source simply do not arise. It's a question, not of truth or correctness, but of perspective. And that marks the distance between my own work and more prevalent critical modes. The difference between traditional criticism and deconstruction is that one thinks a reproduction of the meanings of the original text is possible, while the other does not. But they both take the *attempt* at such a complete and faithful reproduction as the paradigm of the critical act, as the very *ethics* of reading. Whereas I do not. I feel no compulsion to account for every aspect of the text I am discussing.

—Where, then does that leave you? Just what are you trying to accomplish with the texts you are discussing, citing and re-citing, "endlessly elaborating"?

—The best answer I can give is the Wittgensteinian one. The problems of criticism are matters, not of meaning, but of use. Or better, questions of meaning *are* questions of use, and not questions of (adequate or inadequate, proper or improper) representation.

—Questions of use: but isn't Bataille's entire *œuvre* an endeavor to get away from the horizion of utility, to open the perspective of nonutility, of nonproductive expenditure?

—But that's exactly the point. Bataille always insists upon the unsurpassable paradox at the heart of his enterprise, that of trying to "sortir par un projet du domaine du projet [leave the realm of the project by means of a project]" (*OC*, 5:60). Where the existentialists are anguished over the difficulties of inventing, carrying through, and being responsible for, one's own project, Bataille sees precisely the opposite problem: we are stuck in a world in which everything is defined in terms of projects, fixed meanings, responsibilities. Meanings and projects are uses which have become congealed, which no longer have the flexibility which would allow them to change shape, to move elsewhere; which invest only themselves, in a cycle of reproduction on an ever-expanded scale. The realm of utility is predicated on recovery and recompense, a compensation for every loss, the survival of something fixed through every change. And that is why it is also the realm of idealist obfuscation, of the belief in tradition, in essences and archetypes, in hidden meanings which would somehow exist apart from their ever-changing manifestations in use. Utility and ideality are complicit with one another, two sides of the same coin.

—And such a logic is also that of traditional literary criticism. The aestheticism which praises the sublime uselessness of the text, which finds the highest value in its supposed disinterestedness, is generated and supported by practices of appreciation and criticism which strive, precisely, to account for everything, to put the text to work. The New Critic, for example, seeks to unify all the details, to balance or resolve the tensions, to articulate a harmony which would underlie the work of art. And such a neutralization of difference, such a denial of radical heterogeneity in favor of an easily contained pluralism, is what grounds the assertion of the work's transcendent value. How strange, and yet how monotonously predictable, it all is! The sleight-of-hand consists in according the highest market value—whether the market be one of money or of ideas—precisely to that which claims to escape the grubby realities of the market. The disavowal of use, the metaphysical assertion of a transcendent meaning which would remain unsullied by use, is ironically the mark of an economy which puts everything to work, which lets nothing escape, which takes everything into account.

—You seem to be aligning yourself with recent developments in political and social criticism, which question the unity, the value, and the ideology of canonical texts. Yet your own practice as a critic seems as far removed from ideology-critique, or from any "hermeneutics of suspicion," as it is from conventionally idealist modes of discourse. For doesn't ideology-critique still strive to hold the text rigorously to account? It has a different notion than does traditional idealism of what sorts of meaning can be found; but it never abandons the idealist project of the recovery of meaning. It remains committed to the totalization of meaning and truth as its ultimate horizon. Criticism, after Hegel, seeks to situate limited concepts within a larger context of truth. It overturns limits, but only to inscribe a new version of closure. Its operations are recuperated in a final moment of self-contemplating comprehension. Idealist aestheticism and ideology-critique share a fundamental Platonism, in that they both assume the subordination of appearance to truth. It is of little consequence that one praises the work of art for manifesting the truth, and the other blames art for dissimulating the truth, or for failing to conform to it.

—Yes, one might say that ideology-critique remains insufficiently *materialist* as a mode of criticism. One might say about it what Bataille says about the Surrealists.

> La plupart des matérialistes, bien qu'ils aient voulu éliminer toute entité spirituelle, sont arrivés à décrire un ordre de choses que des rapports hiérarchiques caractérisent comme spécifiquement

idéaliste. Ils ont situé la matière morte au sommet d'une hiérarchie conventionelle des faits d'ordre divers, sans s'apercevoir qu'ils cédaient ainsi à l'obsession d'une forme *idéale* de la matière, d'une forme qui se rapprocherait plus qu'aucune autre de ce que la matière *devrait être*. ("Materialisme," *OC*, 1:179)

Most materialists, even though they may have wanted to do away with all spiritual entities, ended up by positing an order of things whose hierarchical relations mark it as specifically idealist. They situated dead matter at the summit of a conventional hierarchy of diverse facts, without perceiving that in this way they gave in to an obsession with the *ideal* form of matter, with a form that was closer than any other to what matter *should be*. (*VE*, 15)

It is surely relevant to note that Bataille's polemic here closely parallels Marx's criticism of Feuerbach: "The chief defect of all hitherto existing materialism—that of Feuerbach included—is that the thing, reality, sensuousness, is conceived only in the form of the *object* or of *contemplation*" ("Theses on Feuerbach," I). Recent Marxist criticism, in its desire to avoid charges of simplistic reductionism, seems ironically to have reverted to a pre-Marxist, and ultimately (by inversion) religious, restricted or contemplative materialism.

—But where does that leave your own critical project? If you refuse to criticize the text, how do you avoid falling into an uncritical, laudatory idealization? Is a thoroughly materialist criticism, of the kind Bataille seems to be demanding, really possible? He calls for "l'interprétation directe, *excluant toute idéalisme*, des phénomènes bruts et non un système fondé sur les éléments fragmentaires d'une analyse idéologique élaborée sous le signe des rapports religieux [the direct interpretation, *excluding all idealism*, of raw phenomena, and not a system founded on the fragmentary elements of an ideological analysis, elaborated under the sign of religious relations]" (*OC*, 1:180; *VE*, 16). But how could such a *direct* interpretation, of *raw* or unmediated phenomena, ever be possible?

—As I've already suggested, I don't think the criterion of *possibility* is at all relevant here. Or, the problem with any appeal to conditions of possibility is that "possibility" is precisely being used as a norm, a criterion. And this is where I return to Wittgenstein, to the invention of multiple uses, rather than the consideration of actual and potential meanings. There are "uses" of the text that return us to the horizon of utility, to the imperialism of the logos, to the capitalization of meanings. And there are "uses" that seek to move us away from such a horizon, that find and amplify the ruptures in this economy. What counts is the orientation of the critical act, and not its "truth," its correspondence to the text, its coherence or completeness or consistency. All too often, even in the best political or deconstructionist criticism, the incongruous, heterogeneous details which the critic so powerfully uncovers merely become the occasion for a new inquisition, something for which the author or the text is to be held all the more rigorously accountable. The critic continues to demand that everything be grounded, explained, accounted for. I consider this to be a reactive, reactionary, idealist use of the text. As far as I'm concerned, there is no need to *account for* anything at all.

—Now you seem to be preaching a silly, and entirely untenable, relativism. Isn't it obvious, as so many philosophers have pointed out, that you cannot propound radical relativism without having recourse, by the very form of your utterance, to precisely those stabilities and conditions of universality whose existence and efficacy relativism seeks vainly to deny? Isn't to communicate relativism, to state it assertively, already to destroy it? Relativism makes a meta-statement even as it denies the validity of meta-statements; it proposes a generalization which exceeds the specificity of any particular perspective, at the very moment that it proclaims the impossibility of ever going beyond particular perspectives.

—I must confess that such accusations have never disturbed me. Indeed, I cheerfully embrace them. Of course, relativism—if that's what you want to call it—cannot be maintained as a doctrine, as a statement of "the truth." But the failure or inefficacy of all such statements (including its own) is precisely relativism's point. You say that it's a point which cannot possibly be made; and yet I have made it. All the arguments against relativism are specious, for they already assume the very standards—criteria of consistency and coherence, for example—which they are trying to prove or to establish. And indeed, in our present social and intellectual life, we are prisoners of these norms and these conventions. We can try to rupture them, but we do not succeed in definitively abolishing them. Relativism remains relative: otherwise, it would no longer be relativism, but a new tyranny of the norm or of the law, of reason or of faith. As Blanchot says of Nietzsche's pseudo-doctrine of the Eternal Return, "la seule faille d'une telle pensée [the sole fault of such a thought]" is that it can *never* be enacted or rendered present. But "ce 'jamais' . . . est aussi sa 'vérification', le signe de son absolu sérieux [this 'never' is also its 'verification', the sign of its absolute seriousness]" (*EI*, 418). This impossibility, this failure ever to be posited as a regulative norm, this refusal to be taken up into the self-reflexive play of thought, is the mark of the limit-experience.

—This point, this limit, has no stability and no identity, and one can only approach it, tirelessly, wearily, hopelessly, again and again. I'm haunted by Bataille's warning, which I've already quoted: "L'existence ne peut être à la fois autonome et viable [existence cannot be at once autonomous and viable]" (*OC*, 6:63). Every assertion, every norm, every totalization must be undone; and yet the relativism which opposes them can never itself be positively asserted. This task can only end in failure; and whatever I write will necessarily fall short. But there's a strange joy in this unending movement, one which I've *also* been trying to evoke throughout this book. And this joy is related to what I've been calling the direction or the use of my own critical writing. An orientation away from the norm, away from homogeneity and utility, away from the standards of accountability and judgment.

—All right, then. So you disclaim all critical responsibility. You are not trying to achieve *adequacy* or *accuracy* in your discussions of Blanchot and Bataille. There is no standard of correctness or completeness. You don't even seek to demonstrate (as deconstructionist critics do) the *impossibility* of fixing meaning, of completing the task of interpretation, of being sure of anything. You simply, and irresponsibly, sidestep the entire issue. Just what do you think you're doing? What is the relation of your own discourse to those you so amply cite throughout the book, to the texts of Blanchot and Bataille?

—A friend (Barry Schwabsky) who read part of this book in manuscript told me that he was "troubled by the ventriloquism of the whole performance—the sense that you are trying to let Blanchot speak through you, or yourself through him, rather than saying your own thing as it were in tandem with an exposition or investigation of his thought." Although he found this "ventriloquism" disturbing, I would say it is a highly desirable (although sometimes embarrassing) position for the critic to be in. It well characterizes my own relation to the texts which I'm discussing: a relation of extreme constraint, and yet at the same time of considerable ambiguity and duplicity. For who is ventriloquizing whom? I am mobilizing, making productive use of, the writings of Blanchot and Bataille; what's important is not the totality of what they actually or potentially say but the new directions they open up, the places they help me get to, the things they can be made to say. I'm using them, abusing them, making them say what I want them to say. But at the same time, this process doesn't seem to me to be voluntaristic, consciously planned and willed, at all. Nothing is freely invented. The texts of Blanchot and Bataille determine my own will while escaping it. They are what I never could have said myself, but what I find myself *compelled* to say. The force of their words within me is that of an obsession, an irrational compulsion. It is the part of me which I cannot think, which is always prior to myself and other than myself. An irreducible opacity which I strive endlessly, stupidly, to master, to illuminate, to reduce; but which fortunately escapes my vigilance, which leads me perpetually elsewhere than ever I could have intended. For finally, there is no mastery. Nothing in this book came out the way I expected. I wrote it this way, about these subjects, because I could not write about anything else.

—One might say, then, that this book is autobiography rather than criticism. But an autobiography of events which never have happened, an account of those occurrences which I am unable to claim or recognize as my own. An autobiography which is secretive, impersonal, and asubjective; not a discovery of self, but the contact of events which can never be recognized by or integrated into that self. I have scorned the claims of objectivity and generality, of scholarly accuracy and philosophical coherence, not in order to arrive at who knows what vague form of self-expression, but in order to clear a path for something which cannot be expressed, and which does not originate from "myself." It is a matter of "something coming from the outside rather than the inside," the point being to say "the thing that you didn't want to say in terms of your own ego—in terms of your image, in terms of your life, in terms of everything" (Jack Spicer, "The Vancouver Lectures," 176–77).

—The outside, as Jack Spicer puts it, the voices of the dead. A ventriloquism of absent or dead voices; yet the relation is more one of parasitism than of ventriloquism. I am the host, and the texts which I cannot help citing are parasites which use my writing in order to communicate their own messages, messages which do not concern me. For Spicer, interiority is like a room with all its furniture; and the outside, the poem, is something radically other, something from elsewhere, something coming into the room, but which does not belong there and does not have a place there. The (living) writer's memories, desires, subjectivity—and even the structures of language which articulate these personal contents of experience—are not what get expressed; they are only the building blocks, the furniture, the raw materials that the voices from outside must use in order to transmit their messages (Spicer, 175–80 passim). The Saying remains exterior to what is said; the outside can speak only by playing with the building blocks, by rearranging the furniture, by using as a medium that which is not its own expression. Yet the message does not exist outside of its medium. All writing is translation, but a translation of that for which there is no original.

—Isn't this also what William Burroughs is getting at, with his dictum that "language is a virus," and indeed, that all human thought is such a parasitic structure, such a virus? "The whole quality of human consciousness, as expressed in male and female, is basically a virus mechanism" (*Cities of the Red Night*, 25).

—Yes, in all these cases what is at stake is the parasitic or ventriloquistic relation between outside and inside, between death and life. Thought and experience are animated only by that which they cannot contain, only by their own deaths, only from outside. The Outside is not a being or substance, not a theological category, not an origin or ground. It is not the Being in which all beings would somehow participate. It escapes any such characterizations; it is never where we find it. It is singular, multiple, perpetually different from itself. It is the limit beyond which there is nothing, and which therefore cannot be crossed, yet which nevertheless has always already been crossed. "La limite ne se conçoit-elle elle-même que par une délimitation qui serait nécessaire à l'approche de l'illimité et disparaîtrait si jamais elle était franchie, infranchissable pour cette raison, toujours franchie cependant parce qu'infranchissable? [Is limit itself conceived only through a definition that is necessary at the approach of the unlimited and that would disappear if it was ever passed—for that reason impassable, yet always passed because it is impassable?]" (*EI*, 632–33; *GO*, 157).

—Agreed, except that after all these pages you still seem to be describing the Outside, or the limit-experience, in merely logical terms—forms of expression, conditions of possibility—when it is reducible neither to logic, nor to the negation, suspension, or paradoxical self-undoing of logic. Isn't it rather a question of what you have been calling *passion*, in the radical sense in which it must be distinguished both from the empirical notion of pleasure (the satisfaction, stimulation, or reduction in tension experienced by an already constituted ego or body) and from the dialectical notion of desire (viewed as a movement in which a subjectivity is constituted, impelled, and transformed by a fundamental negativity or lack)? In the movement of passion, the "subject" is passively submitted to, and yet violently acted or agitated by, the very forces which make impossible its constitution as a subject. Perpetual departure, exile without return, irrecuperable otherness: "Comment ne pas revenir? Il faut se perdre. Je ne sais pas. Tu apprendras. Je voudrais une indication pour me perdre. Il faut être sans arrière-pensée, se disposer à ne plus reconnaître rien de ce qu'on connaît, diriger ses pas vers le point de l'horizon le plus hostile, sorte de vaste étendue de marécages que mille talus traversent en tous sens on ne voit pas pourquoi [How to avoid going back? Get lost. I don't know how. You'll learn. I need some signpost to lead me astray. Make your mind a blank. Refuse to recognize familiar landmarks. Turn your steps towards the most hostile point on the horizon, towards the vast marshlands, bewilderingly crisscrossed by a thousand causeways]" (Marguerite Duras, *Le Vice-consul*, 9; *The Vice-Consul*, 1).

—Passion is exile, deracination. But as Blanchot continually reminds us, exodus, exile, and nomadism are not merely negative concepts. "L'exode, l'exil indiquent un rapport positif avec l'extériorité dont l'exigence nous invite à ne pas nous contenter de ce qui nous est propre (c'est-à-dire de notre pouvoir de tout assimiler, de tout identifier, de tout rapporter à notre Je) [Exodus, exile indicate a positive relation with exteriority, that whose demand leads us not to be satisfied with that which belongs to us (is proper to us)—that is to say, our power to assimilate everything, to identify everything, to refer everything to the 'I']" (*EI*, 186). Passion, exile, is an *other* relation to the Outside, to the real—the loss which it entails is not lack or deprivation, is not merely misery and frustration.

—Yes, and that returns me to a comment made by a friend (Katurah Hutcheson) after reading one of my chapters. She spoke of "that sort of absence and obliteration at the heart of passion—the desire for it—how thought consumes and erases." (Remarks which, I think, would apply equally well to her own work as a photographer.) This continual consuming, this distance, this never-completed obliteration: it is that which moves, which speaks, which is our joy as well as our pain. It is a singing "without human meaning, / Without human feeling, a foreign song. / You know then that it is not the reason / That makes us happy or unhappy" (Wallace Stevens, "Of Mere Being," *The Palm at the End of the Mind*, 398). "Beyond the last thought," the inhuman which impels thought, but which cannot be contained or incorporated by thought. Passion is my "experience" of this inhuman, my impossible relation to "le non-concernant. Non seulement ce qui ne [m]e concerne pas, mais ce qui ne se concerne pas [the non-concerning. Not merely that which does not concern (regard) me, but that which does not concern (regard) itself]" (*EI*, xxiii).

—But here we are reaching the point at which it is no longer possible to think, to speak. And that is why this inhuman affirmation is not the subject of a critical argument, but of an unending cascade, a heterogeneous concatenation, of incomplete, fragmentary voices and quotations. The point being not to master or control these other voices, not to make them something of my own. Neither to venerate these writers and these words, nor to appropriate them, nor to criticize them from a supposedly superior and less mystified perspective. But perhaps to enter the strange space of a nearness and a distance which preclude both subjective identification and critical objectivity. My involuntary relation to these texts is one of love, of passion and obsession, of paranoid delusion, perhaps; but certainly not one of mastery, of knowledge, of comprehension.

—And the writing of this passion, excessive and overwhelming, and at the same time distant, scattered, and indifferent: that is perhaps what I have accomplished in this book (although "accomplishment" is probably not the correct word to use here). At the very least, I have not sought to interpret, to mystify, to demystify, to evaluate. Criticism is not the "same" as literature, just as it is not the same as political action. But as Blanchot suggests (to give one of his texts the last word, there where there can be no final word), critical writing can participate, like literature, and like revolutionary political action, in one of the most urgent struggles of our time.

Et, dans la mesure même où la critique appartient plus intimement à la vie de l'œuvre, elle fait l'expérience de celle-ci comme de ce qui ne s'évalue pas, elle la saisit comme la profondeur, et aussi l'absence de profondeur, qui échappe à toute système de valeurs, étant en-deçà de ce qui vaut et récusant par avance toute affirmation qui voudrait s'emparer d'elle pour la valoriser. En ce sens, la critique—la littérature—me semble associée à l'une des tâches les plus difficiles, mais les plus importantes de notre temps, laquelle se joue dans un mouvement nécessairement indécis: la tâche de préserver et de libérer la pensée de la notion de valeur, par conséquent aussi d'ouvrir l'histoire à ce qui en elle se dégage déjà de toutes les formes de valeurs et se prépare à une toute autre sorte—encore imprévisible—d'affirmation.

And, to the very degree that criticism belongs more intimately to the life of the work, it experiences it as that which does not evaluate itself, it seizes the work as the depth, and also the absence of depth, which escapes from every system of values, being prior to (on this side of) that which has worth, and objecting in advance to any affirmation which would want to take hold of it in order to valorize it. In this sense, criticism—literature—seems to me to be associated with one of the most difficult, yet most important, tasks of our time, one which plays in a necessarily indecisive movement: the task of preserving and liberating thought from the notion of value, therefore also of opening history to that which, within it, is already disengaging itself from all forms of value and preparing for an entirely different—still unforeseeable—sort of affirmation. ("Qu'en est-il de la critique?" *Lautréamont et Sade*, 13–14)

BIBLIOGRAPHY

Althusser, Louis, and Etienne Balibar. *Reading Capital*. Translated by Ben Brewster. London: Verso, 1979.

Barthes, Roland. *Elements of Semiology*. Translated by Annette Lavers and Colin Smith. New York: Hill and Wang, 1968.

Bataille, Georges. *Erotism: Death and Sensuality*. Translated by Mary Dalwood. San Francisco: City Lights Books, 1986.

———. *Guilty*. Translated by Bruce Boone. Venice, Calif.: Lapis, 1988.

———. *Inner Experience*. Translated by Leslie Anne Boldt. Albany: State University of New York Press, 1988.

———. *Œuvres complètes*. 12 vols. Paris: Gallimard, 1970–1988.

———. *Visions of Excess: Selected Writings, 1927–1939*. Translated by Allan Stoekl. Minneapolis: University of Minnesota Press, 1985.

Baudrillard, Jean. *L'échange symbolique et la mort*. Paris: Gallimard, 1976.

———. *Simulations*. Translated by Paul Foss, Paul Patton, and Philip Beitchman. New York: Semiotext(e), 1983.

Benjamin, Walter. *Illuminations*. Translated by Harry Zohn. New York: Schocken, 1969.

Blanchot, Maurice. *Aminadab*. Paris: Gallimard, 1942.

———. *Après coup*. Paris: Minuit, 1983.

———. *L'arrêt de mort*. Paris: Gallimard "L'Imaginaire," 1971.

———. *L'attente l'oubli*. Paris: Gallimard, 1962.

———. *Au moment voulu*. Paris: Gallimard, 1951.

———. *Celui qui ne m'accompagnait pas*. Paris: Gallimard, 1953.

———. *La communauté inavouable*. Paris: Minuit, 1983.

———. *Death Sentence*. Translated by Lydia Davis. Barrytown, N.Y.: Station Hill Press, 1978.

———. *Le dernier homme*. Paris: Gallimard, 1957.

———. *L'écriture du désastre*. Paris: Gallimard, 1980.

———. *L'entretien infini*. Paris: Gallimard, 1969.

———. *L'espace littéraire*. Paris: Gallimard "Idées," 1968.

———. *La folie du jour*. Montpellier: Fata Morgana, 1973.

———. *The Gaze of Orpheus*. Translated by Lydia Davis. Barrytown, N.Y.: Station Hill Press, 1981.

———. *Lautréamont et Sade*. Paris: Minuit, 1963.

———. *Le livre à venir*. Paris: Gallimard "Idées," 1971.

———. *The Madness of the Day*. Translated by Lydia Davis. Barrytown, N.Y.: Station Hill Press, 1981.

———. *Michel Foucault as I Imagine Him*. Translated by Jeffrey Mehlman. In *Foucault/Blanchot*. New York: Zone Books, 1987.

———. *Michel Foucault tel que je l'imagine*. Montpellier: Fata Morgana, 1986.

———. *La part du feu*. Paris: Gallimard, 1949.

———. *Le pas au-delà*. Paris: Gallimard, 1973.

———. *The Space of Literature*. Translated by Ann Smock. Lincoln: University of Nebraska Press, 1982.

———. *Thomas l'obscur* (nouvelle version). Paris: Gallimard, 1950.

———. *Thomas the Obscure*. Translated by Robert Lamberton. Barrytown, N.Y.: Station Hill Press, 1988.

———. *The Unavowable Community*. Translated by Pierre Joris. Barrytown, N.Y.: Station Hill Press, 1988.

———. *Vicious Circles*. Translated by Paul Auster. Barrytown, N.Y.: Station Hill Press, 1985.

———. *When the Time Comes*. Translated by Lydia Davis. Barrytown, N.Y.: Station Hill Press, 1985.

———. *The Writing of the Disaster*. Translated by Ann Smock. Lincoln: University of Nebraska Press, 1986.

Breton, André. *Nadja*. Paris: Gallimard, 1964.

Burroughs, William. *Cities of the Red Night*. New York: Holt, Rinehart and Winston, 1981.

Cameron, Sharon. *Lyric Time: Dickinson and the Limits of Genre*. Baltimore: Johns Hopkins University Press, 1981.

Cixous, Hélène. "Le sexe ou la tête?" *Cahiers du GRIF* 13 (1976): 5–15. [Translated by Annette Kuhn under the title "Castration or Decapitation?" *Signs* 7:1 (1981): 41–55.]

Cohn, Robert Greer. *Toward the Poems of Mallarmé*. Berkeley: University of California Press, 1965.

Deleuze, Gilles. *Différence et répétition*. Paris: Presses Universitaires de France, 1968.

———. *Foucault*. Paris: Minuit, 1986.

———. *Francis Bacon: Logique de la sensation*. Paris: Editions de la Différence, 1981.

———. *Masochism: An Interpretation of Coldness and Cruelty*. Translated by Jean McNeil. New York: George Braziller, 1971.

———. *Nietzsche and Philosophy*. Translated by Hugh Tomlinson. New York: Columbia University Press, 1983.

Deleuze, Gilles, and Felix Guattari. *Anti-Oedipus: Capitalism and Schizophrenia*. Translated by Robert Hurley, Mark Seem, and Helen R. Lane. Minneapolis: University of Minnesota Press, 1983.

———. *A Thousand Plateaus: Capitalism and Schizophrenia*. Translated by Brian Massumi. Minneapolis: University of Minnesota Press, 1987.

De Man, Paul. *Blindness and Insight: Essays in the Rhetoric of Contemporary Criticism*. Minneapolis: University of Minnesota Press, 1983.

Derrida, Jacques. *Parages*. Paris: Galilée, 1986.

———. *Writing and Difference*. Translated by Alan Bass. Chicago: University of Chicago Press, 1978.

Dickinson, Emily. *The Complete Poems of Emily Dickinson*. Edited by Thomas H. Johnson. Boston: Little, Brown, 1960.

Duras, Marguerite. *Détruire dit-elle*. Paris: Minuit, 1969. [Translated by Barbara Bray, under the title *Destroy, She Said*. New York: Grove, 1986.]

———. *La maladie de la mort*. Paris: Minuit, 1982. [Translated by Barbara Bray under the title *The Malady of Death*. New York: Grove, 1986.]

———. *Le ravissement de Lol V. Stein*. Paris: Gallimard, 1964. [Translated by Richard Seaver, under the title *The Ravishing of Lol Stein*. New York: Pantheon, 1986.]

———. *Le vice-consul*. Paris: Gallimard, 1966. [Translated by Eileen Ellenbogen under the title *The Vice Consul*. New York: Pantheon, 1987.]

Emerson, Ralph Waldo. *Selections from Ralph Waldo Emerson*. Edited by Stephen E. Whicher. Boston: Houghton Mifflin, 1957.

Foucault, Michel. "The Discourse on Language." Translated by Rupert Swyer, in *The Archaeology of Knowledge*. New York: Pantheon, 1982.

———. *The History of Sexuality. Volume I: An Introduction*. Translated by Robert Hurley. New York: Vintage, 1980.

———. *Language, Counter-Memory, Practice: Selected Essays and Interviews*. Translated by Donald F. Bouchard and Sherry Simon. Ithaca: Cornell University Press, 1977.

———. *Maurice Blanchot: The Thought from Outside*. Translated by Brian Massumi. In *Foucault/Blanchot*. New York: Zone Books, 1987.

———. "A Preface to Transgression." In *Language, Counter-Memory, Practice*, 29–52.

————. *Sept propos sur le septième ange*. Montpellier: Fata Morgana, 1986.

————. "What Is an Author?" In *Language, Counter-Memory, Practice*, 113–38.

Girard, René. *Violence and the Sacred*. Baltimore: Johns Hopkins University Press, 1977.

Hegel, G. W. F. *Phenomenology of Spirit*. Translated by A. V. Miller. Oxford: Oxford University Press, 1977.

Heidegger, Martin. *Being and Time*. Translated by John Macquarrie and Edward Robinson. New York: Harper and Row, 1962.

————. *Identity and Difference*. Translated by Joan Stambaugh. New York: Harper and Row, 1969.

Hertz, Neil. *The End of the Line*. New York: Columbia University Press, 1985.

Hollier, Denis. *La prise de la Concorde*. Paris: Gallimard, 1974.

Jardine, Alice. *Gynesis: Configurations of Woman and Modernity*. Ithaca: Cornell University Press, 1985.

Kant, Immanuel. *Critique of Judgement*. Translated by James Creed Meredith. Oxford: Oxford University Press, 1952.

————. *Critique of Pure Reason*. Translated by Norman Kemp Smith. New York: St. Martin's Press, 1965.

Keats, John. *The Complete Poems*. Edited by John Barnard. New York: Penguin, 1973.

Klossowski, Pierre. *Nietzsche et le cercle vicieux*. Paris: Mercure de France, 1969.

————. *La Ressemblance*. Marseille: Editions Ryôan-ji, 1984.

————. *Un si funeste désir*. Paris: Gallimard, 1963.

Kojève, Alexandre. *Introduction à la lecture de Hegel*. Paris: Gallimard, 1947.

Lacan, Jacques. *Ecrits: A Selection*. Translated by Alan Sheridan. New York: Norton, 1977.

————. *The Four Fundamental Concepts of Psycho-Analysis*. Translated by Alan Sheridan. New York: Norton, 1981.

————. *Le Séminaire, I: Les écrits techniques de Freud*. Paris: Seuil, 1975.

Laplanche, J., and J.-B. Pontalis. *The Language of Psycho-Analysis*. Translated by Donald Nicholson-Smith. New York: Norton, 1973.

Levinas, Emmanuel. *Sur Maurice Blanchot*. Montpellier: Fata Morgana, 1975.

Libertson, Joseph. "Bataille and Communication: From Heterogeneity to Continuity." *MLN* 89:4 (May 1974): 669–98.

————. *Proximity: Levinas, Blanchot, Bataille and Communication*. The Hague: Martinus Nijhoff, 1982.

Lyotard, Jean-François. *Economie libidinale*. Paris: Minuit, 1974.

————. "One of the Things at Stake in Women's Struggles." Translated by Deborah J. Clarke, Winifred Woodhull, and John Mowitt. *SubStance* 20 (1978): 9–17.

Mallarmé, Stéphane. *Œuvres complètes*. Edited by Henri Mondor and G. Jean-Aubry. Paris: Gallimard-Pléiade, 1945.

Marcuse, Herbert. *Reason and Revolution: Hegel and the Rise of Social Theory.* Boston: Beacon Press, 1960.

Marx, Karl. *Capital.* 3 vols. Translated by Ben Fowkes and David Fernbach. New York: Vintage, 1977–1981.

———. "Theses on Feuerbach." In *Early Writings.* Translated by Rodney Livingstone and Gregor Benton. New York: Penguin, 1975.

Nancy, Jean-Luc. *La communauté désoeuvrée.* Paris: Christian Bourgeois, 1986.

Nietzsche, Friedrich. *The Gay Science.* Translated by Walter Kaufmann. New York: Vintage, 1974.

———. *On the Genealogy of Morals* and *Ecce Homo.* Translated by Walter Kaufmann. New York: Vintage, 1969.

———. *Thus Spoke Zarathustra.* Translated by R. J. Hollingdale. New York: Penguin, 1969.

———. *Twilight of the Idols* and *The Anti-Christ.* Translated by R. J. Hollingdale. New York: Penguin, 1968.

———. *The Will to Power.* Translated by Walter Kaufmann and R. J. Hollingdale. New York: Vintage, 1968.

Poe, Edgar Allan. *Complete Tales and Poems.* New York: Vintage, 1975.

Rorty, Richard. *Philosophy and the Mirror of Nature.* Princeton: Princeton University Press, 1979.

———. "Solidarity or Objectivity?" In *Post-Analytic Philosophy*, edited by John Rajchman and Cornel West, 3–19. New York: Columbia University Press, 1985.

Sartre, Jean-Paul. *Critiques littéraires (Situations, I).* Paris: Gallimard "Idées," 1975.

Spicer, Jack. "The Vancouver Lectures." *Caterpillar* 12 (July 1970): 175–212.

Spivak, Gayatri Chakravorty. *In Other Worlds: Essays in Cultural Politics.* New York: Methuen, 1987.

Stevens, Wallace. *The Palm at the End of the Mind: Selected Poems and a Play.* Edited by Holly Stevens. New York: Vintage, 1972.

Wittgenstein, Ludwig. *Philosophical Investigations.* Translated by G. E. M. Anscombe. New York: Macmillan, 1968.

———. *Tractatus Logico-Philosophicus.* Translated by D. F. Pears and B. F. McGuinness. London: Routledge and Kegan Paul, 1961.

INDEX

Stevens, Wallace, 14, 24–26, 29,
182–83
Surplus value, 42, 54–56

Thomas the Obscure (Blanchot), 7, 28
Trace, 55, 139–40, 150

Transgression, 63–81

When the Time Comes (Blanchot),
142–44, 162–70
Wittgenstein, Ludwig, 4, 30, 74,
153, 175, 177